Haunting Violations

Haunting Violations

Feminist Criticism and the Crisis of the "Real"

Edited by Wendy S. Hesford and Wendy Kozol

University of Illinois Press
Urbana and Chicago

The frontispiece is no. 4 in a series of six gelatin silver prints by
Yong Soon Min entitled *Defining Moments* (1992).

Library of Congress Cataloging-in-Publication Data
Haunting violations : feminist criticism and the crisis of the "real" /
edited by Wendy S. Hesford and Wendy Kozol.
p.   cm.
Includes bibliographical references and index.
ISBN 0-252-02610-1 (hc : acid-free) —
ISBN 0-252-06911-0 (pb : acid-free)
1. Feminist theory. 2. Feminist criticism. I. Hesford, Wendy S.
II. Kozol, Wendy, 1958– . III. Title.
HQ1190.H39   2001
305.42'01—dc21   00-009240

1 2 3 4 5 C P 5 4 3 2 1

To Mia, James, and Paul

Contents

Defining Moments

Wendy S. Hesford

> The importance of history in formulating my own identity is unde-
> niable. Once I felt I had a grasp of alternative history, a history of my
> Korean roots that was denied or suppressed, that there was a role
> model, it gave me incredible strength.
> —Yong Soon Min

Defining Moments #4, which serves as the frontispiece and also appears on the
cover of this book, is the fourth in a series of six gelatin silver prints (1992; 20
x 16 inches each) by Yong Soon Min, a Korean American artist who emigrated
to the United States in 1960. Superimposed on the artist's upper body is a
photographic image of the Kwangju Uprising and Massacre. Superimposing
this historical referent onto the photographic flesh of the artist positions the
material body as a site marked by the trauma of cultural and national conficts.
Yong Soon Min figures her body as an archive of memory, even as she interrogates the dilemma of realist representations by placing the "real" of history
in dialogue with the "real" of the body. Like other contributors to this book,
she forces viewers to confront the paradoxical need to interrogate truth-telling discourses, even as we rely on those discourses to rethink imperialist, ethnocentric, and Western epistemologies.

The uprising and massacre occurred in May 1980 in the southern provin-
cial capital of Kwangju. The uprising began as a peaceful demonstration by
students who were soon joined by large numbers of ordinary citizens as they
protested the South Korean government's military rule and called for democratic elections. The military violently suppressed the demonstrations that
spread across the city, ultimately killing an estimated two thousand civilians.
Yong Soon Min's image depicts a moment when government troops rushed
at a group of protesters in the streets of Kwangju. However, the sign "DMZ"
(demilitarized zone) on her forehead reaches beyond the specificity of the
moment to implicate imperial power and subvert static notions of the nation-

state. More particularly, writing this history on the artist's gendered body turns our attention to the traumatic impact of hegemonic forces on Korean and Korean American women.

Still, Yong Soon Min's gaze is not directed solely at the specter of Eurocentrism and neocolonialism. She also unsettles romanticized, nostalgic images of "the home country" (the United States or Korea or both). The nationalist U.S. slogan "Heartland" bleeds into the image of the Kwangju Uprising and Massacre, seeping into the artist's skin. The disappearance of "land" points to the immigrant experience of cultural dislocation and generational hybridization and to the trauma of historical memory. By marking both geopolitical territories on the body Yong Soon Min creates a context for a transnational feminism that recognizes the relationship of historical identities.

Are we to read this image as a memorial? An elegy? A testimony? Does it call for the viewer to bear witness? If so, are we witnessing the hybridization of identity? The fracturing of the nation-state? The violation of the body of the people? The dilemma of autobiography and historical narration? What is it that haunts the viewing process? What is it that wounds us, that "shoots out of [the photograph] like an arrow and pierces" (Barthes 26–27)?

The historical trauma that haunts the production and reception of *Defining Moments #4* lies in the repetition of the inscription of violence. If photography is, as Barthes suggests, "a figuration of the motionless and made-up face beneath which we see the dead" (32), then we might say that the death of those massacred at Kwangju lies motionless beneath the face of Yong Soon Min. Yet, *Defining Moments* suggests not that one becomes a ghost of oneself—a conception of trauma that limits forgetfulness to individual repression—or that what returns to haunt the subject is the lost referent. Rather it suggests that the archive of traumatic memory "leaves the trace of an incision right on the skin; more than one skin, at more than one age" (Derrida 20). The punctum of *Defining Moments #4* is not only the loss that pierces like an arrow or the absence that lingers like a ghost; it is also the inadequacy of representation— its doubleness. As Patrick Brantlinger puts it in his contribution to this volume, "to resist violence it must give violence expression."

Defining Moments #4 prompts viewers and critics to grapple with the ethical and political questions that arise when we turn to representations of violence, trauma, and oppression. Yoon Soon Min urges us to think about how material bodies take on the function and burden of cultural memory. The image offers a clarifying editorial moment, enabling us to see how political, cultural, and personal violations haunt the crisis of "the real."

Works Cited

Barthes, Roland. *Camera Lucida: Reflections on Photography.* Trans. Richard Howard. New York: Hill and Wang, 1981.

Derrida, Jacques. *Archive Fever: A Freudian Impression.* Trans. Eric Prenowitz. Chicago: University of Chicago Press, 1996.

Acknowledgments

Collaborations are notoriously wonderful and challenging experiences. Like all good collaborators, we were able to draw on each other's different knowledges and perspectives to continually deepen the moral and ethical questions that drive the theoretical and historical analyses of this work. In this regard, we are first and foremost grateful to the contributors of this volume for their rich and provocative insights, which taught us so much, as well as for their willingness to rethink arguments and revise essays. We would also like to thank Dion Farquhar, Sandy Zagarell, and Mary Loeffelholz for their careful and thoughtful readings of parts or all of the manuscript. We gratefully acknowledge Ann Lowry's insightful editorial support and Theresa Sears and Matthew Mitchell's care in bringing the manuscript to publication. We would also like to thank Kelly Wissman for her assistance with the index. Matthew Cariello and Steven Wojtal provided the personal and intellectual support that makes each of our endeavors more meaningful. Our children, Mia, James, and Paul, teach us each day about the performative nature of authenticity and the pedagogical value of the process of questioning the "real."

Introduction: Is There a "Real" Crisis?

Wendy S. Hesford and Wendy Kozol

What is at risk when cultural critics and feminists depend upon realist discourses and notions of authenticity to theorize personal and political agency? How self-consciously are social critics and activists using an uninterrogated site of the "real" to advance particular cultural and political agendas? These questions take on particular urgency when considering representations of trauma, violence, and captivity. For instance, *Calling the Ghosts* (Jacobson and Jelincic), a film about genocidal rape in Bosnia-Herzegovina and Croatia, which features women who remember and retell stories of being raped and tortured at the Serb concentration camp of Omarska, powerfully explores what is at stake in depicting traumatic events. Such retellings cry out for an analysis of the risks of representation and our demand for authentic voices by reminding us of the trauma of memory. As one woman says, "in order to expose the crime, you violate the witness. You don't force her, of course—you beg her to speak, but you make her live through it again." The film problematizes the act of representation in the opening scene when a woman poses the critical question that frames the film: "If I stay silent, how moral would that be? . . . If I speak, how good is that for me?" By envisioning the embodiment of trauma and the violence of memory, *Calling the Ghosts* provocatively challenges our expectations about the ability to represent the "real" story, a problem that haunts history and cultural criticism.

Calling the Ghosts enacts a witnessing of violences hidden from view and a confrontation with the traumas that these women endured. More than an act of recovery, however, is demanded of the viewer when one of the women eloquently states, "when they were killing and raping older women, they were killing and raping living history; when they were raping younger women they were destroying future generations." The ghosts, in this sense, are more than unspoken presences, for calling on them is also a recalling or recasting of history. But how to speak of that history? These women's "real" lives, that is their ordinary, familiar, and routine lives, were suddenly and violently lost as the "realness" of sexual violence reshaped their experiences of self, family, community, and nation.

Rather than explore acts of memory and representation, however, too often politically oriented criticism invokes claims of authentic or "real" experiences to prove the abusiveness of power. Ironically, this dependence takes place even as there is a growing interest in the academy in "truth-telling" discourses, particularly autobiography, documentary realism, and ethnography. These studies have richly criticized assumptions of objectivity embedded in traditional research methodologies and popular cultural representations. Many scholars now recognize the problems with presuming a reality that exists independent of representation. Nonetheless, studies of agency and opposition continue to reproduce a dichotomized view of hegemony wherein resistance remains the uninterrogated site of the real.

Positing a real story against false or ideological positions appears in scholarly debates, especially around contentious issues about what constitutes legitimate knowledge. In the U.S. academy, debates over the "real" infuse discourses surrounding the "culture wars" and "canon wars." Conservatives seek to resecure a traditional canon based on a faith that these championed texts transcend politics or even history. Critics of this position, such as feminists, have rightly pointed out how this "transcendent canon" privileges white, western men. Nonetheless, they too often rely on binary assumptions that promote women's voices as expressions of the authentic experiences of violence, trauma, and resistance.

Calling on the ghosts of memory and representation, however, challenges us to reconsider claims of authenticity and agency. *Haunting Violations* investigates the ways in which cultural discourses mobilize the "real" in struggles over legal rights, definitions of community, historical knowledge, and other assertions of identity. In what ways, we ask, do realist strategies reveal or elide contradictions of power and resistance? What is the relationship between cultural politics and activism, and how does the "real" figure in this relationship?

Haunting Violations thus challenges the presumption that invoking "real" experiences either functions as a tool of hegemonic forces or as an act of resistance. Rather, we are interested in exploring how cultural representations of the "real" negotiate competing interests in the interstices of power, authority, and resistance. These essays focus on a variety of cultural forms and practices such as film, photography, national archives, novels, testimonials, and grassroots activism. Contributors explore how representations of the "real" have been used in different historical moments to construct hierarchies within communities, to silence the views of oppressed groups, or conversely, how ideologies of truth and authenticity are used by marginalized groups to contest dominant narratives and to stimulate resistance. Equally important are the moments that reveal that authenticity cannot secure an absolutely privileged position for either dominance or resistance.

The "Real" Crisis

We invoke the trope of crisis not to manufacture yet another crisis but rather to expose how notions of the "real" structure crisis narratives. The term "crisis" is defined as a turning point or a moment when a decisive change is imminent, especially in times of difficulty or instability. In contrast, the "real" is defined by the Oxford English Dictionary as "having an existence in fact and not merely in appearance, thought, or language, or as having an absolute and necessary, in contrast to a merely contingent, existence." Standard definitions of "crisis" point to change and instability, whereas definitions of the "real" signify stability, a fixed essence. Taken together these terms present a contradiction; the phrase "the real crisis" is an oxymoron. If something is permanently fixed—the real—then how can it change or be in crisis? If "crisis" indicates change, how can it ever be construed as fixedly real? The concept of the "real" as changing and unstable throws a number of other categories into question. If the subject is fractured and no longer unified, as postmodernists suggest, then what happens to notions of experience, subjectivity, and personal and political agency?

Rather than resolve these contradictions, we are interested in exploring them for their pedagogical value. What can they teach us about the links between cultural representations and material conditions, between the performance of historical narratives and realist historiography? What can they teach us about struggles for power and the politics of signification? As feminist critics and teachers, we find ourselves confronting the urgent desire to convey to our students and readers evidence of the traumatic and oppressive conditions faced by women. We frequently rely on empirical data and documentary media to secure a convincing historical narrative about the pervasiveness of domestic violence or the impact of globalization on sex workers. Thus even as we struggle to undermine epistemological dependencies on positivist knowledge claims and to urge our students to engage critically with discursive practices, we recognize our own dependence on them. Likewise, each contributor to this volume has had to address his or her own turn to the "real" as it is known through cultural discourse, a turn that has forced us to rethink notions of evidence, memory, and history. This self-reflexive examination of our own dependence on the "real" also necessitates a questioning of the ethical functions of criticism, especially when addressing violence, trauma, and oppression.

Progressive academics who are committed to social change confront ethical demands when engaged in critiques of representations of trauma and crisis. Our title, *Haunting Violations,* evokes the question of how to teach revisionist histories of imperialism, genocide, or sexual violence without either offering up an alternative "reality" or an uncritical relativism. Why might a critique of a documentary such as *Calling the Ghosts* be needed, and how (ethically) do you conduct such a critique without lessening the horror that the documentary appears accurately and compellingly to depict? How, to put it most bluntly, do you critique a documentary about genocide and state-sanctioned rape that appears to offer a true depiction of this horror? What is it that we want or need to know about such traumas? How do we find the answers in representations that speak from or about those oppressed by violence? The theoretical traditions that contributors to *Haunting Violations* draw on to explore these ethical dilemmas and contradictions, such as postcolonial, feminist, and postmodern theory, are themselves riven with internal debates. With the decline in positivist research paradigms and renewed interest in rhetoric, scholars in the humanities and social sciences are experiencing a crisis of identity and representation. As Roof and Wiegman have asked, who can speak for whom? What does it mean to speak for others? What evidence does one use to document crisis, and how "good" is this evidence? Whose crisis is this anyway? Is the crisis merely academic? Or does it reflect larger social and national crises?

Notably, the crisis of the "real" in the academy emerges at a time when identities are in crisis, as structures of belonging and categories of affiliation such as race, class, gender, sexual orientation, political party, and nation-state are called into question (Mercer). Broad social and cultural changes in the late twentieth century, including shifts from industrial-capitalist mass production to information technologies and a transnational economy dominated by multinational corporations, have led to the proliferation of new identities associated with the politics of personal consumption. Such fragmentation of social identities has prompted a "return to the subjective" and a conceptual shift in our models of the individual subject (Hall 58). As Stuart Hall puts it in "Brave New World," "We can no longer conceive of the 'individual' in terms of a whole and completed ego or autonomous 'self.' The 'self' is experienced as more fragmented and incomplete . . . something with a history, 'produced,' in process" (58–59).

Postmodern theorists point to such fragmentation to argue that modernism has been replaced by the blurring of image and reality, a preference for parody, kitsch, and pastiche over realist modes of representation. Exciting new scholarship has emerged that explores the fluidity of the boundaries between subjectivity, memory, and history. Theorists, however, have not sufficiently addressed the reconfigurations of realist strategies that continue to secure legitimacy for certain truth claims. The vitality that poststructuralism brought to cultural studies, feminist theory, literary analysis, and other humanities and social science disciplines seems to have stalled in recent years over debates about the relative weight of hegemony and resistance, essentialism versus social construction, and the like. This is in part, we argue, because of an uninterrogated dependence on certain kinds of evidence to document oppression, inequality, and resistance. The January 1996 issue of *PMLA*, for instance, focused on the status of evidence in the humanities. Contributors to this special issue offered rich textual analyses that deconstructed foundationalist views of "real" evidence. Yet even here scholars did not question sufficiently how alternative claims of authentic voices also perpetuate idealist notions of agency and resistance. These essays reveal the tensions created when literary scholars and cultural critics reject conventional evidence yet retain respect for the validity of "authentic" experiences by those traditionally excluded from academic inquiry. Skepticism about methodology and evidence has not provoked enough scholarly attention to the heterogeneous nature of "truth-telling" discourses or how constructions of the "real" complicate the debates between constructionist and foundationalist approaches to experience and subjectivity. This lack of attention perhaps results from a discomfort that many scholars find in the contradictions revealed by these intersections and tensions.

Yet it is imperative that we confront and explore the contradictions between concepts of experience and critiques of evidence. We argue, furthermore, that it is virtually impossible to rethink the "real" without also talking about identity, positionality, and the social location of the author and critic (see essays by Sánchez-Casal and Bose and Varghese in this volume). For example, the identity crisis in feminism, or rather the constructed division between cultural and postmodern feminists, is about differing concepts of experience, authenticity, and the "real." Postmodern feminists argue that early feminists, namely those they label as cultural feminists, have reinforced uncritical notions of authenticity and experience in ways that essentialize women based on white middle-class women's conditions. Early feminists called for greater visibility of women's personal experiences and representation of women's accomplishments. Postmodern feminists share with cultural feminists the laudable goal of rendering visible heretofore hidden or marginalized experiences; however, postmodern feminists have complicated the project by focusing on the socially constructed and discursive nature of experience and agency, thus challenging foundational concerns of cultural feminism (Alcoff; Butler; Grosz; Probyn; Scott). Conversely, many cultural feminists have claimed that postmodern feminists objectify women and invalidate their experiences by seeing bodies and material struggles only as another discursive construct. Further, the categories of "postmodern feminism" and "cultural feminism" are themselves contested, as is the constructed opposition between essentialism and social constructionism (see Fuss).

While feminists have long grappled with questions of agency and victimization, they have only begun to explore how a subject's agency is constituted through the negotiation of the material and discursive domains (See Bordo and Jagger; Ebert; Hennessy; Mohanty; Scarry). Feminist debates about agency have turned toward two contrary but equally problematic patterns. These include the problem of the privileged speaking for rather than with the oppressed, thereby situating oneself as an authenticating presence. Conversely, feminists are beginning to question the assumption that the subject can speak only for him- or herself, a stance that ignores how subjects participate in the construction of subject positions. Linda Alcoff, in "The Problem of Speaking for Others," argues that "truth" is not independent of perspectival location and one's social location is not static but multiple, with degrees of mobility (106). Alcoff proposes that scholars consider not only the social location of the speaker or writer but the discursive context into which the utterance or text is projected. In other words, she suggests that we focus on not only who speaks but how one gets heard. *Haunting Violations* takes up the question of evidence and the question of whose speech acts gain legitimacy. These essays explore the tensions between privileging experiential evidence produced or derived from groups historically silenced and theoretical arguments that stress the socially constructed and discursive nature of experience.

Haunting Violations

Key terms in these debates, such as "real," "experience," "evidence," "authenticity," "identity," and "agency," recur throughout the essays in this volume. Rather than offer uniform definitions, the contributors confront and challenge how certain formulations of these concepts shape and limit our understandings of power and resistance. For instance, how can critics and scholars understand the proliferation of representational forms that rely on "real" experiences for their validity in light of postmodern emphases on language and the deconstruction of identity? In what contexts have material bodies or experiences been uncritically positioned as speaking for the "real"? How do subjects' claims of legitimate voice or authentic experience enable or problematize our understanding of agency?

Contributors to *Haunting Violations* are concerned with how subject positions are constituted through and within historically located discourses. The emphasis on history stems from the belief that the "real" is not a fixed essence but a historically formulated epistemology that responds to localized needs and expectations. Much attention is therefore paid to the material body, which is one of the most privileged sites for the production of reality claims because of the presumption that one is one's body, that identity is expressed through the body. Thus definitions of experience and authenticity frequently presume a coherence between subjectivity and the material body. This is most apparent at moments of crisis, for pain occurs not in the abstract but on or in particular bodies. "Haunting violations" refers to both the belatedness of trauma and how representation recasts those violations. How do we remain focused on the body when we interrogate sexual traumas or racialist policies as historically contingent rather than universalized acts of oppression? Does agency emerge through bodies that retain memories, or does it resituate identities by complicating a victimized status? (See essays by Bow, de Alwis, Hesford, and Kozol in this volume.)

These questions locate identity not only in the body but also in political activism and resistance, which means that autobiographical practices are central to these interrogations. Rather than locate autobiography as the site for reifying individualism, however, the essays in this volume examine discursive interrogations of selfhood, identity, and memory through autobiographical moments that contest divisions between fantasy and reality, fact and fiction, and imagined and documentary histories. In this way, *Haunting Violations* locates agency not only in individual subjectivity but also in social structures, cultural politics, and historical relations of power.

The primacy of the body also explains why visual cultures dominate in claims of unmediated expressions of reality. Media critics have increasingly examined the ambiguous power of visual apparatuses to construct ways of seeing that reproduce and/or challenge social relations. Visual culture scholars now argue that a theory of the gaze that relies only on gender dualism excludes race, sexuality, and other key social relations from analysis (e.g., Gaines; hooks; de Lauretis; Pribram; Williams). Moreover, theories of looking need to account for the historical relations of racial, sexual, class, and other forms of privilege that permit certain gazes, while taboos prohibit other gazes. Jane Gaines, for instance, points out that "framing the question of male privilege and viewing pleasure as the 'right to look' may help us to rethink film theory along more materialist lines, considering, for instance, how some groups have historically had the license to 'look' openly while other groups have 'looked' illicitly." (24–25). Exploring the power of the camera's surveilling gaze to classify social groups, for instance, demonstrates how visual cultures are implicated in such processes as class formation and the colonizing power of the nation state (e.g. Alloula; Graham-Brown; Lutz and Collins; Sekula; Tagg). The essays in *Haunting Violations* study the dialogic relationship between visual and written textual performances and material conditions in order to reexamine nationalist anxieties and agendas in discursive claims of authenticity (see essays by Bose and Varghese and Fernandes in this volume).

As *Calling the Ghosts* exemplifies, moments of trauma or crisis most often reveal our dependence on the "real," the authentic, and the truthful, especially when we seek legitimacy or power in response to that trauma. Paradoxically, it is also traumatic moments that most often destabilize and expose the ideological premises underpinning claims to the "real." Each of the following chapters addresses how a reliance on a concept of the "real" mediates these violations. Rather than dividing by discipline or genre, the juxtaposition of essays challenges traditional disciplinary categories. For instance, history and literature are not construed as oppositional, as if history is an objective enterprise and literature subjective. History like literature is a form of representation, a testimony to the "real," which is not transparent but "'reinscribed, translated, radically rethought and fundamentally worked over by the text'" (Felman and Laub qtd. in Friedman 15). This collection intends to make visible the constructed nature of history writing as well as to expose the meaning-making gaze of the literary critic, film critic, and other cultural workers. Moreover, we foreground the historical variability of concepts of power and resistance.

Several chapters in this volume explore how artists or critics contradictorily reinforce and disrupt the naturalizing processes that secure hegemonic power—be it colonialism and its attendant hierarchies of color; assumptions about the deviance of sexuality that secures patriarchal assumptions that rape is women's fault; or the historical erasure of marginalized people's identities, memories, and communities. In each case, the author explores how a writer or filmmaker attempts to disrupt the power of the "real" through challenges to conventions of documentary, genre, and narrative. Wendy S. Hesford argues that the juxtaposition of "real" and "unreal" narratives in *Rape Stories,* a documentary film about one woman's experience of rape, foregrounds the difficulty of representing trauma known in the body but distanced by the logic of dreams and fantasies. Hesford suggests that the revenge fantasy in *Rape Stories,* in which the "victim" kills the rapist, depicts a truth that is perhaps unrepresentable in the realist mode. She argues that rhetorical shifts like those in the film mediate tensions between symbolic and material domains and push beyond realist representation to explore the fluidity of history, memory, and fantasy. Leela Fernandes compares visual representations of Phoolan Devi's life as a legendary female bandit in India in the film *Bandit Queen* with translations of Phoolan Devi's oral testimony in order to examine the modalities of power and resistance produced in each rhetorical site. The disruptive nature of the film speaks to sexual anxieties in Indian culture, anxieties provoked by general cultural acceptance of the film's ability to "represent" a gang rape. Beyond deconstructing assumptions of transparency, however, Fernandes, like others in this volume, argues that visual images do not merely reflect historical conditions but rather mediate those historical forces to shape social understandings of political struggles.

A number of contributors confront and critique theoretical and methodological uses of "experience" that too often reproduce monolithic assumptions about subjectivity. Susan Sánchez-Casal focuses on how the testimonial *I, Rigoberta Menchú* has been appropriated in the U.S. academy as an example of "true" subaltern discourse. Academic uses of this text that promote it as the "real" voice of the Quiché revolutionary Rigoberta Menchú neglect the cultural politics at work in its production and the historical conflicts between the interests of Latin America's middle-class intellectuals and those of its indigenous communities. Julia Watson also explores autobiographical scripts, arguing that identity persists only in being rewritten, that its stories are multiple and often conflicting, and that the only authenticity lies in the performances of what is already disfigured or lost in origin. Watson's insights into the "trauma of authenticity" shed light on Janet Campbell Hale's autobiographical writings about identity, community, memory, trauma, and genealogy. In *Bloodlines: Odyssey of a Native Daughter,* Watson argues, Hale's act of tracing genealogies crisscrosses over her own migratory subjectivity and the bloodlines of her ancestors to create a complex pattern that is both temporal and spatial and that rewrites identity as culturally and historically specific. Purnima Bose and Linta Varghese similarly explore the relationship between social location and the construction of difference in South Asian feminists' responses to Mira Nair's film *Mississippi Masala.* They argue that the film illustrates the extent to which the "real," as a category of experience for diasporic South Asians, has become a site of contestation over identity. Bose and Varghese point out that South Asian feminist critics of the film position themselves as speaking from and on behalf of a coherent, unified "community." As such, they universalize their experiences as the measure of authentic immigrant reality and construct themselves as native informants.

Essays exploring cultural confrontations between social identities and violent historical traumas address how claims of authenticity negotiate the conflicting needs and expectations borne out of violent and/or traumatic confrontations over sexual, racial, gender, and national identities. Leslie Bow interrogates the contradictory embodiment of the immigrant nationalist who negotiates competing histories amid the complex processes of globalization. She examines Le Ly Hayslip's *When Heaven and Earth Changed Places: A Vietnamese Woman's Journey from War to Peace* in light of its activist agenda and the changing tide of Vietnam War representations. Bow argues that the autobiography relies on a gendered pacifism in order to advocate U.S./Vietnam reconciliation at a strategic moment in which Vietnam became open to Western investment. Hayslip's rendering of her experiences in the war zone as a kind of feminine picaresque, a testimony of sexual trauma, resituates her from traitor to nationalist daughter with a healing message. As a "Third-World" commentary, *When Heaven and Earth Changed Places* uses claims of the authentic other not to indict Western neocolonialism but to make a sentimental plea for increased American involvement in Vietnam's modernization. Malathi de Alwis examines the emergence of the Mothers' Front, a grassroots women's group formed in response to political repression in Sri Lanka in the 1980s. Discourses surrounding women's everyday experiences as mothers, especially their tears, produced the mothers as quintessential embodiments of sentiment. Paradoxically, de Alwis argues, such embodiments in turn authenticated the Mothers' Front protest in ways that both enabled and limited transformative politics. Wendy Kozol examines the consequences of documentary in her study of U.S. government photographs of the incarceration of Japanese and Japanese Americans during World War II. Rather than represent them as the enemy, the photographs project an idealized image that routinely emphasizes the commonalities between the internees and other Americans, a representational strategy that denies the trauma of incarceration. To argue, however, that the subjects of the photographs were merely victims captured by the government's gaze ignores the historical struggles of the internees to reclaim citizenship. Instead, Kozol argues, realistic photographic strategies envision social and political struggles between the government and the internees. Two concluding essays by Patrick Brantlinger and Dion Farquhar engage the essays in this volume in a dialogic manner, addressing their larger implications for future feminist, postcolonial, and cultural studies.

Contributors to *Haunting Violations* examine the interconnectedness of cultural forms and material conditions in order to investigate how notions of agency and authenticity have been put to use in the name of political and social struggles for identity, authority, and legitimacy. Our primary goal for this volume is not simply to render nondominant cultural practices visible but to investigate the cultural practices that "create, sustain, or suppress [differences and] contestations over inclusion and exclusion" (Grossberg, Nelson, and Treichler 12). *Haunting Violations* participates in current efforts to reinvigorate cultural and literary criticism in ways that challenge simplistic binaries between hegemony and resistance by reconsidering how such powerful forces are structured by and dependent upon claims of the "real." We hope, therefore, that readers will view the collection as a strategic intervention into rather than a simple chronicle of cultural practices and discourses. As we say this, we are also profoundly aware that cultural theory rarely facilitates radical politics. As Gerald Graff suggests, "'subversive ideas and imagery [often] become fashionable commodities'" (qtd. in Brantlinger 19). This cautionary note raises the question of how can we, as academics, sustain political activism? Can we make effective links between criticism and political solidarity without romanticizing or privileging our own positions? We need to confront such unsettling questions as we investigate the epistemological power of the "real" to shape our knowledge of trauma and those who resist its violences.

Works Cited

Alcoff, Linda Martín. "The Problem of Speaking for Others." In *Who Can Speak? Authority and Critical Identity.* Ed. Judith Roof and Robyn Wiegman. Urbana: University of Illinois Press, 1995. 97–119.

Alloula, Malek. *The Colonial Harem.* Minneapolis: University of Minnesota Press, 1986.

Bordo, Susan, and Alison Jaggar. *Gender/Body/Knowledge: Feminist Reconstructions of Being and Knowing.* New Brunswick, N.J.: Rutgers University Press, 1989.

Brantlinger, Patrick. *Crusoe's Footprints: Cultural Studies in Britain and America.* New York: Routledge, 1990.

Butler, Judith. *Bodies That Matter: On the Discursive Limits of "Sex."* New York: Routledge, 1993.

De Lauretis, Teresa. *Technologies of Gender: Essays on Theory, Film, and Fiction.* Bloomington: Indiana University Press, 1987.

Ebert, Teresa. "Ludic Feminism, the Body, Performance, and Labor: Bringing Materialism Back into Feminist Cultural Studies." *Cultural Critique* (Winter 1992–93): 5–50.

Friedman, Susan Stanford. "Making History: Reflections on Feminism, Narrative, and Desire." In *Feminism Beside Itself.* Ed. Diane Elam and Robyn Wiegman. New York: Routledge, 1995. 11–53.

Fuss, Diana. *Essentially Speaking: Feminism, Nature, and Difference.* London: Routledge and Kegan Paul, 1989.

Gaines, Jane. "White Privilege and Looking Relations: Race and Gender in Feminist Film Theory." *Screen* 29.4 (1988): 12–27.

Graham-Brown, Sarah. *Images of Women: The Portrayal of Women in Photography of the Middle East, 1860–1950.* London: Quartet Books, 1988.

Grossberg, Lawrence, Cary Nelson, and Paula Treichler. "Cultural Studies: An Intro-
    duction." In *Cultural Studies*. Ed. Lawrence Grossberg, Cary Nelson, and Paula
    Treichler. New York: Routledge, 1992. 1–17.

Grosz, Elizabeth. *Volatile Bodies: Toward a Corporeal Feminism*. Bloomington: Indiana
    University Press, 1994.

Hall, Stuart. "Brave New World." *Socialist Review* 21.1 (1991): 57–64.

Hennessy, Rosemary. *Materialist Feminism and the Politics of Discourse*. New York:
    Routledge, 1993.

hooks, bell. *Black Looks: Race and Representation*. Boston: South End Press, 1992.

Jacobson, Mandy, and Karmen Jelincic. *Calling the Ghosts: A Story about Rape, War,
    and Women*. New York: Women Make Movies, 1996.

Lutz, Catherine A., and Jane L. Collins. *Reading National Geographic*. Chicago: Uni-
    versity of Chicago Press, 1993.

Mercer, Colin. "1968: Periodizing Postmodern Politics and Identity Discussion." In
    Cultural Studies. Ed. Lawrence Grossberg, Cary Nelson, and Paula Treichler. New
    York: Routledge, 1992. 424–38.

Mohanty, Chandra Talpade. "Cartographies of Struggle: Third World Women and the
    Politics of Feminism." In *Third World Women and the Politics of Feminism*. Ed. Chan-
    dra Mohanty, Ann Russo, and Lourdes Torres. Bloomington: Indiana University
    Press, 1991. 1–47.

Pribram, E. Deidre, ed. *Female Spectators: Looking at Film and Television*. London: Verso,
    1988.

Probyn, Elspeth. *Sexing the Self: Gendered Positions in Cultural Studies*. New York:
    Routledge, 1993.

Roof, Judith, and Robyn Wiegman, eds. *Who Can Speak? Authority and Critical Iden-
    tity*. Urbana: University of Illinois Press, 1995.

Scarry, Elaine. *The Body in Pain: The Making and UnMaking of the World*. New York:
    Oxford University Press, 1985.

Scott, Joan. "The Evidence of Experience." *Critical Inquiry* 17 (Summer 1991): 773–97.

Sekula, Allan. "The Body and the Archive." In *The Contest of Meaning: Critical Histories
    of Photography*. Ed. Richard Bolton. Cambridge, Mass.: MIT Press, 1989. 342–88.

Tagg, John. *The Burden of Representation: Essays on Photographies and Histories*. Am-
    herst: University of Massachusetts Press, 1988.

Williams, Linda. "Corporealized Observers: Visual Pornographies and the 'Carnal
    Density of Vision.'" In *Fugitive Images: From Photograph to Video*. Ed. Patrice Petro.
    Bloomington: Indiana University Press, 1995. 3–41.

1

Rape Stories

Material Rhetoric and the Trauma
of Representation

Wendy S. Hesford

One day it occurred to me that I would feel a lot better if I got rid of the rapist. So I started fantasizing about killing the rapist. So what I did in my fantasy is I would get into the elevator and I would see the elevator door close, and there I am, I'm in there. I don't look at the rapist's face, though, but I feel the situation. And then when I see the knife I reach my hand out and slowly get the knife away from him. And then he sees me with the knife, and his eyes are really big and scared. And so I slowly take it and stab him, and then I stab him again, and I stab him and stab him until he is dead. And the elevator is a hellhole of blood-spattered walls. So I look down at him and see that he is dead. And I reach up and push the button for the lobby, and the elevator goes down to the lobby. And when the door opens all the people in my building are in the lobby. And they see me standing there all bloody, and they applaud. And then they help me drag his bloody body into my apartment where I stack up all the parts to dry, and then at my leisure I shave off thin slices and put them in envelopes and mail them to all my friends who have been raped, with my condolences.

This revenge fantasy concludes *Rape Stories,* a 1989 autobiographical documentary film about the trauma of rape and the further trauma incurred through its representation. Margie Strosser, a white rape survivor and American filmmaker, is both the subject and the creator of this film. The film traces her experience of the trauma of rape over a ten-year period, including nightmares, phobias, fear of sex, avoidance of men, and fear of empty public spaces—all characteristics of rape trauma syndrome—and ends with a revenge fantasy in which Strosser recasts the rapist as a victim and herself as the victor.[1] This fantasy is a vivid example of how survivors translate private pain into public memory through the appropriation and reversal of culturally dominant rape scripts that presume women's passivity, helplessness, and desire to be raped. I use the term *scripts* to draw attention to how historical, geopolitical, and cultural struggles, narratives, and fantasies shape the materiality of rape and its representation. Cultural narratives and fantasies are not antithetical to material "reality" but fundamental to social and political life (Taylor 30). The revenge fantasy provides an example of how women negotiate, resist, or reproduce rape scripts with their bodies, actions, and narratives.[2] Furthermore, these negotiations raise questions, which are at the heart of this essay, about the representability of the trauma of rape and the purposes of its representation. What is the relationship between material and representational violence? How are we to understand women's agency in the context of sexual violence? What are the risks of representing trauma and violence against women? In what ways do cultural fantasies of domination reduce women to spectacles of victimization and violence? How are representations of rape, trauma, and women's resistance shaped and authenticated by realist conventions?

The critical challenge as I see it is to avoid reproducing the spectacle of violence or victimization and erasing the materiality of violence and trauma by turning corporeal bodies into texts (Fleckenstein). In "Consuming Trauma; or, The Pleasures of Merely Circulating," Patricia Yaeger cautions academics against the co-optation of the suffering of others and commodification of their stories of pain, trauma, violence, and injustice. Yaeger claims that academics are "busy consuming trauma" and "obsessed with stories that must be passed on, that must not be passed over," but are "drawn to these stories from within an elite culture driven by its own economies" (228). "What is *our* stake in their narratives?" she asks; "What is *their* stake in ours?" (230). Yaeger calls for a criticism "nervous about its own certainties" (245), a criticism that considers the relationship between representation and political praxis (236) and the material effects of the rhetoricization of the body (233). She urges critical self-reflexivity, a kind of "textual anxiety" or "discursive doubt" (241). Similarly, Linda Alcoff and Laura Gray-Rosendale in "Survivor Discourse: Transgression or Recuperation?" expose the risks of confessional modes, the sensationalism of survivor's stories, and their potential recuperation by those in positions of power (215). Recuperation can be subverted, they argue, by presenting survivors as subjects, dismantling the victim-expert split, abolishing the bifurcation between experience and analysis, and creating spaces for survivors to theorize their own experience and talk back (215).

Given the dangers of commodification and the risks of retraumatization, how are critics and survivors (roles not exclusive of one another) to proceed? For instance, does the revenge fantasy in *Rape Stories* prefigure Yaeger's warning? Does the fantasy textualize and turn the rapist into a figure? Does the pleasure with which Strosser conveys the fantasy turn her own trauma into a commodity, converting pain into pleasure? The fantasy could be read as a refusal to reproduce images of women as spectacles of victimization. Instead, Strosser's imagined possession and distribution of the rapist's body makes a spectacle of women's revenge. However, like Margaret Atwood's short story "Rape Fantasies," which challenges dominant rape scripts that presume women want to be raped (Jacobsen 74) yet casts the reader as an ally with the listening "you," the potential rapist (VanSpanckeren 82), the revenge fantasy prompts critical anxiety about how resistant representations may reproduce the spectacle of violence by casting viewers into voyeuristic roles. Strosser's imagined distribution of thin pieces of the rapist's dead body among other rape survivors not only speaks to communitarian notions of women's agency and spectatorship (a pattern I discuss in the pages that follow) but also attests to the circulation and consumption of women's trauma.

Notwithstanding Strosser's strategic appropriation of the violence of rhetoric, the revenge fantasy makes me uneasy; it prompts "textual anxiety," a critical nervousness. Strosser's fantasy may challenge dominant rape scripts that construe women as helpless and rewrite women as agents of aggression and anger; however, her counternarrative presents a curious inevitability, an element of futility, which presumes a victim—a raped female body. Despite its cathartic value and reconstruction of the victim as a survivor, the fantasy lacks "discursive doubt"; it does not question the notion that women will be raped. The fantasy is predicated on a cultural rape script that assigns unequal status to women; women are construed as victims and men as ever-threatening rapists (Marcus 392). The revenge fantasy thus illustrates how the language of rape and dominant structures of gendered subjectivity continue to speak through women's resistance and how rape marks the female subject physically and psychologically. As Elaine Scarry says in *The Body in Pain*, "even the elementary act of naming this most interior of events [rape] entails an immediate mental somersault out of the body into the external social circumstances [and discourses] that can be pictured as having caused the hurt" (16). In other words, Strosser's fantasy shows how "rape is not only scripted, [but how] it also scripts" (Marcus 391).

The fantasy of retribution, which Strosser conveys on screen with a sense of pleasure and a subversive smile, sharply contrasts with the austere and realist rendition of the rape that opens the film. Strosser was raped late one evening in the elevator of her apartment building in 1979. As she tells her story, claims are made for its truth-value and historical veracity. "Part of the reason why I wanted to make this film," Strosser explains, was because "I wanted to keep . . . the facts straight, what I did and didn't do." The confessional nature of Strosser's direct address and the handheld camera and head-shots make the story seem all the more "real." The realist narrative purportedly captures a historical truth, whereas the fantasy presumably reveals a psychological truth. The presumption informing both narratives, however, is that by rendering bodily pain and trauma tellable, the survivor can undo "the grasp of the perpetrator and [reestablish] the social dimension of the self lost in the midst of violation" (Culbertson 179). The revenge fantasy could be seen as the equivalent of the talking cure, a speech act that, like an unconscious testimony of a dream, presumably gives access to a psychic reality, in this case the trauma of rape.

The meaning of the term *trauma* has shifted in common and clinical usage from a "stress or blow that may produce disordered feelings or behavior" to a "state or condition produced by such a stress or blow" (Erikson 184). In other words, the term is more often used to refer to the state of mind that ensues from an injury than to the blow itself. The fantasy can be read as an articulation of trauma—a devastating and not-worked-through experience, the more common use of the term—and as an experience lived belatedly at the level of its unspeakable truth (the more specialized notion of trauma in psychoanalytic theory). The fantasy thus beckons viewers into the territory of psychoanalysis to consider the "textual anxieties" surrounding the representation of trauma. One might say that Strosser restages the trauma of rape in order to control what cannot literally be expressed, that which is "not known in words, but in the body" (Culbertson 170). The fantasy situates the viewer as a witness to the "paradox of the distance of one's own experience" (170). In this sense, the fantasy figures trauma's untranslatability, its resistance to yet reliance upon cultural scripting, and thereby illustrates how trauma is imbricated with the imaginary and symbolic and how it "responds to certain expectations of genre and structure" (183). *Rape Stories* thus brings to light the disciplinary and cultural frames available to women to express the painful and personal violation of rape and its traumatic aftermath. Despite structural differences, both the realist narrative and the fantasy implicate the viewer in the "realness" of the narrator's truth through conventions of self-disclosure. *Rape Stories* participates in the feminist proclamation of survivor discourse as a political act against violence—a conception of the personal prevalent in early feminist literature on violence and consciousness-raising groups wherein women's autobiographical stories were positioned as authenticating truths.

Survivor narratives do expose oppressive material conditions, violence, and trauma, give voice to silent histories, help shape public consciousness about violence against women, and thus alter history's narrative. Moreover, there is strong evidence that the process of telling one's story and writing about personal trauma can be essential elements of recovery and that in addition to the integration of the self fractured through intimate violence, such acts also may have lasting effects on the human immune system (Pennebaker). However, as

Linda Alcoff and Laura Gray-Rosendale have perceptively shown, the transgressive effects of the "realness" of survivor discourse are diminished when rescripted by dominant paradigms that code trauma's belatedness through rigid gender ideologies and cultural anxieties over changing gender roles and race relations. For example, the "realness" (believability) of survivor speech is undermined by the categorization of "survivor speech as mad, as evidence of women's or children's hysterical or mendacious tendencies, or even as testimony to women's essential nature as helpless victims in need of patriarchal protection" (205). Survivor narratives often get caught up in discursive practices (legal, religious, and therapeutic) that further individualize violence and trauma and in so doing prompt passive empathy or judgment from viewers rather than a stance of critical witnessing (Boler). For example, the American mass media tends to focus on victims' and perpetrators' psychological states rather than on the sociological, political, and material forces that facilitate and sustain violence. Despite the risks of self-disclosure, however, survivor narratives can affirm oppositional positions. Realist discourses such as autobiography and documentary film are not inherently hegemonic or, for that matter, unequivocally empowering. Rather, they are used in ways that reinforce particular moral, social, and political projects. As Jani Sawicki puts it, "'any practice is co-optable and is capable of becoming a source of resistance'" (qtd. in Smith and Watson 17).[3]

At the heart of the critical project of constructing a material rhetoric of violence and trauma is the crisis of representation prompted in part by the poststructuralist argument that there is no unmediated access to the "real" (historical or psychic reality, categories that are fundamentally interdependent). The postmodern project importantly calls into question the grand narrative of history by displacing realism. As Diane Elam puts it, "realism . . . ceases to be the privileged form of representation for the 'real,' for historical reality" (14). If the task of realism has been a nostalgic recovery of the past, as Elam asserts, how then are we to understand survivors' representations of trauma in the postmodern world? The revenge fantasy in *Rape Stories* provides a partial answer, in that it reveals the underlying paradox of trauma and of realism itself. As Cathy Caruth puts it, "trauma . . . is always the story of a wound that cries out, that addresses us in the attempt to tell us of a reality or truth that is not otherwise available. This truth, in its delayed appearance and its belated address, cannot be linked only to what is known, but also to what remains unknown in our very actions and our language" (4). Strosser invokes certain narrative frames to describe rape trauma, and yet these frames also remind us of those memories that are without language or image (Culbertson 176). In other words, the fantasy reminds us of the limits of narratability.

Together, the framing trauma narratives of *Rape Stories*—the realist version and the fantasy—anticipate a dialogue between what have historically been perceived as antagonistic categories and traditions, namely the materialist "real" (historical reality) and the psychoanalytic "Real" (that which resists symbolization).[4] Thus in formulating a material rhetoric of violence, trauma, and agency we must recognize how survivor narratives (visual and verbal) re-present trauma. In addition, we need to consider how these representations are sustained by realist conventions of documentation and interpretation and the intimate and institutional networks that uphold them (Gilmore 68–69).[5] My goal in this essay is not to look at survivors' representations as mirrors of historical or psychic realities but to consider how realist strategies authenticate survivors' representations. I use the term *realist* in this context to refer to conventions and strategies of representation that signify that which is deemed "true" and presume a measure of objectivity. Thus the "textual anxiety" that sustains this project is the desire to rescue the concept of agency from the antihumanist assaults of poststructuralism in ways that do not configure agency outside of culture and its discourses but reconfigure personal and political agency as embodied negotiations and material enactments of cultural scripts and ideologies. For example, in order to account for the pain that women endure to claim agency in the context of sexual violence, we need to understand rape as both a material and discursive site of struggle for cultural power.

The critical engagement of survivors' representations requires more than "discursive doubt"; it demands an analysis of the material effects of the rhetoricization of the body. As Kristie Fleckenstein puts it, "Reducing materiality to signifiers limits our ability to formulate, recognize, and challenge cultural truths and material conditions" for "It is only *through* the body that competing (con)textualities materialize" (284). The concept of "material rhetoric" highlights the discursivity of the material world as well as the materiality of discourse (Cloud), challenges the idea that corporeal bodies are overdetermined by discourse,[6] and prompts consideration of how individual and collective struggles for agency are located at the complex intersections of the discursive and material politics of everyday life. Material rhetoric enables us to understand how rape survivors' self-representations involve a process of negotiation with prevailing cultural rape scripts and practices. It is precisely because of the risk of producing yet another promise or claim of liberation articulated solely as a cultural politics of representation that I want to retain a materialist edge, while not dismissing the centrality of language and representation in struggles for power. More particularly, material rhetoric is critical for articulating the systematic nature of violence against women and for finding the gaps through which agency can be gained.

Devi's own attempt to stop the film from being distributed and screened in India. Although she had consented to the making of the film, she had not anticipated the visually graphic representation of rape—a portrayal that would violate her sense of honor in the context of hegemonic social norms in India that depict rape victims as figures of shame and dishonor. Moreover, Phoolan Devi's petition accused Kapur of factual misrepresentation and the endangerment of her life since he had depicted her participation in a massacre of upper-caste landlords (*thakurs*) in the village of Behmai.[13] In response to public criticism, Kapur argued that resistance to his film was a manifestation of a middle-class morality that sanctioned public silence about rape. Kapur's position was further complicated by a battle with the Indian state, which attempted to censor nudity in the film's rape scenes.

The film and autobiography raise a number of questions regarding the modalities of power and resistance that are set in motion in each case. For instance, how do they attempt to subvert hegemonic forms of morality, state power, and the policing of women's sexuality in public discourses of women? In what ways do the film and autobiography disrupt or reproduce conventional Western stereotypes of "traditional" Indian society? Does Kapur's representation inadvertently recolonize Phoolan Devi by packaging her as a rape victim? Both representations of Phoolan Devi's life raise complex issues regarding translation, authenticity, and depictions of the "real." My central theoretical endeavor is to contribute to a form of feminist "critical realism."[14] Such a project rests on a recognition of trans/national material, historical, and political relations of inequality and entails a mode of interpretation that includes an analysis of the international political economy of the production and consumption of cultural texts. The first section presents an interpretive reading that locates the film in terms of form and substantive strategies of representation within trans/national relationships of inequality. However, the interpretive dimension of a feminist critical realist approach also demonstrates that such material structures do not predetermine or produce a singular regime of the power effects of these texts in question. The second section examines how the film contains counterhegemonic possibilities within the context of the Indian national public sphere. The third section demonstrates that, while the autobiography and film operate within similar materially based trans/national circuits of power, the autobiography's form and rhetorical strategies are able to disrupt trans/national and national hegemonic discursive frames of reference.[15]

My intention in juxtaposing the film and autobiography is not to make the argument that Phoolan Devi's self-presentation in textual form is more accurate or authentic than Kapur's cinematic representation of her life. My argument—that the contrast between the film and autobiography does not rest on the measurement of the degrees of "truth in representation" but on the contrasting power effects of the texts in question—attempts to move feminist debates on "realism" away from a binary opposition between the politics of representation and methodologies of discourse analysis on the one hand and the politics of authenticity and methodologies of empiricism on the other hand. My methodological approach does not aim to "measure" audience responses in different national contexts but to engage in a transdisciplinary analysis that bridges dichotomies such as structure/representation, political economy/discourse, and real/fictional. My conceptualization of "audience" refers to the national and international cartographies of power within which texts circulate rather than empirically defined audiences at the local level.[16] I use a reading of the two forms of representation of Phoolan Devi as "India's bandit queen" to suggest ways to move toward a trans/national feminist mode of cultural interpretation that recasts the dilemmas of difference, representation, and the "real" from a static problem of untranslatability into a question of the performance of the real through strategies of representation—strategies that are always contingent on the form of representation, the context of reading, and the tactics of rhetoricity deployed in the texts.

Consuming "India's Bandit Queen": Transforming Modernist Authenticity into Cultural Capital in a Postmodern Age

In her essay "Where Have All the Natives Gone?" Rey Chow analyzes a series of discursive and textual forms that attempts to recuperate an originary authentic subject who can escape the structure of imperialist discourse but instead results in the re/production of the objectified figure of the "native" other. Chow examines Malek Alloula's book *The Colonial Harem,* which attempts to produce an anti-imperialist narrative through the presentation of a series of postcards of Algerian women that the French sent home during the colonial period. While Chow acknowledges that Alloula's point is to mark the French colonial construction of the Oriental woman, she argues that "because Alloula is intent on capturing the essence of the colonizer's discourse as a way to retaliate against his enemy, his own discourse coincides much more closely with the enemy's than with the woman's" (40). Her discussion raises critical questions regarding the political implications of witnessing and redepicting forms of power and domination that apply to the production, commodification, and distribution of Phoolan Devi's life history through film and autobiography. Such questions are further complicated by the complexities involved in an analysis of the politics of representing the subaltern woman in a global context of multinational cultural production.

These questions do not signal a call to return to a romanticized notion that presumes that the subaltern woman must speak her own voice and represent herself but ask instead to contextualize depictions of the "real" stories of subaltern oppression within international relations of power that unfold through complex circuits of the production and consumption of the "Third-World subaltern woman." Recent research has begun to analyze the power effects of the recent rise in consumer demand for the "real" stories of Third-World women in the form of testimonials, autobiographies, and documentary film (Grewal and Kaplan; Trinh, *When the Moon*). The production of the figure of India's bandit queen provides a significant site for an interrogation of the production and consumption of the modernist authenticity of the "Third-World subaltern woman" within the shifting, fragmented, and destablized moment of postmodernity in late-capitalist nation-states in the West. I am deliberately deploying the categories "West" and "Third World" in order to foreground the trans/national relationships of power that have governed these constructions. My point is to demonstrate the contradictory power effects of representations without blurring the material historical processes of colonization that have governed relations between the First and Third Worlds (Mohanty; Said; Spivak, "Can the Subaltern Speak?"). My analysis suggests that these processes are marked by three critical characteristics: (1) a process of collaboration that simultaneously marks and seeks to erase relations of power between the First and Third Worlds, (2) a production of a binary opposition between the modern and the traditional, one that temporally places the Third World outside of the historical moment of postmodernity in the West, and (3) moments of subversion within such textual forms that may disrupt or complicate these oppositions.

The film *Bandit Queen* and the autobiography *I, Phoolan Devi* represent in different ways a collaborative project between the First and Third Worlds.[17] While *Bandit Queen* was funded and produced by a British television company, the film cannot easily be classified as a "British film" since it was directed, produced, and shot in India with an all-Indian cast.[18] The autobiography *I, Phoolan Devi* was written on the basis of Phoolan Devi's oral narration of her life story. The text was translated and written by two collaborators since Phoolan Devi is nonliterate and does not speak English. The translation and writing of Phoolan Devi's life story occur through a form of collaboration that defies a clear-cut classification of the book as either "Western" or "Indian." I want to suggest, following the work of Trinh T. Minh-ha, that this very mark of collaboration, which appears initially to interrupt the First World/Third World binary, is a central means for the production and consumption of a modernist Third-World authenticity. As Trinh argues, "Factual authenticity relies heavily on the Other's words and testimony. To authenticate a work, it becomes therefore most important to prove or make evident how this Other has participated in the making of his/her own image" (*When the Moon* 67). The publisher's note at the end of Phoolan Devi's autobiography states that she signed each page of the manuscript to verify and authenticate its truth. This process conforms to the kind of testimonial literature that Carr argues "tracks the international flow of capital, First World/Third World relations and the locus of the borderland of the testimonial" (157).[19] However, the production and extraction of value through the commodification of Phoolan Devi's life story in the postcolonial period departs from the ways colonial discourses constructed the Other. While the French postcards that Alloula compiles from the colonial period presented an objectified view of a silent native woman,[20] in the postcolonial period the native subaltern woman must not only speak her own voice but also be seen speaking in her voice (Trinh, *When the Moon*). Oral testimony and visual spectacle function together in the production of an authentic, realist representation of the "Third-World subaltern woman." The establishment of a collaborative relationship of material production legitimizes this voice in two ways. First, a clear collaboration that can be traced back to India consolidates the local and particular authenticity of the text. Second, an acknowledgment of the boundaries of the Indian nation-state subtly conceals the possibility of a neocolonial relationship that might lurk beneath the collaboration. Phoolan Devi cannot be transformed simply into the bandit queen, she must be represented as "India's bandit queen."[21]

Although the collaboration between First and Third World in making *Bandit Queen* signifies the production of and desire for a Third-World authenticity, the relationships of power inherent in this collaboration are not limited to the material relations of production; they are also simultaneously recoded by strategies of representation. Such representational strategies require the measure of Third-World authenticity to signify a form of difference as otherness. However, this difference can only be produced through an implicit sameness between First and Third Worlds, one that rests on a set of shared humanistic, universal values. This sameness in difference unfolds in *Bandit Queen* through the deployment of images of the modern and the traditional. My aim here is not merely to rehearse a deconstruction of the modernity/tradition binary but to demonstrate how the deployment of "difference" in the film serves to recode trans/national relationships of power. The film casts cultural tradition as the force that explains the caste and gender oppression Phoolan Devi endures and marks this oppression as peculiarly Indian and "different" from the West. Meanwhile, the film continually juxtaposes this tradition with more familiar images that link Indian society with a failed attempt to reproduce universalistic narratives of democracy and modernity. While the sameness of Indian society is marked by such narratives of progress, this sameness is always constructed through difference as otherness (culture) and difference as inferiority (failed modernity).[22]

Bandit Queen casts Phoolan Devi's life story in terms of the problem of "Indian culture" through a series of images that portray the intersection between caste and patriarchy in the everyday life of rural northern India. The film attempts to present an incisive indictment of the reproduction of caste and gender hierarchies in a series of social institutions ranging from marriage and family, community life, state (in the form of the local village government and police), and even the political structure of the dacoit gangs in the northern Indian state of Uttar Pradesh. However, Kapur's depiction inadvertently draws its explanatory power of such social hierarchies from an essentialized conception of Indian tradition. The film highlights particular forms of traditional culture, such as Phoolan Devi's child marriage, caste-based segregation,[23] and passive villagers, which conform well with the Western imagination of oppressive Indian traditions (Mani, "Contentious"). The film juxtaposes such hierarchies with an individualized view of Phoolan Devi's rebelliousness. While the film casts Phoolan Devi as a heroic woman striving against her culture, the audience is not provided with any context in which to place her actions; her rebelliousness is depicted as an aberration within a society that otherwise consists of active oppressors and passive victims.

The difference of gender and caste that marks the boundaries between First and Third World in *Bandit Queen* is also carefully constructed through a framework of sameness that can be used to measure Indian society against the West. This sameness rests on a familiar narrative of modernity that is juxtaposed with the representation of "tradition" in the film. Images of idyllic rural scenery and the rough savage scenes of the ravines and desert where Phoolan Devi and other members of the dacoits are in hiding are juxtaposed with stereotypical urban images of crowds and chaos. Shots of Phoolan Devi bringing her lover and gang leader Vikram to a doctor in Kanpur, one of the major cities in Uttar Pradesh, present a chaotic city in the middle of a public festival with burgeoning crowds and blaring music from a marching band. Moreover, the film presents images that do not merely serve as signifiers of the modern encroaching on a traditional India but as markers of a failed modernity. For instance, all characters representing the modern Indian nation-state, ranging from policemen to doctors to state government officials, are depicted as violent or corrupt. Phoolan Devi is raped by policemen, the doctor who treats Vikram asks for a bribe in order to pay for his daughter's dowry, and the politicians and government officials link their plans to allow Phoolan Devi to surrender alive to the fact that the lower castes vote. These images serve two related functions in the film. First, they serve as signifiers of modernity and democracy that are familiar to Western audiences and therefore facilitate the process of translating Phoolan Devi's "Indian" experience into a language that is comprehensible to Western audiences. Second, the association of such images with corruption and violence clearly projects an Indian modernity marked by a failure to achieve Western standards of progress and democracy. This mark of failure brings us back to the circulation of cultural capital encoded within relationships of power between the First and Third Worlds that shapes the international production and consumption of India's bandit queen. The film does not merely produce an Indian otherness (the traditional) that is dissociated from the West but implicitly reproduces a relationship between India and the West by presenting Indian modernity as a measure of inferiority and failure.

The failure of Indian modernity and democracy has specific political implications within the context of the British production and consumption of the film, given the historical relationship of colonialism. In the world of *Bandit Queen*, Phoolan Devi is trapped by a nation that has neither been able to discard the remnant of its oppressive cultural traditions nor to live up to the modern democratic institutions and traditions that India inherited through the legacies of colonialism. This double bind is depicted in the film by a visual strategy that denotes critical stages of devastation in Phoolan Devi's life by images of travel. The pull of tradition is marked by Phoolan Devi being forcedly taken away on a boat, shot against idyllic images of village India. A journey by boat signifies the first tragic event in the film as she is taken away from her home by her husband. Later in the film, when she is kidnapped by an upper-caste dacoit, she is beaten and taken by boat to the village of Behmai where she is gang raped and paraded naked in front of the entire village in a public demonstration of the brutal violent reprisal for her transgression of caste and gender hierarachies. Such rurally based images of travel are juxtaposed with shots of a speeding train, a classic symbol of modernity that signifies the force of the modern nation-state weighing against Phoolan Devi. A shot of the train prefigures a scene in which Phoolan Devi is arrested and raped by the police in her village after she is falsely accused of burglary by the village district head. Later in the film, when Phoolan Devi's own gang is being hunted down with the full scale of the state government, the shot preceding her surrender to the government is marked by her lying in a crumpled state by the tracks as a train passes by. Such images of movement—whether "regressive" as she is captured and taken by boat back to the confines of oppressive caste and gender traditions or "progressive" as the train marks the coercive recuperation of Phoolan Devi by the Indian nation-state—frame Phoolan

Devi as a nonconsenting victim of the modern and the traditional. These movements, backward into time into the world of repressive tradition or forward into the chronological narrative of a violent, corrupt nation-state, are cast into a singular timeless model of violence and failure.

My analysis suggests that the transformation of difference into otherness and inferiority is achieved not merely through the content of the images that Kapur deploys but also through the form of these depictions. The binary oppositions such as modern/traditional, difference/sameness, and First/Third World are specifically constructed and managed through a trope that interweaves a politics of gender with the visualization of violence. Mainstream Western representations in film, television, and newspapers have a long history of representing the Third World as a site of violence and disorder—whether in relation to ancient primordial religious, tribal, and ethnic conflicts or revolution or state repression (Chow, "Violence"). Such images link the production and consumption of a "Third-World" authenticity to the spectacle of violence. The violent, disordered, and repressive Third World is thus juxtaposed against the civilized, orderly, and democratic West. As Rey Chow has argued in her discussion of U.S. representations of the Tiananmen Square massacre, this is the "cross-cultural syndrome in which the 'Third World,' as the site of the 'raw' material, that is, 'monstrosity,' is produced for the surplus-value of spectacle, entertainment and spiritual enrichment for the 'First World'" (84). Chow's suggestion that we confront "the complicity of our technology, which does much more than enable us to 'see'" (83) points to the ways in which the realist form in cinematic representations can be located historically within the wider genre of the ethnographic film that reproduced relations of race and colonialism through representations of the "primitive," "savage," and "native" (Rony).[24] *Bandit Queen* reworks this genre to some extent, since the depiction of violent rape also foregrounds personalized injury that may invoke empathy. Nevertheless, there is an interesting parallel between the empathy presumed between anthropologist and "native" on the one hand and audience and victimized subaltern on the other hand; more significantly, in both cases empathy is not inconsistent with the power-laden questions of context I am foregrounding. The convergence of specific strategies of representation in the film, the historical tradition of the genre of the ethnographic film, and the political economy of the production and consumption of texts impel *Bandit Queen* to recodify power-laden boundaries between the First and Third Worlds.[25]

Such processes are of particular significance for feminist analysis when the spectacle consists of the image of violence against the "subaltern Third-World woman." I am suggesting that a feminist project of representing violence against women contains within it the potential for reinvoking Orientalist narratives, in particular by marking the Third World as the naturalized site of an unrestrained violence.[26] In *Bandit Queen,* the representation of rape results in a gendered transformation of the Third World into a spectacle of violence. Recent feminist research has demonstrated the ways in which the construction of the paradigm of the Third-World woman as victim serves as the means for the production of a colonial relationship between First and Third World (Mohanty). Building on this research, I argue that such power effects of textual representations are produced not only through representations of Third-World women but also through particular constructions of Third-World men and masculinities. The construction of sexual difference through the deployment of particular meanings of masculinity provides a central mechanism for the articulation of otherness and inferiority of the Third World. In *Bandit Queen,* the oppression of tradition and the failure of modernity in contemporary India are translated through the representation of the intrinsic violence and abnormality of Indian masculinity. Consider the parameters of "good" and "bad" masculinity portrayed in the film. The "bad" men are either violent rapists (upper-caste men, dacoits, police) or weak, passive characters such as the rural villagers who consent to such violence. Meanwhile, the "good" masculine figures are depicted through two characters. The first, Phoolan Devi's lover Vikram, is a dacoit who has transgressed the boundaries of the normal in Indian society. The second, Phoolan Devi's cousin, who helps her at points of crisis in her life, is presented as a bumbling, comic character. More significantly, he embodies a deficient masculinity because he can neither occupy his traditional role as patriarchal figure (he is bullied by his wife and by Phoolan Devi) nor save Phoolan Devi.[27] My reading of *Bandit Queen* shows how a critique of an oppressive culture based on gender and caste hierarchy recodes colonial constructions of otherness and inferiority. The interpretation I have presented presumes an audience located within the West. The effects of the film's textual power shift in important ways when contextualized within hegemonic national discourses in the contemporary Indian bourgeois public sphere.

Disrupting the National Bourgeois Public Sphere: Sexuality, Representation, and Middle-Class Morality in India

The release and distribution of *Bandit Queen* resulted in a sharp public debate centered on the representation of rape in the film. The film presents five incidences of rape in increasing degrees of graphic violence, beginning with the rape of the eleven-year-old Phoolan Devi and culminating with an extended scene of the gang rape of Phoolan Devi in Behmai village. Kapur's use of nudity in representing the rapes is particularly unusual in the context of existing genres of popular Hindi and regional cinema.[28] The controversy surrounding this representation was exacerbated by Phoolan Devi's attempt to stop the film from being screened in India. Her motives were interpreted and represented through widely varying media reports and speculations, ranging from whether she had been paid enough for the film to whether she had been sufficiently consulted during its production. A leading Indian feminist writer, Arundhati Roy, charged Kapur with not consulting Phoolan Devi about the film's representation of her life. A central trope of these discussions was Phoolan Devi's reported opposition to the graphic portrayal of the rapes, as well as her opposition to how the film distorted facts of her life (for instance, by portraying her as the dacoit Vikram's lover). These contestations were further complicated by the Indian state's attempt to censor the film because it contained nudity. Following the film's release, the controversy continued, as reports of male audiences cheering during the rape scenes circulated in television and newspaper reports.[29] Yet at the same time the film was screened with special showings for women-only audiences, opening up spaces for the production of a women's public sphere.[30]

Within the context of the national debate over *Bandit Queen* in India, I argue that the film produced a set of contradictory effects that disrupted hegemonic social codes regarding sexuality and rape within the Indian bourgeois public sphere and reproduced relationships of power that re/colonized Phoolan Devi through the appropriation of her life experiences. In response to the controversy over his representations of rape, Kapur argued that his intention had been to represent rape as a nonsexual act without any hint of sensuality.[31] For instance, in the graphic depiction of Phoolan Devi being raped by the upper-caste dacoit Babu Gujjar, the rape is presented in daylight and the only nudity shown involves the male actor. Kapur argued that although the actual rape had taken place at night he depicted the scene in daylight to avoid any sensual connotations associated with darkness or nighttime. Furthermore, none of the rape scenes depict any female nudity; the only nude shot of the actress playing Phoolan Devi is the scene of the incident when she is paraded naked in Behmai village after she is gang raped. Kapur's representation departs significantly from the usual representations of rape in popular Hindi films, which are generally highly sexualized representations even though they do not include nudity. Typically, the film's hero rescues the heroine from assault. The successive rapes in *Bandit Queen* form a narrative of spiraling violence. The last incident of the gang rape depicts Phoolan Devi being beaten until she is barely recognizable and unable to speak. The representation of rape as a brutal act of violence disrupts public silence on rape and violence against women in India. This disruption is particularly significant given the ways in which public outcries over rape are usually constructed in terms of the loss of honor of the victim and her community (Kumar). The film, in contrast, presents a disturbing vision of the violence the woman experiences. Although for Western audiences *Bandit Queen* reproduces the trans/national power effects in conforming to realist strategies of representation, within the national context of India the film breaks from the conventional strategies of popular films.[32] The strategies of representation in *Bandit Queen* contain counterhegemonic moments when viewed in the context of the Indian national public sphere.

These counterhegemonic effects of *Bandit Queen* in the Indian public sphere are reinforced by the film's representation of rape within a discursive framework that interprets violence against women in terms of the intersections of caste and gender. The film presents a series of images in which upper-caste men in Phoolan Devi's village make remarks that interpret her act of leaving her husband as a sign of her sexual availability and promiscuity. Such scenes set the stage for the events leading to the first rape after she has run away from her husband, setting in motion the subsequent events in her life. The film's narrative interprets Phoolan Devi's final transgression of the law as the bandit queen as stemming from the violent reprisals she faced for her transgressions of gender and caste boundaries. In doing so, the film interrupts the naturalization of caste and gender boundaries within contemporary India. The film calls attention to the ways in which single women are constructed as a sexual and social threat to the moral and social order within India (Fernandes, "Beyond Public"). Kapur's representation also demonstrates that the construction of the boundaries of gender is always contingent on the politics of caste. Phoolan Devi is repeatedly assaulted not only because she has defied hegemonic social norms by leaving her husband but because of a caste-based construction of sexual accessibility where upper-caste men often assert violent sexual access to lower-caste women. Such counterhegemonic effects of the film are also produced by a different subversion of sexual codes in a scene in which Phoolan Devi takes the sexual initiative with her lover, Vikram. The image portrays Phoolan Devi positioned on top of him, making love to him in a sexually assertive manner. As several Indian feminists have argued, the scene represents a positive portrayal of Phoolan Devi's sexuality, one that moves beyond rape, violence, and victimhood.[33]

These counterhegemonic possibilities subvert a common narrative linking the middle classes, consumption practices of cultural forms such as films, and the Indian nation-state. Recent scholars and media critics in India have begun to call attention to the way in which cinema as "an institution of modernity" (Vasudevan 2809) plays a central role in the nationalist imagination. Tejaswini Niranjana has argued that recent popular films have begun to cultivate "an audience primarily composed of the newly articulate, assertive and self-confident middle class that is also claiming for itself the spaces of nation and secularism premised on Hindutva" (79). Niranjana links the production of this new middle-class audience to several interwoven political processes. On one level, the middle classes are presented in a celebratory fashion, invoking images of new lifestyles and consumption practices associated with recent policies of economic liberalization in India (Niranjana; Fernandes, "Nationalizing"). On another level, the "'ordinary' middle-class person is suddenly inserted into a national conflict" and is then projected as the means for restoring or recuperating the modern, secular Indian nation-state (Niranjana 79). In this process, the future of India is reimagined through a lens that rests on the interwoven paradigms of modernity, nationalism, state power, and consumer capitalism.

Kapur's *Bandit Queen* contests such narratives in a number of complex ways. The film disrupts the production of new hegemonic cultural images of India's successful transformation into a consumer capitalist nation competing in a global economy (Fernandes, "Nationalizing"). By foregrounding economic and caste inequalities in rural areas in Uttar Pradesh, the film in effect disrupts the narrative that assumes that the Indian nation has in fact modernized and is now synonymous with the urban middle classes. *Bandit Queen* marks the social fragments that have historically been excluded from the Indian nation as materially and temporally present within the "new" liberalizing Indian nation.

The film produces another narrative that is counterhegemonic in the Indian national context: the means for social justice in the film lie beyond the boundaries of the legal democratic institutions (such as the courts and police) of the Indian state. With this narrative, the film departs from the conventional genre of popular crime films that, as Ravi Vasudevan argues, invoke middle-class anxieties regarding crime while containing these anxieties in an "acceptable narrative of nationalist inspiration, familial re-location and class reproduction" (2813). Phoolan Devi is unable to receive justice through such instruments of India's democracy. The intersections of caste, class, and gender hierarchy produce a situation in which social justice is contingent on Phoolan Devi's transformation into an "outlaw" (Ghosh). In effect, justice and democracy ironically become two poles of a binary opposition.

While *Bandit Queen* subverts hegemonic social codes in contemporary India in many ways, the film's oppositional endeavor nevertheless raises unsettling questions regarding Phoolan Devi's own location in relation to the representation. The fact that she attempted to prevent the screening of the film in India raises the question of whether Kapur's counterhegemonic strategies of representation inadvertently re/colonize Phoolan Devi and position her within new hierarchies of power. Such questions require a focus on Phoolan Devi's location and agency within the politics of representation. I will consider these issues by juxtaposing the film with the depiction of Phoolan Devi's life in the testimonial *I, Phoolan Devi*.

Agency, Authenticity, and Intersectionality

Phoolan Devi's effort to block the film's screening cannot be understood simply as a form of consent to existing silence on rape in the hegemonic public sphere in India. On the contrary, her opposition to the film signals significant paradoxes in the representation of violence against women and the dangers of reproducing a paradigm of victimhood through this representation. The film's emphasis on rape shifts Phoolan Devi from a legendary figure within the Indian context—a woman dacoit, both heroic and notorious, who stole from the rich and distributed wealth to the poor—to the status of a rape victim. The film's presentation of rape as an explanation for her transformation into an outlaw transforms rape into the sole motivation for her subsequent actions. This presents a sharp contrast to the autobiography, which deals at length with a complex conception of social justice that motivated Phoolan Devi's numerous raids on various villages. In her vision of justice, resistance was not merely a retaliation against her own personal experiences of violence but also against the exploitation of lower-caste villagers by upper-caste landlords. Consider the following passage, which begins with Phoolan Devi describing her method of castrating men who were rumored to have raped lower-caste women:

> I heard it often enough. That's why, whenever I heard it, I crushed the serpent they used to torture women. I dismembered them. It was my vengeance, and the vengeance of all women. In the villages of my region there was no justice other than the *lathi* [stick], where *mallahs* (boatmen caste) were the slaves of the *thakurs* [landowning caste]. I dealt out justice. "Who stole from you? Who beat you? Who took your food? Who said you couldn't use the well? Who stole your cattle? Who raped your daughter or your sister or your wife?" The guilty one was brought before my court. He was forced to suffer what he had made others suffer. (370)

In contrast, the only depiction of social justice in the film that does not involve Phoolan Devi's own personal revenge against men who raped her is a scene in which Phoolan Devi gives a small girl a necklace for her dowry during a raid on a village. The film individualizes Phoolan Devi's conception of social justice by casting it within a singular personalized narrative of rape and revenge. Ironically, *Bandit Queen,* in its attempt to call for social justice by revealing the brutal gender- and caste-based violence of rape, does so by silencing Phoolan Devi's own vision of social justice.

My intention in juxtaposing the film and autobiography is not to argue that the autobiography offers us unmediated access to the truth of Phoolan Devi's life. Autobiography is a situated and negotiated text that is constructed through particular strategies of representation. Certainly, as recent research has demonstrated, the decentering of a universalistic Western male subject through autobiography does not serve as a self-evident or transparent means of decolonization but may produce contradictory effects. As Sidonie Smith and Julia Watson argue,

> On the one hand, the very taking-up-of-the-autobiographical transports the colonial subject into the territory of the "universal" subject and thus promises a culturally empowered subjectivity. Participation in, through representation of, privileged narratives can secure cultural recognition for the subject. On the other hand, entry into the territory of traditional autobiography implicates the speaker in a potentially recuperative performance, one that might reproduce and re/present the colonizer's figure in negation. (xix)

Such contradictions are particularly acute when the autobiography in question is characterized by the hierarchies of power inherent in trans/national relations of the translation, production, and consumption of Third-World texts.

I, Phoolan Devi lies in an intermediary space between the genres of autobiography and *testimonio.* While the book is marketed as an autobiography, it was created through methods closer to the testimonial form. I refer to the book as a testimonio to emphasize the contestatory nature of the representation contained within the autobiography. The book was based on taped oral narratives that were translated and transcribed by the book's editors. The book provides no detailed information on the methodological practices used. Readers do not know, for instance, how the editors selected events or made decisions on the order of the narrative, whether all of the tapes were transcribed, what the nature of Phoolan Devi's input was in the editorial process, or what the interaction between Phoolan Devi and the editors was like during the interviews. Unlike *I, Rigoberta Menchú,* Phoolan Devi's testimonio does not contain a formal introduction by the transcribers/editors nor does the reader have any information on the background of these "witnesses" of Phoolan Devi's experiences.[34] The book merely notes that each page was read to Phoolan Devi and signed by her. This designation of her consent only emphasizes the constructed nature of the autobiography. This textual representation of

Phoolan Devi's life history, positioned between the genres of testimonio, autobiography, and ethnographic interview, highlights the performative nature of all representations of the "real." This liminality of form also demonstrates the contradictory processes of the commodification of Third-World women's testimonials (Carr) and the transgressive potential of testimonio (Beverley). The classification of Phoolan Devi's testimonio attempts to contain the representation of her life experiences within the more conventional, individualized form of the autobiography. However, Phoolan Devi's presentation of her experiences in relation to wider structural forms of oppression and the experiences of marginalization of lower-caste and lower-class men and women from her community disrupts this containment. John Beverley argues that "testimonio is an affirmation of the authority of a single speaking subject, even of personal awareness and growth, but it cannot affirm a self-identity that is separate from a group or class situation marked by marginalization, oppression and struggle. If it does this, it ceases to be testimonio and becomes in effect autobiography" (83). *I, Phoolan Devi* transgresses the autobiographical and in the process demonstrates that trans/national materially based structures of the production and consumption of texts do not predetermine the power effects of such textual forms. Thus, while the "autobiography" circulates in the same trans/national circuit of power as the film, the power effects of the representation are not identical.

Particular narratives in the testimonio *I, Phoolan Devi* disrupt binaries such as the modern/traditional or oppressor/victim that the film reinforces. For example, the testimonio contextualizes Phoolan Devi's resistance in relation to her mother's actions and in relation to her own vision of social justice. This contextualization interrupts the process of commodification and consumption of her life as an individualized resistance set against a singularly oppressive culture. Phoolan Devi's words in the book, "I was born with my mother's anger" (11), move the reader away from an individualized vision of her rebellion and compel the reader to view the rebellion in relation to her mother's struggles with and critical consciousness of the socioeconomic hierarchies in her everyday rural life. Such forms of rebellion provide a contrast to the film's presentation of social oppression as a static feature of Indian culture.

Consider another contrast between the film and testimonio. The film begins its narration of Phoolan Devi's story with her parents negotiating her marriage at age eleven to a man three times her age. The negotiations and arrangement present a bleak picture of a hopelessly patriarchal family structure. Her father takes the role of negotiating the arrangements while her mother for the most part stands on the sidelines, watching sadly and silently. Her father protests weakly that she is too young to be taken by her future husband, Putti Lal, but gives in since he has already paid a bride price for her marriage. Phoolan Devi is then taken to her husband's house where she is raped while her mother-in-law stands outside listening passively to her screams. The childhood rape scene is presented before the opening credits of the film and serves as the foundation for the events that unfold in the film's chronology of her adult life. As with the film, the testimonio also opens with a short description of the rape of the eleven-year-old Phoolan Devi. However, the early chapters of the testimonio contextualize the events leading to the rape in ways that disrupt essentialized notions of a static Indian tradition. The testimonio clearly suggests that Putti Lal's insistence on taking Phoolan Devi away at the age of eleven was a violation of customary practice and therefore of Indian tradition. Phoolan Devi states, for instance, that she was told at her wedding that she would leave with her husband in three or four years (65), and she indicates that her older sister did not leave for her husband's village until the age of sixteen (73).

The representation of Phoolan Devi's childhood years and family life presents a striking contrast to the film's depiction of her parental family structure. In contrast to the film's images of Phoolan Devi's silent mother, the testimonio weaves a narrative that presents her mother as a dominant force within the family while her father appears as a passive, weak-willed man who consents to his subjugated social status. Phoolan Devi describes an incident where she is beaten by the village *Pradhan* (district head) because she asked him for a mango. Her mother drags her to the Pradhan's house where she screams at him in rage, "'you think we bring children into the world just to be your slaves? Instead of hitting her like that you should have just killed her! Go on kill her! Then she won't ask you for any more mangoes. Kill her if you want!' When he came home and heard what happened, my father was ashamed. He said it was our duty to serve them. That was the way the world was" (11). While the testimonio implicates Phoolan Devi's mother in the reproduction of gender hierarchy in certain ways (she laments the fact that Phoolan Devi was born a girl and warns her of the danger of female sexuality and the threat of rape), this is complicated by her resistance. Phoolan Devi describes her mother's rejection of God and religion: "She never prayed like my father. She preferred to wail about the misfortunes God had sent her. 'If he would even just give me enough food for all these girls . . . .' Once she took a little statue of one of the gods from our house and threw it down the village well" (12). These anecdotes illustrate contradictory moments in the creation of her mother's social identity. On the one hand, she articulates a form of gendered ideology as she copes with the economic consequences of bearing female children in a patriarchal society. On the other hand, her rejection of God reflects a form of critical consciousness as she rejects a religious order that reproduces her caste location and provides no relief from her class-based poverty. In the process, the testimonio moves away from an assumption that rural Indian society is characterized by a naturalized form of consent to tradition.

The testimonio disrupts particular hegemonic narratives not merely because of a claim to authenticity through the voice of Phoolan Devi but because of specific strategies of representation. It is not simply the empirical fact of the first-person narrative that is at issue here but the way in which the "I" is presented. The effectiveness of such representation centers around the ways in which the translated narrative of Phoolan Devi's life presents her identity in terms of a complex, multilayered form, one that is emblematic of wider structural forms of social oppression.

Throughout the book, Phoolan Devi's narrative of oppression and resistance links social hierarchies within her village to the social relations between landlords and landless peasants. She identifies the origins of her and her family's problems as her uncle cheating her father out of his share of land because her uncle "wanted to be like the rich, like a *thakur*" (51). In her description of her early childhood, her initial rebellions are targeted at her uncle and later her uncle's son as she continually witnesses their ability to use money and upward mobility to cheat her family. It is at this point that Phoolan Devi begins to transgress gender boundaries by openly expressing her defiance against her uncle and cousin. In one such confrontation with her cousin she notes, "Mayadin [her cousin] was learning how to use the power he had inherited from his thieving father. And all the cowering dogs in the village had obeyed him. But he had been red with fury, he was sweating in his fresh clothes and I had seen his eyes blink with disbelief that I had dared to attack him in the absence of my father. I began to calm down as I thought about his embarrassment. It must have infuriated him. He must have thought that I took myself for the head of our household!" (58). This depiction of the unfolding relationship between class, caste, and gender differs from the film's presentation of caste and gender hierarchy in important ways. By depicting her relatives' attempts to improve their social location through land and money and illustrating the ways in which the lure of upward mobility produces class and status hierarchies within Phoolan Devi's extended family, the testimonio counters the notion of caste as a monolithic, unchanging hierarchy.

Phoolan Devi's narrative is also distinctive in terms of her continual references to the complex articulation of the relationship between caste and class in the social relations of everyday life in her village. Her focus on the politics of class is significant not only because it adds another social category to her discussion of oppression but because the category of class disrupts any presumed naturalized boundary between the modern and the traditional. This narrative contests urban middle-class representations of rural India as pre-modern traces lingering within the modernizing consumer capitalist nation. Phoolan Devi's discussion of the links between land ownership and caste highlight the economic bases of power, contradicting the notion that caste is a form of social distinction intrinsic to Indian (Hindu) society. This complex articulation between class, caste, and gender resurfaces later in the testimonio in Phoolan Devi's description of her vision of social justice, which she argues guided the raids she carried out on villages once she had formed her own band of dacoits.

Phoolan Devi's testimonio constructs her identity and experience through a narrative of oppression, agency, and resistance that reveals the complex relationship between caste, class, and gender in contemporary Indian society. In contrast, Shohini Ghosh has presented an incisive analysis of the ways in which Phoolan Devi's agency is foreclosed in the film. Ghosh notes that Phoolan Devi's empowerment is always dependent on male outlaws in the film so that "she is empowered only when she is 'allowed' empowerment by the men around her" (159). More significantly, pointing to a "recurring pattern in the film where oppositional speech is punished repeatedly by assaults on the body," Ghosh argues that "only speech remains her truly autonomous domain of agency and resistance."[35] In the film, Phoolan Devi's speech is defiant yet her actions are individualized and are dependent on a masculine world; the material and "discursive displacements" (Pathak and Rajan 268) that produce her intersectional identity also locate her in a position of disidentification (Alarcon) from either the elites or from the masculine counterhegemonic dacoits. In contrast, in the testimonio Phoolan Devi is able to represent the interests of other marginalized members of her social world—her agency is thus contextualized within and subversive of material structures of oppression; her interwoven identity of caste, class, and gender in this context serves as a potential source for wider social transformation. The testimonio reflects the "critical practice of outlaw genres" that attempt to "shift the subject of autobiography from the individual to a more unstable collective entity" (Kaplan, "Resisting Autobiography" 134).

I, Phoolan Devi is more effective than *Bandit Queen* in disrupting hegemonic relationships between power and resistance because of moments of subversion within the text that prevent a commodification of Phoolan Devi's life into the figure of a victimized "Third-World woman." Such moments allow the testimonio to interrupt the trans/national power relations that shape the translation, marketing, and consumption of the book. A striking example of this type of disruption is evident in Phoolan Devi's response to the public's desire to see her and capture her through visual representations. She vividly describes her resistance to the pressure of the press, as journalists continually attempted to photograph her after her surrender to the police and state governments: "I would charge at them and tear their cameras away from them. I hated being photographed. Every time I heard the click of a camera, I turned into a tigress" (450). The most significant insight into the relationship between power and representation is perhaps captured in the short epilogue to the book: "I had seen all kinds of bandits. Assassins had tried to take my life, journalists had tried to get my story, movie directors had tried to capture me on film. They all thought they could speak about me as though I didn't exist, as though I still didn't have any right to respect. The bandits had tried to torture my body, but the others tried to torture my spirit" (464).

Conclusion

I have argued for a practice of reading that focuses on the power effects of various strategies of representation rather than on a binary approach that either invokes or rejects representations of the "real." My analysis suggests that, although both the film and testimonio are products of collaborative processes between First and Third World that must be located within material relations of production, distribution, and consumption of Third-World texts, the power effects of textual representation are not predetermined by such material relations. On the contrary, a trans/national perspective necessitates a mode of interpretation that pays attention to the contingencies of context and audience.

I have argued that while *Bandit Queen* reproduces hegemonic Western constructs of Indian society, its depiction of rape subverts particular moral and social codes that govern the politics of sexuality in the Indian bourgeois public sphere. The depiction of the "reality" of Phoolan Devi's experiences invokes different modalities of power and resistance that are contingent upon tactics of rhetoricity, form, and context. I suggest that a trans/national feminist perspective on the representation of the Third-World woman does not need to rest on a binary opposition between an authentic speaking subaltern or an unrecoverable subject lost in webs of power and domination. I have presented readings of representations of Phoolan Devi's life experiences that illustrate the trans/national material relationships of power that do govern the circulation of texts and cultural meanings yet demonstrate that such material relations are not necessarily determinate in the last instance. Multinational productions of cultural texts are not intrinsically authentic or resistant because of their presumed hybridity. However, they are also not unitary in the meanings and power effects they produce. As *Bandit Queen* demonstrates, such multinational cultural products do not only represent commodities for First-

World consumption but also circulate and intervene in complex and contradictory ways within the Third-World context in question.

A hypothetical situation in which both the film and autobiography had represented their translations of Phoolan Devi's life as a partial or fictionalized version may have moved us away from the commodification of authenticity but would not necessarily have shifted the threads of power and resistance in the representation and consumption of Phoolan Devi's story. My reading of India's bandit queen suggests that in a consideration of binary oppositions between reality and fiction or truth and partiality, choosing one pole of the dichotomy will not in itself circumvent the problem of power and representation. A rejection of the real in favor of fictionalizing our accounts in film, ethnography, or biography will not, for instance, address questions of who is invoking the real, how it is invoked, and where it is invoked. Rather, a feminist analysis of the trans/national implications of the production, representation, and consumption of the Third-World text necessitates a shift from the "fact" of the (un)translatability of the subaltern Third-World woman (the question of whether she can speak) to questions of how she is being made to speak and in what context her speech is being heard.

Notes

An earlier version of this chapter appeared in *Signs* 25.1 (Winter 1999): 123–54, © 1999 by the University of Chicago. All rights reserved. I am grateful to Harriet Davidson, Wendy Hesford, Wendy Kozol, Laura Liu, Leslie McCall, Rupal Oza, S. Shankar, Caridad Souza, and an anonymous reviewer for their comments on an earlier version of this chapter. Thanks go to Richard Baxtrom and Asha Rani for their efforts in helping me track down source materials.

1. For a critical discussion of an overemphasis on the possibilities of resistance, see Abu-Lughod.

2. I am referring here to current debates over the problems of representing "other" groups—groups marked for instance by class or cultural or national difference.

3. See also John for a discussion of the ways in which theory "travels" across discrepant contexts.

4. I am making two points here. First, in the context of a globalized economy texts that may be produced for a particular national audience are in fact simultaneously consumed within the context of other national audiences. Second, such consumption occurs at the same temporal moment and is not a teleological process in which Third-World countries will eventually consume First-World texts. Note also that this is not limited to texts that are produced in the postcolonial era or about postcolonial subjects. Shakespeare, for instance, is taught within the Indian academy.

5. Phoolan Devi's notoriety in India grew in particular due to what is commonly known as the "Behmai incident." In the northern Indian village of Behmai, she had been gang raped by a group of upper-caste landlords after being captured with the help of an upper-caste dacoit who also served as a police informant. In retaliation, she returned to the village with her gang and killed seventeen upper-caste landowners who had allegedly raped her. The incident caused a national outcry because of the political and social implications of a lower-caste "outlaw" woman attacking landed *thakurs*. Following the incident the state government of Uttar Pradesh launched a full-scale attempt to capture her and ultimately forced her to surrender.

6. Note that prior to the production of the film and the autobiography, Mala Sen's biography, *India's Bandit Queen,* was the key text that claimed to represent Phoolan Devi's life. The film was based on this text.

7. I am drawing here on a Foucauldian analysis of the linkages between power and representation. By using the term "strategies of representation" my aim is to call attention to the performative and constructed nature of textual forms that claim to embody, represent, or speak for "real" experiences of particular individuals or social groups. See Foucault.

8. Note that my point is not to advocate a singular, universal, or "global" feminist approach. Rather, by a trans/national feminist approach I am referring to the need for a feminist analysis of the ways in which the power effects of texts are both contained within and transgress national borders. My use of a slash in the term "trans/national" attempts to signal the simultaneity of power effects within and across nations.

9. Both the film and autobiography claim to represent the true life story of Phoolan Devi. While the film begins with the caption, "This is a true story," a short note of a page and a half at the end of Phoolan Devi's 463-page autobiography indicates that the book (based on two thousand pages of transcribed interviews) was read out to her and that "she approved each page with her signature, still the only word she knows how to write" (468). The note ends with the words, "After everything she lived through, she deserved to be given the chance to tell her story herself" (468).

10. For a more general and comprehensive collection of women's writings in India, see Tharu and Lalitha.

11. See for example the volume of testimonials by the feminist collective Stree Shakti Sangathana documenting the experiences of women's participation in an armed struggle against landed interests in the princely state of Hyderabad between 1948 and 1951, a movement that later brought its participants in direct confrontation with the Indian army.

12. Although rape scenes are common in commercial Hindi films, such films do not depict any form of nudity.

13. Since Phoolan Devi was charged with these crimes, the film's representation could potentially have served as "evidence" of her acknowledgment that she committed the crime.

14. This approach distinguishes between empiricism and notions of the real. See Bhaskar; Barad.

15. In other words, the relationship between structural location (where the text is produced) and representation (the power effects of the text) is not predetermined.

16. A project that analyzes fractured audience responses to the film within India and Britain is an important endeavor but is not relevant to the theoretical or methodological project of this chapter. Such a project is currently being carried out by Shohini Ghosh. In "Deviant Pleasures and Disorderly Women," Ghosh discusses the acclaim *Bandit Queen* received at international film festivals and in reviews in Europe.

17. I am specifically foregrounding the multinational nature of this production for two reasons. First, to point to the material basis of the production of such texts; second, to interrogate the implications of this multinational character. One possible interpretation could cast this as another manifestation of an international (neo)colonial relationship. A second interpretation could cast this as an intrinsic sign of authenticity or subversive hybridity. Recent anthropological debates, for instance, have discussed the possibility of including the "native's" authorship as an experimental subversive strategy. During the course of this chapter, my discussion of the film and autobiography will complicate this binary opposition while recognizing the *material* basis of such collaborative processes. See Behar for a complex discussion of such issues. Note also that in the case of the film *Bandit Queen,* the British production company Channel IV retained joint control with Shekar Kapur over the film's content. In this case the material collaboration directly shaped the representation. In other cases such "shaping" is often indirect or implicit.

18. Furthermore, the script was written by Mala Sen, Phoolan Devi's biographer.

19. Note that Phoolan Devi's location in many ways corresponds to Gloria Anzaldua's conception of the borderland since the intersections among caste, class, and gender place her at the margins and in-between spaces of Indian society.

20. See also Spivak, "Can the Subaltern Speak?" and Visweswaran for discussions of the ways in which silence becomes the marker of the colonial subaltern woman.

21. See Jameson and Ahmad for an exchange regarding the ways in which Western scholarship recasts Third-World literature within allegories of the nation.

22. See Trinh, *Woman/Native/Other,* for a discussion on the ways in which difference is deployed in ways that re/produce hierarchies of power.

23. See Appadurai for a discussion of the ways in which caste has been constructed as an essentialized marker of social organization and hierarchy in India.

24. Such questions regarding cinematic form have also been addressed in relation to the category of gender (see Kaplan, *Women*). This raises important questions for future research regarding the parallels and intersections between the spectacle of race, the spectacle of woman, and of "woman of color."

25. Such categories thus continue to have salience in cultural analysis (even while we deconstruct them) not merely as analytical tools but because they are reproduced through practices of cultural production.

26. Such processes are not only linked to the Third World. Consider for instance the racialized, gendered politics of images of black men and the politics of lynching in the United States (see Hall).

27. For a historical discussion of such colonial ideologies of masculinity, see Stoler.

28. Popular films do not generally depict nudity and until recently did not depict explicit sexual intimacy, including kissing.

29. Such reports were often tinged with particular class narratives and the deployment of stereotypes of "uncivilized" working-class men who cheered at such violence.

30. Such special screenings are not new or unique to *Bandit Queen* and can be traced back historically to the early twentieth century. See Vasudevan.

31. All references to Kapur's perspective are based on a televised interview on the interview program *In Focus* (Home TV channel, India, 10 June 1996).

32. Note that the film also presents a gendered reworking of a significant genre of popular commercial Hindi films which depicts the "male outlaw figure," for instance, through representations of male dacoits or the male working-class hero who transgresses the law.

33. For strong negative reviews, see Roy; Kishwar.

34. Contrast this to the careful strategies of representation in Ruth Behar's *Translated Woman*, particularly in relation to the ways in which Behar makes explicit her role as (privileged) witness.

35. For an interesting interrogation of the relationship between speech and subjectivity, see Pathak and Rajan.

Works Cited

Abu-Lughod, Lila. "The Romance of Resistance: Tracing Transformations of Power through Bedouin Women." *American Ethnologist* 17.1 (1991): 41–55.

Ahmad, Aijaz. "Jameson's Rhetoric of Otherness and the 'National Allegory.'" *Social Text* 17 (1987): 3–25.

Alarcon, Norma. "The Theoretical Subject of *This Bridge Called My Back* and Anglo-American Feminism." In *Making Face, Making Soul: Haciendo Caras.* Ed. Gloria Anzaldua. San Francisco: Aunt Lute Press, 1990. 356–69.

Alloula, Malek. *The Colonial Harem.* Trans. Myrna Godzich and Wlad Godzich. Minneapolis: University of Minnesota Press, 1986.

Anzaldua, Gloria. *Borderlands/La Frontera: The New Mestiza.* San Francisco: Aunt Lute Press, 1987.

Appadurai, Arjun. "Putting Hierarchy in Its Place." *Cultural Anthropology* 3.1 (1988): 37–50.

Barad, Karen. "Meeting the Universe Halfway: Realism and Social Constructivism without Contradiction." In *Feminism, Science, and the Philosophy of Science.* Ed. L. H. Nelson and J. Nelson. Boston: Kluwer Academic Publishers, 1996. 161–94.

Behar, Ruth. *Translated Woman: Crossing the Border with Esperanza's Story.* Boston: Beacon Press, 1993.

Beverley, John. *Against Literature.* Minneapolis: University of Minnesota Press, 1993.

Bhaskar, Roy. *Reclaiming Reality: A Critical Introduction to Contemporary Philosophy.* London: Verso, 1989.

Butler, Judith. *Gender Trouble: Feminism and the Subversion of Identity.* New York: Routledge, 1990.

Carr, Robert. "Crossing the First World/Third World Divides: Testimonial, Transnational Feminisms, and the Postmodern Condition." In *Scattered Hegemonies: Postmodernity and Transnational Feminist Practices.* Ed. Inderpal Grewal and Caren Kaplan. Minneapolis: University of Minnesota Press, 1994. 153–72.

Chow, Rey. "Violence in the 'Other' Country." In *Third World Women and the Politics of Feminism.* Ed. Chandra Mohanty, Ann Russo, and Lourdes Torres. Bloomington: Indiana University Press, 1991. 81–100.

———. "Where Have all the Natives Gone?" In *Writing Diaspora: Tactics of Intervention in Contemporary Cultural Studies.* Bloomington: Indiana University Press, 1993. 27–54.

———. *Writing Diaspora: Tactics of Intervention in Contemporary Cultural Studies.* Bloomington: Indiana University Press, 1993.

Clifford, James. *Routes: Travel and Translation in the Late Twentieth Century.* Cambridge, Mass.: Harvard University Press, 1997.

Devi, Phoolan. *I, Phoolan Devi: The Autobiography of India's Bandit Queen.* London: Little, Brown, and Company, 1996.

Fernandes, Leela. "Beyond Public Spaces and Private Spheres: Gender, Family, and Working-Class Politics in India." *Feminist Studies* 23.3 (1997): 525–47.

———. "Nationalizing 'the Global': Cultural Politics, Economic Reform, and the Middle Classes in India." *Media, Culture, and Society* 22 (Nov. 2000; forthcoming).

———. *Producing Workers: The Politics of Gender, Class, and Culture in the Calcutta Jute Mills.* Philadelphia: University of Pennsylvania Press, 1997.

Flemming, Leslie. "Between Two Worlds: Self-Construction and Self-Identity in the Writings of Three Nineteenth-Century Indian Christian Women." In *Women as Subjects: South Asian Histories.* Ed. Nita Kumar. Charlottesville: University Press of Virginia, 1994. 81–107.

Foucault, Michel. *Power/Knowledge: Selected Interviews and Other Writings, 1972–1977.* Trans. Alan Sheridan. New York: Pantheon Books, 1980.

Ghosh, Shohini. "Deviant Pleasures and Disorderly Women: The Representation of the Female Outlaw in *Bandit Queen* and *Anjaam.*" In *Feminist Terrains in Legal Domains: Interdisciplinary Essays on Women and Law in India.* Ed. Ratna Kapur. New Delhi: Kali for Women, 1996. 150–83.

Grewal, Inderpal, and Caren Kaplan, eds. *Scattered Hegemonies: Postmodernity and Transnational Feminist Practices.* Minneapolis: University of Minnesota Press, 1994.

Hall, Jacquelyn Dowd. "The Mind That Burns in Each Body." In *Powers of Desire: The Politics of Sexuality.* Ed. Ann Snitow, Christine Stansell, and Sharon Thompson. New York: Monthly Review Press, 1983. 328–49.

hooks, bell. *Yearning: Race, Gender, and Cultural Politics.* Boston: South End Press, 1990.

Jameson, Fredric. "Third World Literature in the Era of Multi-National Capitalism." *Social Text* 15 (1986): 65–88.

John, Mary. *Discrepant Dislocations: Feminism, Theory, and Postcolonial Histories.* Berkeley: University of California Press, 1996.

Kaplan, Caren. "The Politics of Location as Transnational Feminist Practice." In *Scattered Hegemonies: Postmodernity and Transnational Feminist Practices.* Ed. Inderpal Grewal and Caren Kaplan. Minneapolis: University of Minnesota Press, 1994. 137–52.

———. "Resisting Autobiography: Out-Law Genres and Transnational Feminist Subjects." In *De/Colonizing the Subject: The Politics of Gender in Women's Autobiography.* Ed. Sidonie Smith and Julia Watson. Minneapolis: University of Minnesota Press, 1992. 115–38.

Kaplan, E. Ann, ed. *Women and Film: Both Sides of the Camera.* New York: Methuen, 1983.

Kapur, Shekar. *Bandit Queen.* London: Film Four International and Kaleidoscope, 1994

Kishwar, Madhu. "Review of *Bandit Queen.*" *Manushi* 84 (Sept.–Oct. 1994): 34–37.

Kumar, Radha. *The History of Doing: An Illustrated Account of Movements for Women's Rights and Feminism in India.* New York: Verso Press, 1993.

Mani, Lata. "Contentious Traditions: The Debate on Sati in Colonial India." In *Recasting Women: Essays in Colonial History.* Ed. Kum Kum Sangari and Sudesh Vaid. New Brunswick, N.J.: Rutgers University Press, 1989. 88–126.

———. "Multiple Mediations: Feminist Scholarship in the Age of Multinational Reception." *Feminist Review* 35 (1990): 24–41.

Menchú, Rigoberta, with Elisabeth Burgos-Debray. *I, Rigoberta Menchú: An Indian Woman in Guatemala.* Trans. Ann Wright. London: Verso, 1984.

Mohanty, Chandra. "Under Western Eyes." In *Third World Women and the Politics of Feminism.* Ed. Chandra Mohanty, Ann Russo, and Lourdes Torres. Bloomington: Indiana University Press, 1991. 51–80.

Niranjana, Tejaswini. "Interrogating Whose Nation? Tourists and Terrorists in 'Roja.'" *Economic and Political Weekly* 29.21 (1994): 79–82.

Pathak, Zakia, and Rajeswari Sunder Rajan. "Shahbano." In *Feminists Theorize the Political.* Ed. Judith Butler and Joan W. Scott. New York: Routledge, 1992. 257–79.

Rony, Fatimah. *The Third Eye: Race, Cinema, and Ethnographic Spectacle.* Durham, N.C.: Duke University Press, 1996.

Roy, Arundhati. "The Great Indian Rape Trick." 2 pts. *Sunday,* 22 Aug. and 3 Sept. 1994.

Said, Edward. *Orientalism.* New York: Pantheon Books, 1978.

Sen, Mala. *India's Bandit Queen: The Story of Phoolan Devi.* New York: Harper Collins, 1991.

Smith, Sidonie, and Julia Watson, eds. *De/Colonizing the Subject: The Politics of Gender in Women's Autobiography.* Minneapolis: University of Minnesota Press, 1992.

Spivak, Gayatri Chakravorty. "Can the Subaltern Speak?" In *Marxism and the Interpretation of Culture.* Ed. Cary Nelson and Lawrence Grossberg. Urbana: University of Illinois Press, 1988. 271–97.

———. "The Politics of Translation." In *Destabilizing Theory: Contemporary Feminist Debates.* Ed. Michele Barrett and Anne Phillips. Stanford, Calif.: Stanford University Press, 1992. 177–200.

Stoler, Anne. "Carnal Knowledge and Imperial Power: Gender, Race, and Morality in Colonial Asia." In *Gender at the Crossroads of Knowledge: Feminist Anthropology in* a *Postmodern Era*. Ed. Micaela di Leonardo. Berkeley: University of California Press, 1991. 51–101.

Stree Shakti Sangathana. *'We Were Making History': Women and the Telangana Uprising*. New Delhi: Kali for Women Press, 1989.

Tharu, Susie, and K. Lalitha, eds. *Women Writing in India: 600 B.C. to the Present*. 2 vols. New York: The Feminist Press, 1993.

Trinh T. Minh-ha. *When the Moon Waxes Red: Representation, Gender, and Cultural Politics*. New York: Routledge, 1991.

———. *Woman/Native/Other*. Bloomington: Indiana University Press, 1989.

Vasudevan, Ravi. "Film Studies, New Cultural History, and Experience of Modernity." *Economic and Political Weekly* 28 (4 Nov. 1995): 2809–14.

Visweswaran, Kamala. *Fictions of Feminist Ethnography*. Minneapolis: University of Minnesota Press, 1994.

3

I Am [Not] Like You

Ideologies of Selfhood in *I, Rigoberta Menchú:
An Indian Woman in Guatemala*

Susan Sánchez-Casal

> As we listen to her voice, we have to look deep into our own souls for
> it awakens sensations and feelings which we, caught up as we are in
> an inhuman and artificial world, thought were lost forever. Her story
> is overwhelming because what she has to say is simple and true.
> —Elisabeth Burgos-Debray, introduction to *I, Rigoberta Menchú*

> Please do not idealize us, because we are not mythical beings from the
> past nor the present. We are active communities. And as long as there
> is one Indian alive in some corner of America or of the world, there
> will be a spark of hope and an original way of thinking.
> —Rigoberta Menchú Tum, in *When the Mountains Tremble*

I, Rigoberta Menchú: An Indian Woman in Guatemala[1] is undoubtedly the most
widely read testimonial "autobiography" in the U.S. academy. The 1996 anthology *Teaching and Testimony: Rigoberta Menchú and the North American Classroom* (Carey-Webb and Benz) demonstrates the broad, interdisciplinary ap-
plication of this noncanonical text across the humanities curriculum as well
as the predominant ways in which it is being interpreted in the critical languages of anthropology, sociology, political science, women's studies, history,
and literature.[2] In North American college and university classrooms the testimonial genre has revitalized the study of subaltern communities by creating a new site of enunciation, placing center-stage the previously muted voices
of Latin America's most marginalized and oppressed peoples. Emerging in the
post–Cuban Revolution era in Latin America, the *testimonio* challenges the silences and distortions inherent in the traditional codes of literary, historical,
and anthropological discourses by foregrounding the subaltern as subjects of
history and agents of their own destinies. Testimonial literature thus becomes

the polyphonic companion to polygraphic testimonial artifacts such as the *arpilleras*[3] and in this sense interrupts both the exclusion of the popular in canonical aesthetic expression and the univocal representation "from above" of heterogeneous historico-political processes. Testimonial narratives like *I, Rigoberta Menchú* act as forms of cultural and political archeology that excavate and display an elided and distorted chunk of Latin American history, constructing and situating that history at the level of the native eyewitness.[4]

My desire in writing this essay is to contribute to the intense discussion on *I, Rigoberta Menchú* and women's testimonial literature in general by developing a critical/theoretical language that focuses not only on what this text means but also *how* it means, specifically on how the intrinsic elements of this testimonio dismantle its explicit intention of creating a unified autobiographical subject and a monological "native" discourse of truth and authenticity. My point of departure is the critical premise that *I, Rigoberta Menchú* is a conflictive textual space where a dialogical struggle for knowledge and autobiographical voice is staged, a struggle in which the voice of the representative, plural Quiché "I" is challenged by instances of the individual, radical voice of the "inappropriate other," a space where a discourse of national unity (the traditional Quiché culture) collides with a modern language that, by its appropriation of the discourses of feminism, Marxism, and Liberation Theology, dislocates traditional cultural forms and processes. I will argue that these juxtaposed and sometimes oppositional views of and positions in the world are not subjective contradictions but the thing itself: the subjectivities that emerge in the fragmented spaces of these changing, flexible discourses suggest that the textualized Menchú is an epistemological traveler in the process of being. I borrow María Lugones's metaphor of "world-traveling" to describe the ways in which Menchú's chronotopic shifting allows her to assume and accommodate multiple languages and how this metaphysics of reality creates a speaking subject who is ontologically plural:

> The shift from being one person to being a different person is what I call "travel." This shift may not be willful or even conscious, and one may be completely unaware of being different than one is in a different "world." Even though the shift can be done willfully, it is not a matter of acting. One does not pose as someone else, one does not pretend to be, for example, someone of a different personality or character or someone who uses space or language differently than the other person. Rather one is someone who has that personality or character or uses space and language in that particular way. (396)

Since many testimonial critics have constructed Menchú as a nonideological subject whose relationship to experience, knowledge, and truth is transparent and immediate, my view of her shifting epistemic "traveling" requires a rethinking of agency and notions of authenticity.[5] I argue that Menchú's shifting subject positions and the ways in which these shifts bear on truth and meaning in her narrative are crucial to the specificity of her agency. Simultaneously, her destabilizing gestures render implausible critical claims of her absolute representativeness of the indigenous communities of Guatemala. Given that the narrator's locus of knowledge production is fluid and mutable, claims for authentic (read immediate, unnegotiated, and stable) and representative selfhood can only be sustained by noncritical readings, by deliberately looking at the text through what Elzbieta Sklodowska calls "testimonio-seeing eyes" ("Spanish American" 35).[6]

In this essay I will expose and interpret certain textual and narrative strategies that construe Menchú's agency and explore how these strategies are grounded in uncritical and constricting notions of the "real." I hope to show that in the interplay of the narrative itself, fixed or stable images of Menchú, her community, traditional native discourses, and outside constituencies (ladinos,[7] Catholic clergy) become scrutinized, complexified, and ambiguous. For example, at the end of the narrative the notion of homogeneous community presented by the editor in the introduction (and by Menchú in the course of her narrative) has been shaken: the logic of closed indigenous communities that prohibit or limit contact or coalition with ladinos gives way to the new knowledge that cross-cultural, political, heterogeneous communities that link the oppression of Guatemalan Indians to that of the ladinos are crucial for indigenous survival. Similarly, despite the claims for native authenticity presented in the introduction and in Menchú's transcribed testimony, the narrator emerges at the end of the text as a multiply situated, nonunified self, a revolutionary survivor of and witness to a historical cataclysm whose experience and agency has been equally marked by material structures and by exceptional, transgressive, individual choices.

The three major textual and narrative strategies I refer to place themselves in tension with the intrinsic action of the text itself, attempting to construct a seamless, monolithic notion of native selfhood by constricting or concealing Menchú's exceptional subject positions: 1) the excision of ethnographic markings, 2) the prescriptive frameworks for reading offered in the editor's introduction, and 3) the testimonial narrator's explicit negation of her singularity. I will argue that the ideological specificity of this testimonio lies in its supreme ambiguity: the text fails to resolve the tension between its presentation of the life-story of an epistemically privileged native woman and its simultaneous insistence on reducing her exceptionality to the traditional outlines of authentic Quiché selfhood. By marking the contours and the excesses of the textual spectacle, I aim to examine this book as artifice, to call attention to its seams and fissures, to the places where unity of subject and discourse disintegrates, and thereby to allow its complexities and contradictions to speak in their own, new multiple tongues.

To write about the discursive tensions and contradictions that emerge in women's testimonial narratives necessarily draws one into highly charged territory. Given that the explicit political intention of Latin American women's testimonials is the retelling and revisioning of histories of domination from the perspectives of oppressed indigenous communities, much has been written about this genre's ability to deliver "the real thing." A great majority of teachers and scholars approach and appropriate this text as the unmitigated offering of previously suppressed "truths," bypassing the text's rich layers of epistemological negotiations and confrontations and fixing the testimonial speaker in a static subject field.[8] Like these educators and critics, I value the function of women's testimonial narratives in recasting indigenous peoples as the subjects of Latin American history, in naming the sinister omissions of official history, and in reproducing the literary voice of those who have been absent from or distorted in the literary pantheon. Yet no matter what significance one assigns to its political project (and I, for one, believe in the urgency and legitimacy of the testimonio's political intentionality), can this genre somehow escape the semiosic[9] mediations of language and interpretation? Can testimonials possibly be, as Jara has problematically claimed, an uninterpreted "imprint of the real"? (2).[10]

For U.S. Third-World feminists like myself, women's testimonios provide a more democratic inscription of subaltern subjectivities, histories, belief systems, and modes of imagination, yet in a conflicting way these texts may present us with as many critical, theoretical, and ethical problems as they solve. The predominant critical interpretation of the autobiographical subject of *I, Rigoberta Menchú* as "collective" and "impersonal," for example, can only be sustained through a selective reading of the text that ignores its discursive complexities and tensions and highlights only one of its multiple subject positions, obscuring other, less stable or classifiable positions. For critics like myself, hungry for the materiality of the indigenous woman's word, of her work in communities of resistance, of her interpretation of her own history and that of her people, it feels almost blasphemous to approach the pages of the testimonio with the poststructuralist tools of the academic investigator. And yet if we avoid critical engagement with women's testimonial narratives we run the risk of remystifying the "woman-native-other," of rejecting former unacceptable models of monolithic native subjectivity only to refashion the figure of the Third-World woman into a new monolith, one more suited to our progressive or radical purposes.

Since the late 1980s a number of Latin Americanists in the U.S. academy have begun to problematize the arguments of testimonial editors and critics who advance essentialist notions of subaltern subjectivities and who insist upon transparency between signifier and signified, between text and referent, and between a fabricated human image and immediate subjective presence.[11] Yet even today those of us who choose to scrutinize how the function of writing conditions and manipulates the testimonio's construction of the "real" and the reception of these narratives as transparent "truth-saying" are often seen as uninvited, awkward intruders who question not only the genre's ability to deliver the "real truth" but also its intended function as a political tool of resistance. To consider truth and authenticity as effects and not conditions of these texts is to acknowledge within them the presence of artifice, of fiction, and therefore to reject the static notion of the testimonial as a waiting vehicle for the overwhelming truth of the referent and to reject at the same time the possibility that the text can deliver the "simple," "true" voice of the indigenous testimonial informant. The ethnographic project, as Clifford has argued (7), will always produce a partial or interested truth no matter how democratic the exchange between ethnographer and informant. Trinh's argument that the ethnographer must "acknowledge the irreducibility of the object studied and the impossibility of delivering its presence, of reproducing it as it is in *its truth, reality and otherness*" (*Woman* 70; emphasis added) can and should be directed at editors and literary critics of testimonials as well. *I, Rigoberta Menchú* is not a neutral space into which the constituted, unified subject Rigoberta Menchú pours her self but a dynamic discursive and symbolic field that produces a new subject mediated heterogeneously by power, location, and discourse, a new native self whose rich complexities and ambiguities compel the critical reader to question every previous definition of native selfhood posited in and outside the text.

The Editorial Construction of Native Authenticity

> ... nothing was left out, not a word, even if it was used incorrectly or was later changed. I altered neither the style nor the sentence structure. . . . I soon reached the decision to give the manuscript the form of a monologue. . . . I therefore decided to delete all my questions. By doing so I became what I really was: Rigoberta's listener. I allowed her to speak and then became her instrument, her double by allowing her to make the transition from the spoken to the written word.
>
> —Elisabeth Burgos-Debray, introduction to *I, Rigoberta Menchú*

Many readers, including myself, find this introduction infuriating and offensive. Burgos-Debray represents her relation with Menchú in sentimental and paternalist terms that imply the very attitudes of racial and class superiority Menchú is combating, both in Guatemala and among Metropolitan readers.

—Mary Louise Pratt, "*Me llamo Rigoberta Menchú:* Autoethnography and the Re-coding of Citizenship"

I, Rigoberta Menchú was edited and introduced by the Venezuelan ethnographer Elisabeth Burgos-Debray and first published in Spanish as *Me llamo Rigoberta Menchú y así me nació la conciencia* in 1982. This testimonial narrative is the product of over twenty-four hours of recorded interviews conducted by Burgos-Debray with the twenty-three-year-old Quiché informant Rigoberta Menchú. The text produces multilayered discourses and human images: a selective native account of the customs, traditions, laws, and spiritual belief systems of the Quiché, an exceptional protagonist who offers a first-person account of her life story and the history of her community, an accounting of historical grievances that outlines and analyzes the systems of indigenous oppression, and an equally detailed and compelling history of indigenous resistance to genocide.

Although *I, Rigoberta Menchú* is the product of ethnography, it was constructed, published, and received as the autobiography of the 1992 Nobel Prize recipient, Menchú. The marketing of all editions of the text has also promoted its reception as Menchú's autobiography by featuring an image (photograph or drawing) of the lone Menchú on its front cover. So powerful is the image of the real-life Menchú as the author of her life story that I would label this phenomenon a "normalized error of perception," a false conclusion that, by nature of its overwhelming presence in readers and critics of this text, functions as a "truth."[12] The notion of Menchú's authorship is so pervasive that North American libraries catalog the text under Menchú's name, and she is almost exclusively listed as the author of the text in bibliographical citations.[13] The ethnographer/editor Burgos-Debray and many testimonial critics have minimized the editorial function in *I, Rigoberta Menchú,* considering the authorship of this text as negotiated between editor and informant—Menchú is frequently referred to as Burgos-Debray's "co-author."[14] At one level, the notion of negotiated authorship is supported by explicit political solidarity between the editor and informant: Burgos-Debray identifies herself in the introduction as a supporter of indigenous resistance in Latin America, criticizing the role of "we Latin Americans" in reproducing for indigenous communities the social and political relations created in colonial rule. Burgos-Debray clearly intends her text to function as a tool of resistance that will help end centuries of oppression wrought upon the Quiché and other indigenous groups in Latin America.[15] In Burgos-Debray's language, her text is a space where Menchú can "tell of the oppression her people have been suffering for the last five hundred years, so that the sacrifices made by her community and her family will not have been made in vain" (xii). In this sense, the shared goals of ethnographer and testimonial informant support the idea of collaborative authorship.[16]

At another level, the editorial decision to eliminate the ethnographer's questions from the body of the text supports the "false-truth" of Menchú's authorship by minimizing—almost erasing—the presence or juxtaposition of native Other and colonial self in the pretextual encounter. In doing so, Burgos-Debray guides the reader away from the heteroglossia[17] inherent in the ethnographic interview and toward a seamless presentation of autobiographical native discourse. Especially significant here is the way in which Burgos-Debray's excision of colonial signs and subsequent presentation of Menchú's testimony as autonomous monologue heightens the reader's sense of the text's authenticity; ironically, this effect is achieved only by concealing the impure or real conditions of the text's production.[18] This textual strategy attempts to persuade the modern reader that what he or she is about to read is "the real thing."

Burgos-Debray explains in the introduction that her decision to remove the framing questions was motivated by the desire to represent more authentically the dynamics present in the interviews with Menchú, during which Burgos-Debray claims to have mutated from ethnographer to mere listener. This statement is of course strikingly paternalistic, but even more remarkable than its paternalism is the implicit acceptance of this assertion in predominant readings and criticisms of the text. By asserting that Menchú is the singular generator of her own image and meaning and that any listener, any ear would have elicited the same answers, responses, and stories from the informant, Burgos-Debray again reinforces the idea of Menchú's authorship and at the same time bypasses the perturbing history of cultural politics and struggle present in this new encounter of native informant and Latin American intellectual. Moreover, this assertion invites us to move away from the more unstable zones of contact in the ethnographic encounter, namely that conflictive space in which a dual process of reading and positioning occurs between Burgos-Debray and Menchú (the dominant reading the Other/the Other reading the dominant). This process, although most evident during the interview, also precedes it. Fischer has argued that "the ethnic, the ethnographer, and the cross-cultural scholar in general often begin with a personal empathetic 'dual-tracking,' seek-

ing in the other clarification for the processes of the self" (199). This is evident in Burgos-Debray's introduction, where she acknowledges that she "seeks" in the "simple, true" voice of Menchú what she and the reader have "lost" ("sensations and feelings which we thought were lost forever") (xiii). She does not, however, give uptake to the complex functions of her empathetic and romantic interests in seeking knowledge of the indigenous Other nor to how her desire and needs may shape and bind intrinsic textual images and subsequent readings of Menchú. We must also consider that just as Burgos-Debray seeks nostalgically for the "real" in the background of the Other, so Menchú must seek her own image in the historically punishing mirror of "we Latin Americans" of whom Burgos-Debray is the embodiment.

In the cultural context of the ethnographic interview, Menchú offers testimony to one who represents those who have dominated and exploited her, a group whose power and pluralities she has come to know and engage through the experience of operating in their worlds. Without trivializing the significant political difference that characterizes the coexistence of Burgos-Debray and Menchú in the Paris apartment where the interviews take place, we must also consider the haunting parallel between this new coupling of upper-class woman and indigenous woman and the historically antagonistic coupling of the *patrona/sirvienta* (mistress/servant). Even more significant for my analysis is the consideration that although Burgos-Debray stands in for the historical figure of the patrona in whose world Menchú conversely assumes the disempowered role of indigenous servant (the text, in fact, includes a chapter that details Menchú's work as a domestic servant in an upper-class household in Guatemala City), the editor's account of the ethnographic encounter fails to address the compelling material and ideological differences that characterize it. Burgos-Debray's silence around the conflictive relationship that she and Menchú symbolically reenact during their cohabitation in Paris serves to collapse opposing identity categories and to support her underlying argument that she and Menchú constitute a utopic "double" subject. In this textual performance the ethnographer constructs the real upon a seamless—if dubious—edifice of sameness:

> I think it was mainly the fact of living together under the same roof for a week that won me her trust . . . . A woman friend had brought me some maize flour and black beans back from Venezuela . . . . I cannot describe how happy that made Rigoberta. It made me happy too, as the smell of *tortillas* and refried beans brought back my childhood in Venezuela, where the women get up early to cook *arepas* for breakfast . . . . The first thing Rigoberta did when she got up in the morning was make dough and cook tortillas for breakfast; it was a reflex that was thousands of years old. (xv–xvi)

By framing Menchú's actions within the instinctual "reflex" of an essential indigenous identity, Burgos-Debray effectively negates the informant's cross-cultural agency by flatly categorizing all of her actions as "native" ways of being. In other words, it is also possible that Menchú gets up and makes tortillas because she wants to be a thoughtful guest or because, as an act of kindness, she wishes to please Burgos-Debray by making foods to which the ethnographer has little access in Paris. Burgos-Debray's romantic representation of Menchú takes place in spite of what the ethnographer already knows about Menchú's heterogeneous cultural experience (by the time the interview takes place, Menchú has become an international spokeswoman for the political and armed struggle of indigenous communities in Guatemala), and most significantly, it negates the activity of choice in the informant's life. Burgos-Debray freezes Menchú in time and space, fixing her in mythical, monocultural stasis by situating all of her actions—past and present—within the essentialized logic of what Burgos-Debray considers traditional, authentic Quiché culture.

Regardless of what Menchú may have felt as she made breakfast for herself and Burgos-Debray, this description also fails to consider or problematize how Menchú's daily preparation of tortillas is a "reflex" embedded in five hundred years of colonial history and ruthless exploitation of indigenous labor. By glossing over the fact that in privileged Latin American households the "women" who get up early to cook arepas or tortillas for breakfast are often Indian servants, Burgos-Debray avoids the unsettling implications of race and class tensions present in this unequal field of domestic production, creating a universalizing community of women in which Menchú's work loses its racial marker and becomes purely feminine and cultural (in the most ossified sense). Rendering neutral the perturbing ghosts of colonial history and her own relational position within that context, Burgos-Debray thus neglects to consider in what ways Menchú's responses to her questions may have been shaped or censured by the informant's awareness of and response to Burgos-Debray's privileged location within those historical tensions. By representing Menchú as a truth-sayer, Burgos-Debray downplays her informant's rich history and epistemological complexities as a "world-traveler," the fact that Menchú—who, unlike Burgos-Debray, has operated in both the context of indigenous worlds and the context of the colonizer—is not only object but agent of perception who is acutely aware of the material differences between the two women. Lugones's theory of the double edges of perception and subjectivities allows us to complexify the interaction of dominant and native agencies in the ethnographic interview and to debunk Burgos-Debray's essentializing representation of Menchú: "We can also make a funny picture of those who dominate us precisely because we can see the double edges, we can see them doubly constructed, we can see the plurality in us and in them. So we know truths that only the fool can speak and only the trickster can play out without harm. We inhabit 'worlds' and travel across them and keep all the memories" (398). How can Burgos-Debray, as Trinh has asked of the traditional ethnographer, write the indigenous Other, not knowing how the Other has read into her?

The consequences of the presence of the colonial body in the testimonial negotiation is further demonstrated by the editor herself, when she explains that during the process of transcribing the interview tapes and selecting and ordering segments of response-stories she ultimately decided to correct Menchú's spoken "mistakes" of gender usage, arguing that "it would have been artificial to leave them uncorrected and it would have made Rigoberta look 'picturesque,' *which is the last thing I wanted*" (xxi; emphasis added).[19] She neglects to say for whom this would be unnatural or artificial, but one can assume that she isn't thinking of Menchú nor of other Quiché Indians who have access to the colonial tongue. Burgos-Debray corrects Menchú's speech in order to engage the needs of the implied reader of the text—a reader whose cultural proximity to Burgos-Debray is paralleled by his or her cultural distance from Menchú—and to support her claim that to tame Menchú's Quiché tongue is *naturalizing* but to let it speak wildly, to allow Menchú's oral performance to announce her cultural difference and distance from the reader, would be "picturesque." In other words, in order to construct for the reader what she deems an authentic native image, Burgos-Debray decides to alter "the real thing." Menchú's appropriation of Spanish—just as it is in her own truth and reality—will not constitute the authentic native presence that Burgos-Debray is after. Because of Menchú's historical experience as a Quiché, a foreigner to the master language of both Burgos-Debray and the reader, the authenticity of her textualized identity must rely on artifice. That truth and authenticity are the effects of writing is clear in this example. What is also clear in Burgos-Debray's editorial decisions is that in "allowing her to make the transition from the spoken to the written word," in facilitating the metamorphosis of Menchú from oral respondent to written autobiographical subject, Burgos-Debray shapes the specific image of nativeness presented in the text: the ethnographer chisels away undesirable signs of Menchú's cultural difference before allowing her to enter the colonizing territory of the reader.

A critical reading of Burgos-Debray's introduction casts a spotlight on the ideologically charged cultural and racial tensions between editor and indigenous informant and also indicates the degree to which Burgos-Debray's authorial decisions manipulate the performance of "the real." As the writer of this native testimony, Burgos-Debray's main tasks are to provide clear links between Menchú's life story and the history of indigenous oppression in Latin America since the Spanish conquest, to mediate the semiosic distance between Menchú and the text's implied reader, and to persuade the reader that Menchú's unmediated access to knowledge and language allows her to be a nonideological "truth-sayer." From this perspective, it becomes clear that Burgos-Debray functions not as Menchú's double but as the reader's, making editorial decisions that take into account the cultural and linguistic interpretations of "we Latin Americans," inviting the powerful authority of the colonizer/reader to condition the text's representation of native selfhood and native community: which elements go in, which come out, which are repeated, and which are modified from their "true" version. Although Burgos-Debray attempts a disappearing act by excising significant ethnographic markings, the presence and authority of her colonial self remain encoded throughout the text.

The prescriptive framework of the prologue, the romanticizing of the native informant, the removal or concealment of both colonial and "undesirable" indigenous signs, the editor's discourse of justification for the selective use of artifice, and the occulted use of artifice itself all contribute to the promotion and consumption of this text as the authentic voice of Rigoberta Menchú.

Shifting Subject Positions and Configurations of Agency

> The moment the insider steps out from the inside she's no longer a mere insider. . . . She is, in other words, this inappropriate other or same who moves about with always at least two gestures: that of affirming "I am like you" while persisting in her difference and that of reminding "I am different" while unsettling every definition of otherness arrived at.
> —Trinh T. Minh-ha, "Not You/Like You: Post-Colonial Women and the Interlocking Questions of Identity and Difference"

I, Rigoberta Menchú opens with the famous passage in which Menchú establishes an exclusively representative politics of experience and identity that authorizes her to speak for her community:

> My name is Rigoberta Menchú. I am twenty-three years old. This is my testimony. I didn't learn it from a book and I didn't learn it alone. I'd like to stress that it's not only my life, it's also the testimony of my people. It's hard for me to remember everything that's happened to me in my life since there have been many very bad times but, yes, moments of joy as well. The important thing is that what has happened to me has happened to many other people too: My story is the story of all poor Guatemalans. My personal experience is the reality of a whole people. (1)

This testimonio is widely regarded by critics as a text that provides a corrective to the objectification of the native in traditional anthropology by democratizing the ethnographic process and allowing Menchú to speak not only for herself but for her people as well. By situating herself and her experiences within the communal history of indigenous struggle for survival in Guatemala, Menchú establishes authority and authenticity as the nonexceptional, collective "I"-witness, subject and object of the historical events related in the text. Menchú, alongside her people, has witnessed and suffered the brutal consequences of the political technologies of genocide: gross exploitation of indigenous labor, subhuman working and living conditions, systematic and violent theft of indigenous land, rape, torture, and mass murder. Because Menchú regards her own life story—"what has happened to me"—as a representative experience of all indigenous communities in Guatemala, the telling of her individual story is inextricably bound to the telling of the collective story of the whole *pueblo* (people or community). Positioning herself within the historical polarity of indigenous peoples versus the state (what has happened to *us* because of *them*) Menchú's "I" becomes interchangeable with the "we" of the entire Quiché community.

Critical claims for Menchú's authenticity have supported the correlative claim (advanced by Menchú herself) about the narrator's status as an indigenous woman whose life story is representative of other lives in her community. Doris Sommer, in "Not Just a Personal Story," has analyzed the representational or metonymic relationship of Menchú to her community, arguing that this lateral representation dismantles the dichotomy established in Western bourgeois autobiography of individual versus collective experience (narratives in which the superior speaking "I" metaphorically replaces the inferior "you"). While I agree that the organization of the text and Menchú's narrative itself locate the narrator's agency within this lateral or representative function, a critical reading clearly indicates that this subject location is not fixed: Menchú as indistinguishable insider constitutes only one instance of the multiple subject identities constructed throughout the text. I argue that the specificity of Menchú's agency is configured in the motivated relationship between the needs of the "I" and those of the "we" and in the complex effects of Menchú's epistemological travel between these two locations. In other words, the specific human image of Menchú constituted in the text is produced in the uneasy conjunction of representative and exceptional (individual) sites. Moreover, the effects of sustaining these two positionalities will eventually lead Menchú to rethink and rewrite indigenous ways of being, something that dismantles the very notions of native authenticity laid down in the text. As the autobiographical voice moves through textual time and space, Menchú's dual gestures as "insider" and "outsider"—the narrator's exceptionality, her preoccupation with self, her appropriation of modern discourses and practices, her criticisms and redefinitions of Quiché beliefs and customs, her regret at having lost the "pure vision" of those who have never left the community—generate a heterogeneous, unstable image of Menchú: that of Trinh's "inappropriate other" or "inappropriate same" whose shifting identities emerge in the ideological and epistemic borders of the different and even opposing worlds he or she inhabits ("Not You" 375). The complex agency of Rigoberta Menchú materializes in this shifting chronotope of the self.

Menchú's agency is successively recoded through her reactions and responses to the material conditions of indigenous life. By closely following the text's chronotopes and the narrator's changing placement within them, it becomes possible, in Betty Bergland's language, to decenter the essentialized autobiographical self (in this case Menchú as unified, authentic native) and to read a speaking subject dynamically positioned in multiple, sometimes conflicting discourses (134). Reading Menchú's narrative chronotopically allows us, as Bergland has argued generally for autobiographies of the cultural Other, to "read differently—to apprehend the effect of discourses in which the autobiographer is situated by examining the subject's temporal and spatial placement in the world" (156). Approaching the study of Menchú's agency through the analysis of chronotopic and subjective shifting also allows us to bring to the surface and to critique ideologies of authentic native selfhood that emerge in the global production of the text and in Menchú's narrative segments. My analysis of the subject's chronotopic shifting is crucial to an understanding of Menchú's agency because it exposes the processes by which Menchú acquires the collective consciousness announced in the title of the text and shows that this process of *concientización* (coming to consciousness) is not a priori to the life story, nor is it Menchú's essential ontology but the consequential effects of her conflictive, ambivalent movements and of the subjective activity of choice. In her testimony, Menchú alludes to the ways in which her eventual representativeness is contingent upon her unique, deliberate desire to link the "I" to the "we": "I have to tell you that I didn't learn my politics at school. *I just tried to turn my own experience into something which was common to a whole people.* I was also very happy when I realized that it wasn't just my problem; that I wasn't the only little girl to have worried about not wanting to grow up. We were all worried about the harsh life awaiting us" (118; emphasis added). Particularly significant in this passage is Menchú's acknowledgment that her "collective consciousness" is born from both necessity and choice, from her desire to make sense of her own experience by politicizing it and linking it to the experience of "a whole people." Thus, although Sommer's critical claim that Menchú's "singularity achieves its identity as an extension of the collective" ("Not Just a Personal Story" 108) appropriately theorizes the relationship of the collective "I" as it appears in representative subject positions, this assertion downplays the presence and significance of narrative linking of individual and collective positionalities and Menchú's subsequent shifting between these two positions. Because the text exhibits a motivated relationship between the effects of individual suffering and the process of how Menchú's collective consciousness is born and how it evolves, it is perhaps more accurate to say that Menchú's collective identity emerges only as an extension of her singularity. By staying close to shifting subject positions, we can expose the significant causal link between "I" and "we" and at the same time challenge exotifying readings of the text that have viewed Menchú's collective consciousness as essential native selfhood. These shifts and links are crucial to an understanding of the specificity of Menchú's political trajectory (the specific configuration of her actions) and of the text itself: Menchú's agency and conscious location within the collective struggle is represented as the historical and diachronic consequence of her movements through and engagement with the worlds and temporal zones of the text. Additionally, if we consider that the narrative continually reconfigures Menchú's community, unwriting the monolithic notion of indigenous collective and redefining it according to political alliances that cut across ethnic barriers, the issues of Menchú's identity and agency become even more complex, since the collective within which she defines herself will eventually include a tense but crucial relationship with ladino communities.

As Menchú's textualized life story unfolds, the chronotopes that are most significant for the narrator's developing consciousness are the *finca* (plantation), the *altiplano* (the mountainous region in northwest Guatemala where most of its indigenous communities live), and Guatemala City; each of these spaces and moments creates specific challenges and opportunities for the protagonist in terms of physical and psychological survival as well as changing historical consciousness and action. Menchú locates the birth of her political consciousness in her childhood experiences in the finca. Witnessing her mother's back-breaking labor in the fields produces a deep sense of helplessness and personal responsibility in Menchú: "watching her made me feel useless and weak because I couldn't do anything to help her except look after my brother. That's when my consciousness was born" (34). Significantly, in this chronotope Menchú begins to question and rebel against the systematic brutalities of indigenous exploitation by articulating the needs of the individual "I" who seeks personal escape from this cycle of oppression. Menchú states that "from that moment, I was both angry with life and afraid of it, because I told my-self: '*This is the life I will lead too; having many children, and having them die*'"(41; emphasis added).

Menchú anguishes over her mother's suffering not only on her mother's behalf but also because she fears that she will eventually become her moth-er's double, watching her own undernourished children die, working to ex-haustion in subhuman conditions, and suffering malnutrition, hunger, and misery. When Menchú's friend dies of pesticide poisoning, her narration again shifts from the description of the hardship of those around her to the expres-sion of moral outrage and fear for her own life:

> I hated it [the finca] because my friend died there and two of my brothers died there. My mother told me that one of my brothers died of intoxication as well and I saw another of them die of hunger, of starvation. I remembered my mother's life; I saw her sweat and work but she never complained . . . . One month she said we hadn't got a single centavo: "What were we to do?" This made me very angry and I asked myself what else could we do in life? *I couldn't see any way of avoiding living as every-one else did, and suffering like they did.* I was very anxious. (88–89; emphasis added)

These passages articulate not only the brutality of institutionalized racism and its effects on the life of Menchú and of indigenous peoples in Guatemala but also the individual nature of her early accounting of this savage reality. Clear-ly, the narrator's collective consciousness is not yet developed in these chro-notopes. The desire to escape the communal fate of those like her leads Menchú to exclaim, "*I* don't want to suffer like *they* do." Feelings of fear, anger, worry, and desire serve as sites of utterances for this distinguishing "I" or individual consciousness of the narrator. These sequences in which Menchú inquires about her singular condition or seeks individual salvation generate complex images of the self by positioning it within the mutating temporal plane of ontological and political being. Moreover, telling the story this way establish-es a causal link between Menchú's preoccupation with individual survival and her eventual awareness that her personal suffering is part of the collective con-sequences of systematic structures of oppression. We can argue, then, that Menchú's ability to act effectively, to become an agent of political resistance, is contingent upon an initial and sustained preoccupation with salvation of the self. Menchú states: "I started analyzing my childhood, and I came to the conclusion that I hadn't had a childhood at all. I was never a child. I hadn't been to school, I hadn't had enough food to grow properly, I had nothing. I asked myself: 'How is this possible?'" (117).

Menchú's narrative focuses on her relentless drive to give meaning to her individual predicament, to find a political means of identifying herself that will allow for a coherent accounting of the social conditions of her life, and for an answer to her compelling question about indigenous oppression, "how is this possible?" This personal preoccupation with the external conditions in which the self operates propels the narrator into "world-travel," as she searches for knowledge and fights for survival. Her progressive circuit of travel to other indigenous communities, to the capital, and later to sites of political organization that include poor ladinos will begin to provide answers to urgent questions about the root causes of her individual condition. By establishing a motivated relationship between the exceptional and the representative Menchú, the text demonstrates that the needs, desires, and actions of the personal "I" are a necessary precondition for the progressive emergence of the narrator's collective consciousness: her individual rejection of the fate of her community will progressively lead her to seek collective identity and solutions.

Through her contact with the Achi and Mam Indians, with radical Catholic clergy, and with the ladino man who teaches her Spanish, Menchú will eventually come to identify the cause of both indigenous and ladino suffering as the struggle for the land. As the narrative progresses, Menchú's initial linking of the fate of the "I" to that of the "we" not only signals her changing placement within the Quiché collective but also her new relational identification with poor ladinos. Menchú later states that "to bring about change we had to unite, Indians and ladinos" (168). This new knowledge will propel her to forge political alliances with a group despised by her community and regarded as a threat to indigenous survival. In this sense, the "we" of her narrative becomes heterogeneous and complex, fracturing the facile, monolithic construction of an "authentic native world" while pointing to the genesis of a tense cross-cultural, cross-ethnic collective whose survival depends on a new, radical definition of native selfhood and community.

Exceptionality, "World-Traveling," and *Concientización*

> I wanted to know what the world was like on the other side.
> —Rigoberta Menchú, *I, Rigoberta Menchú*

Since the textualized image of Rigoberta Menchú has been categorized and utilized in critical discourses as a representative image of a people or community, critical focus on the text's construction of Menchú's exceptionality has been sparse. The neorealist project of constituting Menchú as a woman capable of standing in for fixed indigenous communities seems to have precluded a discussion of her relative privilege and exceptional subject locations as well as how these locations and practices undermine notions of authentic native community. I believe that the exceptional actions and development of the narrator of *I, Rigoberta Menchú* offer a compelling interpretation of the changing political needs and practices of the Quiché community, mapping out the fracturing and transformation of the "authentic" native world alluded to by Burgos-Debray in the introduction and the birth of a new, modern, heterogeneous notion of community. In this sense, as Negrón-Muntaner has argued, Menchú "speaks more 'for' a coherent, albeit changing, contemporary political project than for a 'people,' an ethnic group or a culture" (240). Although I will discuss this point more extensively in the conclusion, I would like to mention here that I consider the debate over Menchú's exceptionality to be crucial not only for a more democratic understanding of her agency and her community but also for making visible and critiquing the ideological limits of predominant readings of Menchú's subjectivity by Western intellectuals.

The text produces images of Menchú's exceptionality in multiple ways by organizing her life story around: 1) the idiosyncrasies of an ambitious self who engages in the relentless pursuit of knowledge, 2) Menchú's privileged status within the Quiché community and later as a cross-cultural political organizer and leader, and 3) the ontological, epistemological, and political consequences of Menchú's "world-travel." While these categories overlap and cannot be neatly separated, I will attempt to put flesh on each one while also considering their relational function.

Menchú's exceptionality is clearly borne out by her genealogy and by the distinguishing role she assumes (inherits) in the community: her parents were the community's elders, "the most important people in the village" (105). She was her father's favorite, traveled extensively with him as a young girl, and was directed by him to follow his footsteps as one of the community's most important leaders: "When you're old enough, you must travel, you must go around the country. You know that you must do what I do" (31). Menchú becomes an active and well-known catechist, ultimately teaching the synchretic and revolutionary Christian doctrine of Liberation Theology to her own community and later to others. She becomes a roving political leader and eventually develops extensive and ever-increasing contact with the international world ("I learned a lot from my mother, but I also learned a lot from other people, especially when I had the opportunity of talking to women who aren't from our country" [221]). Menchú actively pursues education, theorizing and learning from her own experience but also from books ("I was by now an educated woman" [169]), and becomes an independent, critical thinker who appropriates certain feminist postures, deciding that marriage and motherhood are choices for women and not predestined roles to be accepted passively, even though the rejection of these traditional roles for women in her community directly violates the most sacred Quiché ancestral teachings. Menchú is a *guerrillera* (guerrilla leader), a teacher, an interpreter, and a storyteller, and she eventually becomes the most renowned international figure in the struggle for indigenous rights in Guatemala and all of Latin America. As she travels through the course of the narrative, she emerges as an organic intellectual who appropriates[20] the political and theoretical languages of Liberation Theology and Marxism to make vital connections between individual and collective experiences of suffering and to provide answers to the questions that direct the movements of her life story, the development of revolutionary consciousness and agency, and her transforming subjectivity: "What are the root causes of my/our suffering?"; "Can revolutionary violence be justified in the eyes of God?"; "Who is the enemy?"

In Menchú's subjective trajectory the two projects of survival and knowledge are inextricably linked by the convergence of her historical and ontological needs: from the outset, the text casts Menchú as an extraordinarily complex self who cannot be fully actualized in any one world. In the flow of her narrative, Menchú continually redefines her tendency to grasp for the "outside," sometimes by denying that distinguishing desire, other times by recoding it within the logic of revolutionary liberation. For example, her desire to know what is outside her experience—to learn how to read, write, and speak Spanish—is at first represented as an individual or personal project by virtue of which she proposes to transcend the limits imposed upon her as a member of the Quiché. Her quest to speak Spanish is subsequently redefined as a response to life in the finca, where the inability to communicate with other ethnic groups complicates daily life, impedes interethnic cooperation, isolates one group from another, and allows the indigenous to be swindled by ladinos. As the text progresses, however, her desire to learn Spanish and to read and write are represented as practices that support the collective project of liberation. After her father is imprisoned, she redefines her desire in relation to indigenous survival: learning Spanish will enable her to broaden coalition among linguistically diverse indigenous groups as well as among politically organized ladinos.

Menchú's singularity is increasingly marked by her unique access to restricted Quiché spaces and her travels to outside "worlds." Whereas Quiché tradition sharply limits the movement of women within the community and severely restricts their contact with spaces outside the family home, Menchú inherits from her mother the unusual freedom of travel. The dialogical circuit of movement within her own community provides access to experience and knowledge that would otherwise be denied her, and her ability to travel to and from different cultural zones provides the necessary condition for her development as a privileged interpreter or messenger who brings back news of the outside to the Quiché community. Menchú's relationship with her father and his exceptional role in the community are the means by which she first engages the capital, which will become one of the text's most significant sites of subjective transformation:

> My first visit to the capital was a very big step in my life. I was my father's favourite; I went with him everywhere . . . . It was the first time that I'd been in a truck with windows. We were used to traveling in closed lorries . . . . I hardly slept at all looking at the countryside we passed through from Uspantán to the capital. It impressed me very much, it was wonderful to see everything along the way—towns, mountains, houses very different from our own . . . . When we reached the capital, I saw cars for the first time. I thought they were animals just going along. It didn't occur to me that they were cars . . . . It was all so amazing for me. I remember when I got home telling my brothers and sisters what the cars were like, how they were driven, and that they didn't crash into one another or kill anyone, and a whole load of other things as well. I had a long tale to tell at home. (31)

Menchú's exuberant description of her first trip to Guatemala City at age seven announces the beginning of her distinguishing adventure into world-travel, and initiates the circuit of inside/outside movement that organizes textual structure and subjective transformation. This passage clearly communicates Menchú's personal joy in experiencing foreign worlds and at the same time represents her as one who mediates cultural dichotomies for her community (the capital/the altiplano; ladino world/indigenous world). The access to travel establishes her as a privileged witness who sees that which is hidden, outside, or inaccessible to others in her community. The narrator's exceptional role as intratextual mediator or interpreter parallels the intertextual function of the testimonial narrative itself: the protagonist Menchú interprets outside (ladino) worlds for the Quiché just as *I, Rigoberta Menchú* interprets inside (native) worlds for the reader of the text.

Menchú's exceptionality is further demonstrated as her transgressions against traditional patriarchal Quiché authority and wisdom become textual repetitions that announce her shifting subject positions and heterogeneous knowledge base. Moreover, her progressive subversion of traditional patriarchal Quiché authority and wisdom not only constitutes her exceptional relationship to the community but also serves as evidence that the transparent relationship between native and authentic native world has been irretrievably fractured. These repetitive sequences create an image of a protagonist whose unsinkable ambition to learn and to travel is supported by a desperate desire to escape the miserable conditions imposed on indigenous women. Chapter

13, "Death of Her Friend by Poisoning in the Finca," presents three archetypal actions that form the basis of the narrator's individual impulses to move through different worlds in search of what the narrator terms "una salida" (an exit or escape): 1) the narrator's emotional reaction to the violence of her everyday life, 2) her desire to speak Spanish as a tool to acquiring liberating knowledges and practices, and 3) her transgressive choices and departure into "world-travel." The chapter opens with a description of Menchú's trip to the finca at the age of fourteen, then recounts her grief and desperation at the tragic death by pesticide poisoning of her friend, María. Her friend's death initiates for Menchú a frantic desire to escape a similar fate by making radical life choices:

> I was afraid of life and I'd ask myself: "What will life be like when I'm older?" And that friend of mine had left me with things to think about. She used to say that she would never get married because marriage meant children and if she had a child she couldn't bear to see him die of starvation or pain or illness. This made me think a lot. I drove myself mad thinking about it. . . . And when my friend died, I said: "I'll never get married," because that's what she'd said. I didn't want to go through all the grief. My ideas changed completely; so many ideas came to me. *"What am I going to do?"* (88; emphasis added)

First presented here as a choice that supports individual survival, Menchú's decision to reject marriage and motherhood—sacred and mandated roles for women in Quiché ancestral law—is eventually rewritten in her narrative as a choice that directly supports the collective struggle. However, in this sequence the narrator implicitly challenges the Quiché order of things by situating herself outside of its traditional logic and allowing the authority of her experience and desire to guide personal decisions about her life.

Chapter 13 continues to create an exceptional image of the narrator's selfhood by focusing on Menchú's desire to learn. Following the discussion about the brutalities of life for indigenous women, Menchú recounts how her desire for formal education was for many years thwarted by her father. Like Sor Juana Inés de la Cruz, whose access to formal education and the written word was ultimately revoked by the patriarchal structure of late-seventeenth-century Mexico's Catholic hierarchy, Menchú's access to multiple knowledges, to speaking, reading, and writing Spanish, is for many years denied by her father and his fear that she will become ladinized and leave the Quiché collective to secure personal gains. Whereas Sor Juana's genius and adventure into knowledge was perceived by the male hierarchy of the church as a threat to the edict of "holy ignorance" imposed on women, Menchú's becomes a threat to ethnic unity and strength. Yet in spite of these pressures and Menchú's sympathy for them, her narrative voice traces her decision to stop at nothing and to continue to nurture her ambition to learn outside the linguistic and cultural borders of the Quiché community: "I had a lot of ideas but I knew I couldn't express them all. I wanted to read or speak or write Spanish. I told my father this, that I wanted to learn to read. *Perhaps things were different if you could read.* . . . But my father said he didn't agree with my idea because I was trying to leave the community, to go far away, and find what was best for me. He said: 'You'll forget about our common heritage. If you leave, it will be for good. If you leave our community, I will not support you'" (89; emphasis added). Even after her father threatens to withdraw his support for her, Menchú remains determined: "My father explained all this to me, but I said: 'No, I want to learn, I want to learn,' and I went on and on about it" (89); "I had to learn Spanish and to read and write" (156). Menchú's father both opens and closes the door to her "world-traveling": he nurtures his daughter's exceptionality by obliging her to speak and to assume authority in the community, yet at the same time he tries to confine that movement to cultural spaces and practices that appear to be free of the threat of acculturation and that support the Indian/ladino dichotomy. Thus Menchú's relationship with her father distinguishes her as an exceptional self in two conflicting ways; she is like him and not like him. Menchú inherits her father's privileged place in the community and accepts its related responsibilities, but she distinguishes herself by rejecting his authority when it interferes with personal/political ambitions that go beyond the dictates of traditional Quiché wisdom. As in her rejection of motherhood, Menchú's singularity is coded in her tendency to sustain individual desires and to say "no" to voices of authority that attempt to limit her qualitative movements away from the inside. Significantly, the narrator's obstinate refusal to accept her father's decision reinforces the text's development of Menchú as an extraordinarily unique Quiché woman while it simultaneously foregrounds the disintegration of traditional Quiché logic: the daughter, not the male elder, possesses a superior knowledge whose implementation may provide a route to survival—Menchú's desire to learn Spanish is revealed in her narrative as a crucial step in the eventual political coalition of indigenous and nonindigenous groups.[21]

Chapter 13 ends with Menchú's departure for Guatemala City. She is offered twenty *quetzals* a month to be a maid in the capital, but the narrator reports that her father "was very worried because he never wanted us to go to the capital to be maids. He thought that our ideas would be all distorted afterwards. He was afraid that we would forget all the things he and my mother had taught us since we were little" (90). Despite her father's fears, Menchú accepts the offer. So determined is she in her desire for knowledge that in response to her father's report that her sister is suffering miserably working as a maid in the capital, where she is being "treated like dirt by the rich,"

Menchú responds: "I said it didn't matter if they treated her badly, if she could learn Spanish and learn to read. That was my ambition. . . . I wondered how it could be harder than our work, because I always thought that it would be impossible to work harder than we did" (90). Textual sequences like this one construct a headstrong, unyielding protagonist whose ambition to learn (and to leave) exceeds her own fears about becoming a ladinized outsider. Additionally, Menchú's experience in the capital eventually marks another crucial site of concientización, as the deplorable conditions of her work as a maid in an upper-class household provides new knowledge about the racist worldview of the Guatemalan elite, something that fuels her transforming revolutionary consciousness and refines her understanding of the role of social class in the ladino/Indian struggle. Menchú's defiance of her father's prophecy that she will leave the community for good or forget what she has been taught sketches both the exceptional agency of the narrator and the limits of Quiché nationalist knowledges: once outside her community she assumes even more effective leadership as she begins to understand the systematic nature of her suffering and thereby to formulate new theories of oppression that redefine and resituate her own community's needs. Thus Menchú's life story inscribes an uncommon and extraordinary bios and at the same time represents the making of a new world, a world in which disobeying the ancestors becomes both the singular mark of the protagonist's agency and a necessary condition for indigenous survival.

Struggling for Inscriptions of Self: Menchú as Insider/Outsider

> . . . it becomes imperative to develop a theory of autobiography that acknowledges the importance of marginalized voices, but avoids essentializing individuals and groups; that takes into account complex relationships between cultures and discourses that produce the speaking subject, but avoids viewing language as a transparent representation of the imagined real.
> —Betty Bergland, "Postmodernism and the Autobiographical Subject: Reconstructing the 'Other'"

A critical reading of *I, Rigoberta Menchú*, performed without the positivist-realist complicity of "testimonio-seeing eyes," produces radical new definitions of native selfhood and native community. The ontological and epistemological consequences of Menchú's entrance into outside knowledges and "world-travel" place the narrator in what Trinh refers to as "the undetermined and constantly shifting threshold of 'insider/outsider,'" a space where Menchú redefines and transforms not only her self but her place within the Quiché culture and her interpretation of its needs, practices, and beliefs. As Negrón-Muntaner argues:

> it is evident from Menchú's narrative that the "world" she is sharing has suffered deep transformations as a result of war, ideological conflict, and contact with other countries and groups. Within the flow of her narrative, the narrator also questions, re-defines, and transforms her "world" almost beyond recognition. . . . Menchú's narrated subjectivity is a "site" of continuous conflict and negotiation between various discourses where "success" is primarily measured by the ability to build coalitions for survival beyond the ladino/Indian dichotomy. (244)

In this sense, *I, Rigoberta Menchú* represents the unmaking of the "authentic" native world posited by realist strategies of reading and writing and portrayed in the introduction and in segments of Menchú's narrative. The plane of narrative content itself rejects ossified notions of native experience, actions, and imagination as it presents us with definitive evidence of the deep epistemic fissures in the indigenous world in which Menchú develops. I argue that Menchú's narrative serves as testimony not to the unchanging indigenous world and its indistinguishable representative (as presented by Burgos-Debray) but to the thrusting of that ever-changing world and its exceptional protagonist into a cataclysmic relation with modernity. The text chronicles not only Menchú's exceptional efforts to resist the campaign of genocide waged against the indigenous by the Guatemalan government but also her efforts to transform the Quiché community along political and cultural lines that disarticulate traditional notions of "us versus them" and promote the entrance of the indigenous world into the ambivalent but necessary realm of the ladino.

Despite the text's radical reworking of native subject and community, the positivist-realist strategies present in the introduction's prescriptive framework and in prominent readings of the text are supported within the text itself by the narrator Menchú, who makes explicit claims about her status as a purely representative Quiché woman, downplaying or criticizing what might be interpreted as transgressive moments of radical individuality or epistemic shifting. Although, as we have seen, the text continually negotiates the representative and exceptional subject positions of the narrator, at the explicit level of utterance Menchú (like Burgos-Debray before her) does not accommodate the complexities of her heterogeneous languages and actions nor consider how these plural positions may inscribe new native subjectivities. In other words, the conflictive and multiple gestures constructed in the narrative exceed the narrator's ability or willingness to translate those actions intelligibly into a new definition of native selfhood and native world.

We have seen that the text organizes Menchú's life story upon repeated temporal sequences of her intractable pursuit and appropriation of distant and/ or forbidden experiences and knowledges, yet at the synchronic level Menchú appropriates her father's initial logic and traditionalist Quiché beliefs by repeatedly emphasizing the dangers of cultural disintegration implicit in her contact with the outside—the finca, the capital, ladino schools, the Spanish language, intellectual discourses, and Catholic missionaries. The narrator attempts to muffle the excesses of her movements and identities with explicit utterances about the "disgusting" (61) nature of the ladino world, yet the text subverts these claims by juxtaposing the autobiographical subject's unbridled ambition to leave the center of the Quiché world in search of knowledge and change—historical, linguistic, cultural, ideological, political, and metaphysical. Although Menchú denounces the city as the punishing world of ladinos, asserting that "the city for me was a monster, something alien, different" (32), she is ambivalently and persistently drawn to know and understand the manifestations of its monstrousness, asserting that after her first trip to Guatemala City, "every time my father went to the capital, I wanted to go with him" (32). While the city is unequivocally characterized by the narrator as a site of degradation and misery, she returns to the capital many times, as her desire and need for other worlds directs her out of the indigenous community and into the heterogeneous sphere of the ladino.

The consequences of the narrator's "world-travel" produce ambivalent textual effects that point to an internal struggle for images of native selfhood: at one level the text produces a narrator who is epistemically privileged, whose extraordinary ability to appropriate diverse knowledge bases and to situate herself coherently in heterogeneous worlds allows her to achieve success, both in individual and collective terms. But at another level these new and flexible subject positions conflict with Menchú's ideological construction of self, in which she denounces her ontological plurality and radical agency as a deformation of authentic Quiché knowledge and selfhood. It is within this tense ambiguity between what the narrator does and what she thinks about herself that the speaking "I" develops:

> In my community's terms, I was already a grown woman, and I was very ashamed at being so confused, when so many of my village understood so much better than I. But their ideas were pure because they had never been outside their community. We'd been down to the *fincas,* but *they* hadn't known anything different. Going to the capital in a lorry brings about a change in an Indian, which he suffers inside himself. That's why my little brothers and my brothers [*sic*] and sisters understood more clearly than I did. (121)

The shift in subject positions—from "world-traveler" to "authentic native woman"—is quite clear in this passage. While recounting a life story in which her exceptionality—and the very ground of her bios—is largely defined by a passionate, relentless desire to apprehend the distant and the unknown, Menchú simultaneously degrades the specificity and the success of her agency by idealizing those who have been denied the experience of travel, considering them free of the contamination brought about by contact with difference (the very contact she has been forcefully seeking throughout the text). That Menchú considers impurity and confusion the consequences of her progressively evolving ideas and actions attests to her multiple (and uneasy) positioning in the dynamic zone between the discourses of the "authentic native world" and those of the "fractured acculturated worlds" of ladinos and "world-travelers" like herself. Throughout the text, she laments her own condition as an indigenous woman whose experience between two worlds has resulted in an ontological deficiency and epistemic loss, yet the text clearly demonstrates how her movement between the Guatemalan altiplano and the finca, the altiplano and the capital, and later between Guatemala and Mexico provides the necessary conditions for malleable, changing inscriptions of self and potentially for the survival of Guatemala's indigenous communities. By recounting the story of her desire for diverse knowledges and experiences and its relationship to revolutionary change, a desire that is eventually fulfilled in the text, yet at the same time denouncing those like herself who move away from traditional cultural practices and linguistic codes, the speaker positions herself in the impasse between two opposing ways of seeing and being in the world. These instances of discourse never openly confront one another, nor are they ever resolved. Yet it is here, "looking in from the outside and out from the inside," that the ambivalent narrator of *I, Rigoberta Menchú* materializes.

Conclusion: Post-Positivist Realist Strategies and the Construction of Otherness

> The fullest account of decolonization should include a vision of the possibilities that human agents have for living their lives according to principles and values that they choose through rational deliberation and can thus call their "own." . . . Beyond this starting hypothesis lies the difficult but necessary job of specifying commonalities and articulating disagreements and of learning from one another.
> —Satya P. Mohanty, "Colonial Legacies, Multicultural Futures:
>   Relativism, Objectivity, and the Challenge of Otherness"

My desire in this essay has been to bring into conflictive counterposition the discursive and ideological complexities of *I, Rigoberta Menchú* and the reductive interpretive practices of its creators, critics, and readers. Whether or not Rigoberta Menchú consciously constructs for her interviewer the image of "authentic" native self and world or whether she *is,* as Lugones would say, "two different native women" whose shifting cosmovision is a manifestation of ontological plurality, Menchú's idealizing statements (as rendered by Burgos-Debray) about authentic native selfhood have clear effects on the reader. Although during the course of the narrative Menchú dismantles notions of homogeneous native subjectivity and traces the fracturing of the traditional Quiché community and its knowledge bases and ideologies, the explicit romanticized insistence of both Menchú and Burgos-Debray on native authenticity and truth-saying encourages the reader to posit within the text an essentialist epistemology of "the real."

While some critics of the testimonio have sidestepped the more critical ambiguities emerging in testimonial narratives, muting a critical discussion of native exceptionality or radical individuality by asserting that "it does not matter who speaks," clearly it not only matters but plays a determining role in the commodifying of texts for the international market and in the testimonio's function as a political tool—think of how the singular image of Menchú has been exploited to facilitate the sale and circulation of *I, Rigoberta Menchú* and to attract the focus of international attention to the systems of oppression directed by the Guatemalan state.

The awarding of the Nobel Peace Prize to Menchú in 1992, which in Arturo Arias's opinion allowed her to return to Guatemala as a respected indigenous leader and "gave her the power to publicly articulate critical perspectives on the rights of the indigenous population, the continuing violation of human rights in the country, the lack of social or economic justice, and the need for a new consciousness to confront the nation's crises, without being harmed or silenced and while being treated as an honored dignitary for verbalizing such views" (39), indicates the degree to which the indigenous community represented in the text has been supported by the insistence on Menchú's iconic singularity and visibility as a spokeswoman for indigenous justice. Additionally, the question of collapsing the difference of the individual native speaking subject into the polyphonic but textually absent voices of the collective may work well for Western critics whose goal is the dismantling of Western philosophical dichotomies (the individual versus the collective), but for indigenous communities it prematurely forecloses the literary and historical inscription of individual native subjectivities and ignores the text's exigency that the reader detain him- or herself in the specific, complex, and unique image of Otherness it generates.

The advent of testimonial narratives has reframed an intense discussion about how to read cultural Otherness and, perhaps more importantly, about

the need to read critically the discourse of the Other. In order to apprehend
the dynamic, discursive images of Rigoberta Menchú and to analyze the ways
in which the changing political and social relations presented in the narrative produce a new native subject, we must abandon the colonizing desire to
posit within the text an already constituted native subject and we must reject
the mystifying idea that the testimonio is a "neo-realist super-genre, a model
of an 'authentic narrative' for witnessing the unspeakable and narrating the
unspoken experience of the Latin American subaltern" (Sklodowska, "Spanish American" 43).[22] Editorial constructions notwithstanding, *I, Rigoberta
Menchú* presents us with the opportunity to learn about the Other by reading and interpreting a text that presents a compelling revision of indigenous
self and world, yet I would argue that many of "us" did not learn from
Menchú's narrative, finding in the text only what we wanted to find, what we
already knew and wanted to know before we read the first page. By reading
the narrative critically, by problematizing, for example, the way its ideological production limits Menchú's political agency (I refer to her negative interpretation of her own multiple subjectivities), we practice respect for Menchú
as a producer of knowledge and as a complex and contradictory subject and
place her interpretive practices in an equal field with our own. If, however, we
remain uncritical about the ideological content of the discourse of the Other, exotifying rather than critiquing difference, we may certainly avoid tense
discussions and ethnocentric mistakes—as Satya P. Mohanty points out—but
at the expense of eliminating "the possibility that they [the Other] will ever
have anything to teach us" (112). To move forward with the project of recon-
stituting epistemic relations between "us" and "them" will allow us to apprehend our historical tendency to reproduce monolithic models of native Otherness while allowing us to consider new indigenous inscriptions of the
transforming relationship of the individual to the collective, so that we may
create and sustain new ways of thinking about these complex, multiply determined positionalities. In this way we can truly practice the work of decolonization by unsettling and making visible our own mystifying constructions
of Otherness.

Notes

I would like to thank my good friend and colleague Amie Macdonald for helping me
to think through many of the ideas in this essay and for her moral support throughout the process. I am also very grateful to the editors of this volume, Wendy S. Hesford and Wendy Kozol, for their close and challenging readings of an earlier version
of this piece and for their invaluable editorial suggestions.

Regarding the second epigraph that opens this chapter, Menchú expresses this wish in the final minutes of *When the Mountains Tremble,* a videorecording originally released in 1983 and rereleased in a post–Nobel Peace Prize version in 1992. This new version contains footage of Menchú receiving the prize as well as a voice-over that explains what she was feeling and thinking at the time. Her message in Spanish reads: "Sólo lo único que puedo pedir es que no nos idealicen, porque nosotros no somos mitos del pasado ni del presente, sino somos pueblos activos. Y mientras que haya un indio vivo en cualquier rincón de América y del mundo, hay un brillo de esperanza y un pensamiento original." In translating this piece of monologue, I had to give much thought as to how to translate the word *original,* which in Spanish can mean both "new" and "authentic." Menchú could have used the Spanish word *auténtico* (authentic) but she didn't, and therefore the responsibility rests with the translator to resolve this very fruitful ambiguity. I decided to leave the word as a cognate for the English "original," which I believe most closely maintains the instability and tension between the possible signifieds of her utterance.

1. In September 1998 Rigoberta Menchú and the text *I, Rigoberta Menchú* were thrust into controversy. In a recently published book by the anthropologist David Stoll, *Rigoberta Menchú and the Story of All Poor Guatemalans,* key parts of Menchú's testimony have been called into question. An interview conducted by the *New York Times* in September 1998, following up on Stoll's claims about the falseness of Menchú's testimony, confirmed Stoll's evidence that in her testimony to Elisabeth Burgos-Debray, Menchú fabricated and misrepresented key "facts." While academics are taking sides on this shocking development, most professors who use the text in their classrooms are arguing that Menchú's personal "lies" are unimportant since her testimony represents the truth of the larger collective struggle against indigenous oppression in Guatemala. When questioned about Stoll's book and the growing awareness that she lied about the nature of her father's struggle for land rights, about having been deprived of an education, and about the details surrounding the deaths of her father, mother, and brother, Menchú has maintained that the details are unimportant and that her testimony is still "true." For those critics invested in the testimonio's access to the verifiable "real truth" and in Menchú's transparency as a native "truth-sayer," these new disclosures would seem to dismantle the very core of their poetics for the genre. For those of us who have scrutinized the relationship between testimony and truth, who have worked to foreground the ambiguities, contradictions, and complexities of the genre, in short, those who have studied this genre as *writing,* Menchú's "lies" actually lend support to our claim that the testimonio—regardless of the significant historical "truths" it may produce—should be studied as a discursive world.

2. Allen Carey-Webb asserts that by the mid 1990s this text, the winner of the Casa de las Américas Prize as the outstanding testimonial of 1983, had achieved the status of a "minor classic" (4).

3. *Arpilleras* are embroidered patchwork tapestries that protest and denounce human rights violations in Latin America (in the 1980s arpillera workshops became sites

of organized resistance to political oppression; their production flourished in Chile, for example, during the seventeen years of the fascist dictatorship of Augusto Pinochet). The arpillera is a graphic testament that not only documents the hidden crimes of the state against its people but also urges those who view the storytelling tapestry to remember and to name those crimes and their victims. These artifacts are especially crucial in political situations in which historical memory itself is an act of subversion.

4. The most prominent form of testimonio is the collaborative form, such as *I, Rigoberta Menchú,* in which an intellectual in solidarity with a member of an oppressed constituency elicits, records, and transcribes the native informant's testimony. Other notable collaborative women's testimonial narratives published between 1969 and 1986 include *Hasta no verte Jesús mío* (Elena Poniatowska), *"Si me permiten hablar . . .": Testimonio de Domitila, una mujer de las minas de Bolivia* (Domitila Barrios de Chungara with Moema Viezzer), *No me agarran viva: La mujer salvadoreña en lucha* (Claribel Alegría and D. J. Flakoll), *Historias de vida: Hebe de Bonafini* (Hebe de Bonafini with Matilde Sánchez), and *Doris Tijerino: Inside the Nicaraguan Revolution* (Margaret Randall).

5. For critics who constitute Menchú as a nonideological subject see Beverley; Fernández Olmos; and Yúdice. Additionally, many of the essays in the Carey-Webb and Benz collection—with some notable exceptions—fail to problematize the projected transparency of Menchú's testimony.

6. Sklodowska follows Greimas in asserting that the modern testimonial reader has to be persuaded to interpret discourse as truth-saying. According to Greimas, truth believing involves the active and deliberate complicity of speaker and reader, "'thus creating a tacit agreement, a veridiction contract between the speaker and the addressee'" (qtd. in Sklodowska, "Spanish American" 35). This theory works well with my own analysis of the intention and function of Burgos-Debray's introduction, which attempts to persuade the reader that Menchú's words do not require critical interpretation, since they are "simple and true."

7. *Ladino* is an identifying term applied to mestizos (mixed-blood people) of Guatemala who define themselves in opposition to indigenous peoples and indigenous practices and belief systems. Ladinos are distributed in all social classes but, given the economic condition of Guatemala, most are poor. *Ladino* may also apply to indigenous people who have left indigenous communities and who reject identification as Indians; these ladinos usually reside in the poorest and most exploited sectors of Guatemalan society.

8. In addition to the essays I have listed, my own observations at my institution (and others) support this assertion. I am sometimes asked to lecture on the testimonial genre and Burgos-Debray's text in particular in the classes of colleagues in other disciplines, and invariably these colleagues are surprised (and sometimes confounded) by my critical focus on the complexities and problematics of testimonial transcription, reception, and representation of Otherness.

9. Semiosis is the terminology of the American school of semiotics as outlined by John Deely in *Basics of Semiotics.* "Semiosic process" is a more rigorously applied term

than "semiotic process," since it refers specifically to the relational process of sign activity itself, while "semiotic" refers to the study of that activity. This distinction made by the American school reflects a rejection of anthropologocentrism, as semiosis is a process that also (and more often, in fact) takes place outside of human perception, human activity, and human language (e.g., zoosemiosis, phytosemiosis).

10. I am not suggesting that any text should or could escape its status as an unstable sign system whose meanings are largely dependent on the interpretations of readers; Jara's assertion robs the text of its multiplicity and indeterminacy—which are the specific markings and richness of literary discourse—but at the same time, and even more problematically, it relieves the reader of his or her responsibility in the act of reading and interpreting from situated cultural and ideological locations. In spite of these glaring issues, this unsustainable assertion was widely held in the first wave of testimonial criticism, something that may point to a critical nostalgia for positivist notions of realist discourse, namely that we can gain immediate access to the "real" through the causal reconstruction of verified facts that "speak for themselves." René Jara, for example, claims that the testimonio is "a trace of the real" (2). See also Kearney and Gugelberger; Marín; and Gugelberger.

11. See Sklodowska, "Spanish American" and Testimonio; Negrón-Muntaner; Vera-León; Amar Sánchez; Luis; Millet; and Pratt.

12. Both Dinesh D'Souza and Mario Vargas Llosa attack the political ideas expressed by Menchú in the text; they make no distinction between narrator and real-life informant, which clearly establishes their acceptance of Menchú's status as autobiographer. In his article that comments on this ultraconservative targeting of the real-life Menchú, Gene Bell-Villada further supports the idea of Menchú's authorship when he states that "by encountering her as the narrator of When the Mountains Tremble, and as the direct or indirect target of conservatives both in the U.S. and in Peru, American undergraduates are afforded the opportunity to 'experience' Rigoberta, more variously and vibrantly, outside the pages of her own book" (79; emphasis added).

13. The standard library catalog entry for I, Rigoberta Menchú lists Menchú as the author and Burgos-Debray as having "edited and introduced" the text. However, I have on rare occasion found Elisabeth Burgos-Debray listed as author of the text (with no mention of Menchú) and have also encountered some bibliographic listings where the title of the text is listed first with subsequent reference to Burgos-Debray as editor and author of the introduction (again, no mention of Menchú). Since one of the main goals of this essay is to highlight the determining ways in which Burgos-Debray functions as author and as producer of the text's "truths," I had listed Burgos-Debray as the author in my works cited section. I was subsequently asked by the editorial staff of the University of Illinois Press to conform to the more standard bibliographic listing with Menchú as author and Burgos-Debray as editor.

14. Judith Thorn discusses Menchú's role in helping Burgos-Debray edit the final manuscript of her testimony (which was reportedly read aloud to her in its entirety). While this inclusion of Menchú in the selection process democratizes and recodes the traditional role of "native" informant, most of the determining functions of author

remain entrusted to Burgos-Debray. As Sklodowska has argued, despite its commitment to democratization the testimonio remains a discourse of the elite, and its production and dissemination rely on the support of intellectual institutional apparatuses that are designed to "accommodate" within an elite order of production and reception the voice of the subaltern Other (*Testimonio* 86). Menchú herself has objected to the attribution of authorship to Burgos-Debray. In a 1993 interview with Alice Brittin and Kenya Dworkin, Menchú asserts that in order to correctly represent the authorship of the text it should be listed as "shared" (214). However, when questioned in September 1998—after the release of David Stoll's book—about the alleged misinformation in her testimony, Menchú is quoted as saying: "I am the protagonist of the book, and it was my testimony, but I am not the author" (Rohter).

15. The linking of the testimonio and native survival has been overstated in predominant criticism. As Negrón-Muntaner states, while the text *I, Rigoberta Menchú* may have played a part in saving Rigoberta Menchú's life, the Guatemalan and United States governments responded quickly and effectively to international attention drawn by the publication of the text. Fearing "another Nicaragua," the United States supported centrist-right regimes and the Guatemalan army "stopped random persecutions and torture and returned to selected and minimal targets, established model villages to simulate capitalist and non-threatening forms of economic organization, and pitted communities against each other and against guerrillas, through civilian patrols" (261). While international response to this testimonio intervened in the politico-military strategies of the United States and Guatemala, the new tactics adopted by both governments continue to plunder native communities, and the relationship of the testimonio to native survival remains irresolvable. At the same time, it is important to consider the role that Menchú has played in consolidating political identity and coalition among disparate Mayan groups in Guatemala (which comprise 55 percent of the national population). Arturo Arias asserts that "Menchú's role as a living icon and a spokesperson for all Mayan peoples has . . . given [the Mayan peoples] new hope, new means of political enfranchisement and a new pride" (43).

16. Burgos-Debray's self-conception as Menchú's political comrade is supported by Achugar's development of the concept of the "letrado solidario" (the intellectual in solidarity with the informant) who, together with the testimonial witness, produces the transmission of the testimony. Achugar defends the "translation" or manipulation of the informant's testimony (which he refers to as an "adecuación sintáctica" [syntactical adaptation]) as a crucial form of eliminating "noise" or "interference" (*ruidos*) that would decrease the flow of the transmission of the testimonio. In his view, these manipulations of the raw material function to preserve the voice of the Other. Although Achugar's interpretation is far from my own, it is important to note that he is not arguing for a transparent or nonmitigated voice of the informant, an uninterrupted presentation of "the real," but instead situates collaborative testimonials "as a discursive space that presents a *struggle for power* of those social subjects who question the discursive hegemony . . . of dominant social and ideological sectors" (57; my translation; emphasis added).

17. By utilizing Bakhtin's theory of heteroglossia I wish to emphasize not only the multiple conditions and effects of dialogue between Burgos-Debray and Menchú, which transform the production of the informant's raw testimony, but also the specific context of cultural power in which Menchú's utterances are delivered and received (in other words, the range of interactive material and discursive forces present in the event of the interview and the unique meanings that this collision helps to produce).

18. Curiously, in "Rigoberta's Secrets," Sommer argues that the responsibility for creating and sustaining the illusion of immediacy "between the narrating 'I' and the readerly 'you'" rests solely on the shoulders of the Western reader. We can therefore infer that in her view the illusion of transparency bears little if any relation to the function of Burgos-Debray's introductory framework nor editorial manipulations.) Sommer argues that it is the Western reader's insistence on projecting "onto the persona we are hearing a present and knowable self, despite being told that the voice is second or third hand" that collapses the critical distance between narrator and reader. She states that these projections allow the reader to appropriate the voice of the other unproblematically, something that "closes off the distance between writer and reader" (32). I argue that the unproblematic appropriation of Menchú's voice does indeed occur in readers but that this kind of uncritical consumption must also be read as one of the effects of the editor's persuasive introduction; in other words, it is a sympathetic projection supported by the construction of the "real" in the text itself.

19. Spanish is a Romance language (evolved from Latin) whose nouns are usually either masculine or feminine; Burgos-Debray's allusion to the narrator's gender "mistakes" refers to Menchú's tendency to combine masculine articles with feminine nouns (or vice versa). It is important to stress that these "transgressions" of the European linguistic code form part of the regularized speech of Spanish-speaking indigenous communities in Latin America (they are not "mistakes," nor random usage) and that Burgos-Debray's correction of this usage actually makes Menchú's oral performance less "authentic."

20. For an excellent discussion of Menchú's specific appropriation of Liberation Theology, see Negrón-Muntaner.

21. Over the course of the narrative, Menchú (and her father) discover that native survival depends upon what her community has traditionally considered an impossible coalition of Indians and ladino *campesinos*. However, the early admonitions of her father are, in one sense, borne out by the action of her life story: Menchú's increasing contact with outside worlds and knowledges constitutes a qualitative departure from traditional Quiché ways of seeing and being in the world—in addition to making personal decisions that violate ancestral teachings, in the course of her narrative Menchú adopts an increasingly critical posture toward Quiché practices that she views as counterproductive and retrograde.

22. Sklodowska goes on to say that she believes that most critics who have insisted on the testimonio's transparent deliverance of the "real" "did not read testimonial texts—they read the official voice of these texts, confusing the tongues of the editor and his/her surrogates" ("Spanish American" 43). John Beverley corroborates this view

in his well-circulated essay "The Margin at the Center: On Testimonio (Testimonial Narrative)," leveling the charge of "liberal individualism" at Kitty Millet for her insightful analysis of the testimony *Los sueños de Lucinda Nahuelhaul,* while admitting that he "can't comment on the specifics of Millet's critique," since he hasn't read the text in question!

Works Cited

Achugar, Hugo. "Historias paralelas/historias ejemplares: La historia y la voz del Otro." *Revista de Crítica Literaria Latinoamericana* 36 (1992): 49–71.

Alegría, Claribel, and D. J. Flakoll. *No me agarran viva: La mujer salvadoreña en lucha.* Mexico City: Ediciones Era, 1983.

Amar Sánchez, Ana María. "La ficción del testimonio." *Revista Iberoamericana* 151 (1990): 447–62.

Arias, Arturo. "From Peasant to National Symbol." In *Teaching and Testimony: Rigoberta Menchú and the North American Classroom.* Ed. Allen Carey-Webb and Stephen Benz. Albany: State University of New York Press, 1996. 29–46.

Bakhtin, M. M. *The Dialogic Imagination.* Ed. Michael Holquist. Trans. Caryl Emerson and Michael Holquist. Austin: University of Texas Press, 1981.

Barrios de Chungara, Domitila, with Moema Viezzer. *"Si me permiten hablar . . .": Testimonio de Domitila, una mujer de las minas de Bolivia.* Mexico City: Siglo XXI, 1977.

Bell-Villada, Gene. "Creating a Context for Rigoberta Menchú." In *Teaching and Testimony: Rigoberta Menchú and the North American Classroom.* Ed. Allen Carey-Webb and Stephen Benz. Albany: State University of New York Press, 1996. 73–80.

Bergland, Betty. "Postmodernism and the Autobiographical Subject: Reconstructing the 'Other.'" In *Autobiography and Post-Modernism.* Ed. Kathleen Ashley, Leigh Gilmore, and Gerald Peters. Amherst: University of Massachusetts Press, 1994. 130–66.

Beverley, John. "The Margin at the Center: On Testimonio (Testimonial Narrative)." *Modern Fiction Studies* 35.1 (1989): 11–28.

Bonafini, Hebe de, with Matilde Sánchez. *Historias de vida.* Buenos Aires: Fraterna/Del Nuevo Extremo, 1985.

Brittin, Alice, and Kenya Dworkin. "Rigoberta Menchú: 'Los indígenas no nos quedamos como bichos aislados, inmunes, desde hace 500 años. No, nosotros hemos sido protagonistas de la historia.'" *Nuevo Texto Crítico* 6.11 (1993): 207–22.

Burgos-Debray, Elisabeth. Introduction to *I, Rigoberta Menchú: An Indian Woman in Guatemala,* by Rigoberta Menchú with Elisabeth Burgos-Debray. Trans. Ann Wright. London: Verso, 1984. xi–xxi.

Carey-Webb, Allen, and Stephen Benz, eds. *Teaching and Testimony: Rigoberta Menchú and the North American Classroom.* Albany: State University of New York Press, 1996.

Clifford, James. "Introduction: Partial Truths." In *Writing Culture: The Poetics and Politics of Ethnography.* Ed. James Clifford and George E. Marcus. Berkeley: University of California Press, 1986. 1–26.

Deely, John. *Basics of Semiotics*. Bloomington: Indiana University Press, 1990.

D'Souza, Dinesh. *Illiberal Education: The Politics of Race and Sex on Campus*. New York: Random House, 1992.

Fernández Olmos, Margarita. "Latin American Testimonial Narrative, or Women and the Art of Listening." *Revista Canadiense de Estudios Hispánicos* 13.2 (1989): 183–96.

Fischer, Michael M. J. "Ethnicity and the Post-Modern Arts of Memory." In *Writing Culture: The Poetics and Politics of Ethnography*. Ed. James Clifford and George E. Marcus. Berkeley: University of California Press, 1986. 194–233.

Gugelberger, Georg. "Introduction: Institutionalization of Transgression: Testimonial Discourse and Beyond." In *The Real Thing: Testimonial Discourse and Latin America*. Ed. Georg Gugelberger. Durham, N.C.: Duke University Press, 1996. 1–19.

Jara, René. "Prólogo." In *Testimonio y literatura*. Ed. René Jara and Hernan Vidal. Minneapolis: Institute for the Studies of Ideologies and Literature, 1986. 1–6.

Kearney, Michael, and Georg Gugelberger. "Introduction: Voices of the Voiceless in Testimonial Literature." *Latin American Perspectives*. Special issue: "Voices of the Voiceless in Testimonial Literature." Ed. Georg Gugelberger and Michael Kearney. 18.70.3 (Summer 1991): 3–14.

Lugones, María. "Playfulness, 'World'-Traveling, and Loving Perception." In *Making Face, Making Soul: Haciendo Caras*. Ed. Gloria Anzaldúa. San Francisco: Aunt Lute Press, 1990. 390–402.

Luis, William. "The Politics of Memory and Miguel Barnet's *The Autobiography of a Runaway Slave*." *MLN* 104.2 (1989): 475–94.

Marín, Lynda. "Speaking Out Together: Testimonials of Latin American Women." *Latin American Perspectives*. Special issue: "Voices of the Voiceless in Testimonial Literature." Ed. Georg Gugelberger and Michael Kearney. 18.70.3 (Summer 1991): 51–68.

Menchú, Rigoberta, with Elisabeth Burgos-Debray. *I, Rigoberta Menchú: An Indian Woman in Guatemala*. Trans. Ann Wright. London: Verso, 1984.

———. *Me llamo Rigoberta Menchú y así me nació la conciencia*. Barcelona: Seix Barral, 1982.

Millet, Kitty. "Framing the Narrative: The Dreams of Lucinda Nahuelhaul." In *Poética de la población marginal*. Ed. James Romano. Minneapolis: Prisma Institute, 1987. 395–428.

Mohanty, Satya P. "Colonial Legacies, Multicultural Futures: Relativism, Objectivity, and the Challenge of Otherness." *PMLA* 110.1 (1995): 108–18.

Negrón-Muntaner, Frances. "Discursive Tensions and the Subject of Discourse in *I, Rigoberta Menchú*." *Dialectical Anthropology* 21.3–4 (1996): 239–63.

Poniatowska, Elena. *Hasta no verte Jesús mío*. Mexico City: Ediciones Era, 1969.

Pratt, Mary Louise. "*Me llamo Rigoberta Menchú*: Autoethnography and the Re-coding of Citizenship." In *Teaching and Testimony: Rigoberta Menchú and the North American Classroom*. Ed. Allen Carey-Webb and Stephen Benz. Albany: State University of New York Press, 1996. 57–72.

Randall, Margaret. *Doris Tijerno: Inside the Nicaraguan Revolution*. Trans. Elinor Randall. Vancouver: New Star Books, 1978.

Rohter, Larry. "Nobel Winner Finds Her Story Challenged." *New York Times,* 15 Dec. 1998, A1+.

Sklodowska, Elzbieta. "Spanish American Testimonial Novel: Some Afterthoughts." *New Novel Review* 1.2 (1994): 31–47.

———. *Testimonio hispanoamericano.* New York: Peter Lang, 1992.

Sommer, Doris. "Not Just a Personal Story: Women's Testimonios and the Plural Self." In *Life/Lines: Theorizing Women's Autobiography.* Ed. Bella Brodzki and Celeste Schenck. Ithaca, N.Y.: Cornell University Press, 1988. 107–30.

———. "Rigoberta's Secrets." *Latin American Perspectives.* Special issue: "Voices of the Voiceless in Testimonial Literature." Ed. Georg Gugelberger and Michael Kearney. 18.70.3 (Summer 1991): 32–50.

Stoll, David. *Rigoberta Menchú and the Story of All Poor Guatemalans.* Boulder, Colo.: Westview Press, 1999.

Thorn, Judith. *The Lived Horizon of My Being: The Substantiation of the Self and the Discourse of Resistance in Rigoberta Menchú, M. M. Bakhtin, and Víctor Montejo.* Special Studies no. 29. Tempe: Arizona State University Center for Latin American Studies Press, 1996.

Trinh T. Minh-ha. "Not You/Like You: Post-Colonial Women and the Interlocking Questions of Identity and Difference." In *Making Face, Making Soul: Haciendo Caras.* Ed. Gloria Anzaldúa. San Francisco: Aunt Lute Press, 1990. 371–75.

———. *Woman, Native, Other: Writing Postcoloniality and Feminism.* Bloomington: Indiana University Press, 1989.

Vargas Llosa, Mario. "Questions of Conquest." *Harper's,* Dec. 1990, 45–54.

Vera-León, Antonio. "Hacer hablar: La transcripción testimonial." *Revista de Crítica Literaria Latinoamericana* 36 (1992): 181–200.

When the Mountains Tremble. Updated Nobel Prize edition; Reissue of 1983 production. Videorecording. Skylight Pictures. New York: New Yorker Films, 1993.

Yúdice, George. "Testimonio and Postmodernism." *Latin American Perspectives.* Special issue: "Voices of the Voiceless in Testimonial Literature." Ed. Georg Gugelberger and Michael Kearney. 18.70.3 (Summer 1991): 15–31.

Zimmerman, Marc. *Literature and Resistance in Guatemala: Textual Modes and Cultural Politics from El Señor Presidente to Rigoberta Menchú.* Vols. 1 and 2. Athens: Ohio University Press, 1995.

———. "Testimonio in Guatemala: Payeras, Rigoberta, and Beyond." *Latin American Perspectives.* Special issue: "Voices of the Voiceless in Testimonial Literature." Ed. Georg Gugelberger and Michael Kearney. 18.71.4 (Fall 1991): 22–47.

4

Writing in Blood

Autobiography and Technologies of the Real in Janet Campbell Hale's *Bloodlines*

Julia Watson

> You must teach your children that the ground beneath their feet is the ashes of our grandfathers. So that they will respect the land, tell your children that the earth is rich with the lives of our kin. Teach your children what we have taught our children, that the earth is our mother. Whatever befalls the earth befalls the sons of the earth. If men spit upon the ground, they spit upon themselves. This we know, all things are connected like the blood which unites one family all things are connected.
>
> —Chief Seattle, 1854

> Once I longed to belong to the family I came from. Not anymore. I'm one of its broken-off pieces now.
>
> —Janet Campbell Hale, *Bloodlines*

Janet Campbell Hale is an American Indian writer known for her 1985 novel *The Jailing of Cecelia Capture,* which depicted issues confronting a contemporary American Indian woman and was subsequently made into a well-received film. Her 1993 autobiographical narrative, *Bloodlines: Odyssey of a Native Daughter,* has been less enthusiastically received.[1] *Bloodlines* writes against the grain of much contemporary Native American writing, situating its stories paradoxically in a collective cultural past and a world of "real" experience where that past is lost and irretrievable. Its exposé of tensions in a family made dysfunctional by alcohol and violence coupled with its celebration of Indian heritage has seemed contradictory to readers. But Hale, I will argue, reconstructs American Indian identity by employing contemporary dominant-American practices of identity formation to contest the terms through which

other American Indian writers have sought to write "authentic" autobiographical narratives embedded in traditional stories.[2]

The multiple voices that her narrative takes up are not presented as those
of a chorus of characters but are all assembled under the sign of "I." This practice contrasts with the use of polyphonic voices that characterizes much Native American autobiography, such as Leslie Marmon Silko's *Storyteller*. As
Arnold Krupat notes, "There is no single, distinctive, or authoritative voice in
Silko's book nor any striving for such a voice (or style); . . . Silko will take pains
to indicate how even her own individual speech is the product of many
voices. . . . [It is] a strongly polyphonic text" (*Voice* 163). While Hale also constructs a dialogic text, it is of a different sort, with stories filtered through dis-
cordant voices—some sharp with the trauma of remembered pain, others
reflective on the ironies of her family's generations or angry about the system-
atized racism against Indians uncovered in her retelling of collective history
through personal stories. To use Mae Gwendolyn Henderson's term, Hale's
plurality of voices is a "glossolalia," speaking in the tongues of diverse languages of public discourse (347). *Bloodlines* thus lacks an authoritative voice.
Its multiple "I"s take up a range of voices in constructing a personal, even
transgressive, family history.

Perhaps because of Hale's candor about her Indian family, *Bloodlines* has
been skeptically received among literary publics. The South African critic Frederick Hale, who wrote an extensive review of the book and included discussion of it in a monograph, *Janet Campbell Hale (JCH)*, for the Western Writers Series, faults *Bloodlines* for not living up to his concept of how a memoir
should reveal the "real" truth of a life. It is "a carelessly written book" (*JCH*
49), he alleges, with several inaccurately cited dates in her personal history and
poor editing, and says little about "her evolution as a literary artist" and "the
impact of recent Native American history on [her] literary career" ("Tradition"
74–75). He finds Hale's memoir to be "sketchy and anecdotal," "leav[ing] the
impression of unreliability" (78–79). It does not correspond to or flesh out the
sketch of her life or match his idea of how an autobiographical account ought
to illuminate the larger history and contexts of Native American life ("Tradition"). He finds *Bloodlines* conventional and "hardly one of Hale's best works
as a literary artist" (*JCH* 44). While he acknowledges that Janet Campbell Hale,
as a mixed-blood writer, attempts to "come to grips with the dysfunctionality
which she believes has been passed from her miscegenated family of origin to
her own life" and "tries to understand her estrangement from her Coeur
d'Alene tribal heritage," the text is too personal and "therapeutic" ("Tradition"
78), an "account . . . dictated from a psychiatrist's couch" (*JCH* 47). In effect,
Frederick Hale faults *Bloodlines* for being too American and confessional as

well as insufficiently indigenous. For him, Janet Campbell Hale is one of those "Native Americans who have taken their cultural cues chiefly from Euroamerican civilization [and] write according to the conventions of Western autobiography" ("Tradition" 70). That is, not only has she ignored the tradition of Native American men's *coups* tales by writing a personal and subjective narrative, which he acknowledges some American Indian women writers do, but she has ignored the generic requirements of the Euro-American memoir as well. Frederick Hale sees autobiography as self-written biography fulfilling the expectations of biography but written in the first person.[3] He does not consider that Janet Campbell Hale might have chosen to write another kind of autobiographical narrative or to make a hybrid of several incompatible kinds of writing.

To the contrary, I would argue that she attempts, in the text's eight titled chapters, to narrate her life as embedded in collective Indian multigenerational history but "tellable" only in the terms of contemporary American discursive practices of identity. By taking up dominant-cultural terms, *Bloodlines* creates discursive "tools" for telling cultural stories that can intervene in the life scripts of indigenous Americans on the cultural margin. It is implicitly a "how-to" narrative for changing that story. Hale, then, practices a kind of "strategic essentialism" from her position as a mixed-blood American Indian writer, educator, and mother. At the same time that she celebrates her indigenous bloodline, she acknowledges its devastating cost to American Indians in a heritage of dispossession, from colonialism to the present, that has induced internalized anger and pain.[4] By identifying with her heritage while critiquing its deterioration and abuses in her own "blood" or family history, Hale comes up against a narrative crisis: the dilemma of "telling" as "telling on." To celebrate her Indian identification she must also castigate it, refusing to be simply either victim or hero.

Like much multicultural autobiography, *Bloodlines* stands in a problematic relationship to the "real" as it both marks out the difference of its cultural subjects and writes back to a history of their erasure. For some readers it is not factual enough in documenting Indian history, and for others it is insufficiently "authentic" ethnically because it "tells on" and exposes abuses of alcoholism and abuse resulting from a climate of poverty and racism generated in her family's lives by government appropriation of their homes. Frederick Hale, for example, finds the candor in her representation of Indians "to a great extent unflattering" ("Tradition" 74). In telling on as well as telling personal history, *Bloodlines* diverges from the contemporary autobiographical practices of such American Indian writers as N. Scott Momaday, Leslie Marmon Silko, Joy Harjo, and James Welch and is at odds with the norms of traditional oral literature of the northwest plateau in its focus on the personal (Kinkaid 40). Although a highly educated bicultural woman, Janet Campbell Hale casts her life in terms that address American Indians whose everyday concerns exceed the traditional stories in many of what Arnold Krupat calls "autobiographies by Indians."[5] While Silko, in *Storyteller* or her novel *Ceremony*, argues for the power of stories to re-member a present generation to its mythic history and ancestors, Hale is interested in stories that address and challenge community norms.

Hale's writing of an Indian woman's autobiography thus implicitly challenges critical assumptions usually ascribed to the genre. Hertha D. Sweet Wong, for example, has argued that the self-narratives of Native American women are communal and collective in their strategic production of contextually relational selves. But in *Bloodlines* Hale upholds the notion of ethnic community and dissociates herself from what she represents as the abusive stranglehold of family. This practice is also at odds with how Gretchen M. Bataille and Kathleen M. Sands have characterized American Indian women's autobiography: "the multigenre form . . . a recent innovation by . . . creative writers . . . who mix oral tradition, personal narrative, fiction, and poetry into works that might best be called cultural memoirs" (189). While their definition acknowledges that American Indian women who narrate their personal experiences can find themselves in "double jeopardy," being misread by both Indian and dominant-culture readers, Bataille and Sands do not explore the consequences for writers and readers of "telling on" the family (189–90). Hale confronts this situation in *Bloodlines* as she asks that her autobiographical narrative be read through everyday practices of American culture, including family genealogy, trauma stories, and family photos, along with the mythic and collective discourses of American Indian identity.

Technologies of the "Real"

Hale's divergent narrative strategies in *Bloodlines* include telling stories of reservation poverty, alcoholism, violence, and abuse as seen from the point of view of the scapegoated daughter and teenaged welfare mother she presents herself as before she gained, bit by bit, a college education. In such contexts, Indian identity is represented as fractured by social trauma and the experience of forced migrancy. The turn to narrative becomes potentially a rehabilitative act, both personally and collectively. By naming and addressing fissures in her experiential world she voices sites of revaluation and transformation for Indian identity, if its legacy of blood, memory, and community is to become a source of collective healing. Hale's narrative thus reads differently than we may expect an autobiography to, as its narrative "I" is recast through a network of relationships, a bloodline.

The sociologist Ken Plummer's concept of autobiography may be more productive than the usual notion of "self-biography" for reading *Bloodlines*. Plummer reframes autobiographical writing as acts of personal storytelling directed to communities that "are part of wider habitual or recurring networks of collective activity" (22). Performing or challenging cultural "scripts," the autobiographer is also spoken through them, encoded within the often conflicting limits of particular, varied identities. In these terms Hale is both encoded in the cultural scripts of "autobiographies by Indians" and writing against them by employing what I will call "technologies of the real." This concept of "technologies" derives from Foucault's argument that discourses for constituting the self—through practices of truth-telling about internal feelings, thoughts, and desires, particularly those prohibited by sexual inter-dictions—became organized and brokered as "technologies" (Foucault 16). My notion of "technologies of the real" extends this analysis to suggest that the personal is also constituted from the proliferating discourses of contemporary social practice that interpolate subjects and require the taking up of specific, situated identities. That is, we are required to construct our social identities differently in everyday discursive realms such as the doctor's office, the wel-fare office, the curriculum vitae, or a date, and we must shift and modify these self-presentations rapidly. Subjectivity in contemporary America is anything but a unified process.

Not only are acts of personal storytelling generated in social communities, but cultural scripts, in Plummer's terms, are multiple and changing. Hale, for example, in different chapters presents her personal stories through scripts drawn from the contemporary practices of twelve-step programs, genealogy discussions, scrapbooks, and other oral modes for reciting everyday life. In-novating upon mythic storytelling in autobiographies by Indians, she employs such scripts as technologies of the real for retelling her family's life stories as implicated in the cultural identity of an indigenous past and the outsider sta-tus imposed by poverty, racism, and abuse. She casts her narrative in various frames: as a trauma narrative of family dysfunction; a coming-of-age "video montage" of life on the run; a narrative of a welfare mother; a reader and sub-ject of family photographs in an imagined album of a Native American blood-line without access to such documents; a writer of a dry-eyed, caustic mem-oir of her mother; and a genealogist of her family's fragmented and ethnically mixed history. Hale's many kinds of personal storytelling are mixed into a heterogeneous narrative that resists distillation into a unitary "life." Her stories are linked to objects of personal experience that seem to guarantee the narrative's validity: family photographs, albums, Bibles, records, and heirloom objects, as well as "technological technologies" such as the video montage. These "real" signifiers of the family's past, while not a formal archive, serve to authenticate an enduring family bloodline, yet one that exists only in her writing of it. Residues of experience, they evoke memories and sustain collective memory. Different in kind from personal memory because they are both shared and symbolic, such objects and stories of family are established collaboratively and in continuing negotiation by family members.

Of course many autobiographers integrate references to life memorabilia into their narratives to verify their stories—photographs of family members may include heirlooms, pets, or homesteads as authentication.[6] Although Hale's narrative conspicuously lacks a single photograph, she describes from memory several that hung on walls or sat in drawers as evidence that her stories originated in the "real." And her text is dense with verbal maps of birthplaces, homes, and the travels of family members as well as the names of relatives, towns, schools, employers, and historic sites. This materiality of Hale's text becomes its autoethnographic signature, not only recalling but re-membering as vital and constitutive the stories and practices of everyday life erased or fractured by the brutalities of history.

Although Hale's modes of telling are multiple and materially embedded, her narrator hesitates frequently over the question of which story to tell, marked by her frequent shifts of voice. Reflecting on her first novel, *The Owl's Song,* she observes: "I was torn between writing a novel that was true to my own vision and one that presented a positive image of Indian people" (*Bloodlines* xxii). The story she wants to tell conflicts with those she feels she should tell in the service of presenting Indians as authentic people of the earth. In many ways the pages of *Bloodlines* are haunted by her conflicts in trying to tell, as an Indian-identified woman, about her culture at the same time that she vindicates her sense of self from her family's belittling abuse of her.

Complicating the notion of technologies of the real in Hale's narration is her employment of the mythic discourse of the bloodline. The trope of blood and memory, also taken up in many other autobiographies by Indians, provocatively asserts a continuous line of descent and affiliation linking family across generations in shared experience despite government expropriation of their lands, forced assimilation of native peoples, and distance from reservation life. Hale announces her purpose at the start of *Bloodlines:* "The book is in part an effort to understand the pathology of the dysfunction, what made my family the way it was. I examine my own life in part, but reach beyond what I personally know or could know . . . . Back along my bloodlines to imagine the people I came from in the context of their own lives and times" (xxii). In recollecting that history, memory moves from a private, introspective process to a collective project of symbolic reappropriation of land and reaffirmation of blood ties, with the intent of revitalizing indigenous culture. "Blood," "land," and "memory," terms that have become widely used to mark ethnic and national identities, are presented as givens; but in fact they are part of a process or project of construction that produces indigenous identity by marking origin, heritage, and cultural landscape.[7]

The rhetoric of the bloodline may seem hyperbolic in a successful writer such as Hale, who has lived for over a decade in New York City and lacks a current connection to her reservation. Yet her reading of the bloodline through technologies of the real insists that her family has maintained kinship unconsciously despite itself, that its history can be recast as a line of continuous and meaningful descent, and that in her own dreamlife the bloodline remains alive. Hale's mythic story of dreaming in 1987 of the return of the Turtle Clan of the Kootenay, to which her father's family belonged, is emblematic of this: "The dream was saying that our family only appeared to be dead, stepped on, broken into a million little pieces. The family—or the power of the family—lives on in some form and is strong" (xxxi). Her story becomes an autoethnographic act of both resisting and taking up the identity of a Coeur d'Alene Indian in its shifting historical meanings.

In the narrative's hybrid character as an orally oriented, contemporary woman's story of coming to terms with her experience of poverty, racism, and abuse as well as a mythic call to reaffirm a transpersonal ethnic bloodline, Hale questions notions of American Indian identity as a fixed essence. While her hybrid narrative entangles personal experience, collective history, and tribal myth, it insists that these modes are implicated in one another through her subjectivity. Her argument for the continuity of blood—in memory, dream, image, prophecy, and experience—from generation to generation is presented as radically literal.

This concept of the bloodline may seem anachronistic to a postmodern view of the subject. In "Blood (and) Memory," however, Chadwick Allen has argued compellingly that the signature trope of blood memory in Native American writing can be read as a process of "conflating . . . storytelling, imagination, memory, and genealogy into the representation of a single, multifaceted moment in a particular landscape" (94). The use of blood or the bloodline as memory, Allen points out, is a site of multiple interpretations in American Indian discourse: It is celebrated in the stories and essays of N. Scott Momaday, attacked by the critic Arnold Krupat as "racist," and complicated in the trickster discourse of Gerald Vizenor. As the U.S. government historically has regulated Indian identity exclusionarily by blood quantum, the debate about blood memory needs to be understood as part of a response by Indian people to who and what "counts" or is included as indigenous. The claim for memory through the bloodline, Allen argues, occurs in a textual process of constructing identity by appeal to and innovation upon the material reality of blood networks rather than as the naive invocation of a preexistent faculty particular to American Indians (96). The bloodline is, in short, a trope for making a relationship. In this view, Hale's autobiographical narrative, employing technologies of the real to trace the trope of the bloodline, becomes a rhetorical practice of hybridity, anchoring her writing of American Indian identity to an investment in monumental practices of American culture, such as reading, writing, and teaching, and kinds of oral narrative that innovate on autobiographical storytelling.

By mapping routes of memory, including what she has not personally experienced, Hale attempts not only to remember but to re-member herself to an originary tribal identity no longer available in the "real" world and able to be invoked only textually. She presents herself in diverse, even contradictory, ways—as group member, as gendered body, as cultural inheritor of a set of indigenous traditions, as a raced and classed subject, and as a subject marked by history experienced as loss or deferral, in tension with national boundaries and histories. Her assemblage of family stories thus creates a context in which she can situate herself as a minoritized subject shaped by the outsider status of migrancy, poverty, and her experience of white "othering" of her "dark" skin. But another story also emerges, of her education and success in publishing *Bloodlines* with a major publisher and her professional status as a writer and sometimes professor of creative writing, which suggests that she has become a metropolitan subject. Writing a "how-to" for recovering the imaginary bloodline of a past family in a textual "land" where the "blood" connections of a collective identity that eludes her may be a risky, even contradictory, project; but it is also one that does important cultural work.

A Pre-Text for Telling

In 1990 Janet Campbell Hale was the lead author of *Native Students with Problems of Addiction,* a manual for community educators in a Native Adult Education Resource working with rural Canadian Indians in British Columbia. In the process of describing how "to help adult-education instructors deal with addictive or preaddictive behavior in their Native American students," it suggests methods and a rationale for reconstructing Indian identity.[8] "Broader issues such as cultural identity, ethnic pride, self-confidence, and self-esteem" need to be addressed, it argues (1). The section on "Indian Identity" critiques previous programs of assimilation in Canada (and implicitly the United States). Throughout, the manual situates Indian identity as a project of recovering and articulating a preestablished heritage by a process of critiquing stereotypes of Indians and defining the terms of a positive ethnic identity (95). For example, it presents the story of "Wynette," a female wino in the Bay Area drifting into alcoholism whose story parallels some details of Hale's own narrative in *Bloodlines*. Arrested for drunk driving, Wynette is sent to a treatment center where she confronts the history of violence and abuse in her family; in deep denial, she resists identifying with other alcoholics and beginning a treatment program. Students are invited, in questions after the story, to identify Wynette's blind spots and name potential steps for her healing. That is, students are asked to rewrite the story of dysfunction she cannot script as a way of learning to author life stories of their and their families' crises.

Telling personal narratives, the manual suggests, is a therapeutic way for students to engage their histories of addictive behavior collectively, through ethnic identification. Alcoholics Anonymous twelve-step program practices are adapted to the cultural context of rural reservation Indians. The manual frames illness as a cultural sickness stemming from historical crisis and requiring changes throughout the community. Childhood trauma is particularly important: "Addictive tendencies develop when children experience emotionally painful events such as sexual abuse, physical abuse, neglect . . . . Examples of frozen development in Native culture have occurred in children taken from their lands and families to residential schools [where] Native languages and traditions were abandoned . . . [and] children were required to deny their culture and numb feelings toward their family and heritage" (19). For Hale the erosion of community tradition and subsequent history of addiction are linked directly to the relocation of Indians during the western conquest of the nineteenth century. The loss of land weakened blood ties, producing cultural amnesia and self-destructive behavior. Her call to healing requires remembering pain and reactivating ethnic bonds if behavior is to be successfully changed. In this model an ethnic community is reconstructed from its fragmented parts precisely through the shared illness of its members and their need for support. As Jack David Eller has noted in discussing the characteristics of ethnic communities, "an ideology of continuity with the past" has to be posited for the group to cohere; and "the group is based more on its 'consciousness' or 'awareness' of difference and shared traits and past than on the objective quality of those traits" (559). In the manual, telling personal stories of addiction becomes a means not only to gain relief but to create an ethnic community through a process of "telling on" the community.

The manual as a pre-text allows us to read Hale's autobiographical narrative as an exploration of the relationship between personal experience and public history that revalues and rewrites markers of difference. This self-examination, both personal and collective, resists the unity and coherence of biographical stories, probing the interfaces of discourses of illness and healing, community and alienation, bloodline and estrangement that are parts of how the "story" of American Indian experience is currently being renegotiated. My reading of *Bloodlines* consequently focuses on Hale's writing voices and strategies in different chapters rather than arguing for a cumulative self- or collective portrait. Hale's modes of storytelling in *Bloodlines,* encompassing trauma narratives, genealogy, travel accounts, a verbal photo album, and essays on mixed-blood heritage, comprise a process of experiments in voicing identity variously and contradictorily rather than as a composite portrait. But its "self-tryouts" may be grouped into three rubrics: autobiographical essays primarily on writing and subjectivity where the voice of the present-time narrator predominates; an extended trauma narrative of Hale's relationship with her mother; and three essays on historical and cultural contours of the bloodline.

Telling Writing

The narrator of *Bloodlines* struggles with a primary question: Whose story and which story to tell? The book's epigraph from Wallace Stegner insists that the posing of urgent questions about identity rather than the rehearsal of conventional or fixed identity motivates autobiographical storytelling: "The guts of any significant fiction—or autobiography—is an anguished question."[9] In juxtaposing the paradoxical discourses of a mythic bloodline to technologies of the real, Hale takes up this stance of inquiry.

The initial chapters recall autobiographical moments. Each engages one or more technologies of self-presentation to evoke childhood memories—the truth in/of the photograph, a sibling's story, the autobiographical dimension of fiction—that are contradicted by other memories of her past. How to tell her story is intimately linked to the question of which story to tell. The hybrid character of Hale's text results in part from her recording of these discrete and fragmentary moments of memory that refuse to cohere as a collective and transformative story.

In the introduction to *Bloodlines,* "Circling Raven," the trope of spiraling figures what Hale sees as the irreconcilably fractured parts of her life narrative. "Circling Raven" traces ever-smaller circles around the familial bloodline. Its oscillating movements interweave historical and mythic moments, beginning with the history of the Kootenay nation since the coming of colonialism when, according to their stories, three circling ravens presaged the coming of three black (Jesuit) fathers, nominally as mediators. This myth of her family's origin overwrites her mother's mixed-blood heritage and their separation from the Coeur d'Alene (northern Idaho) reservation, despite being at the end of the Coeur d'Alene Turtle Clan. But in the logic of the spiral that ending is potentially a new beginning of re-membering, connecting to the bloodline as an ideal of family in clan, tribal collective, and regional landscape.

Moving from collective to personal history and subjective memory, the narrative describes a photograph of her family (not included in the text) that was taken in 1946 when she was a baby. The image is, deceptively, of "a happy, handsome family" (xxx). Her mother, mixed American Indian and Irish, looks pretty and in love with her ruggedly handsome Indian father; her three older sisters look fresh and innocent; and she is a bright-eyed baby, secure and happy. But the serene faces of her parents and her sisters in the image contradict her earliest memories of the family as a tense, dysfunctional group torn by poverty and abuse, united only in their scapegoating of her (xxix–xxx). Rather than being an autobiographical point of entry, the photograph is a documentary dead-end, its script of the happy family a lie. Her autobiographical storytelling, the narrator decides, has to trace a different itinerary of a family history played out in anger and hostility and re-membered only in the dream-myth of a blood it no longer recalls.

If "Circling Raven" traces a downward spiral of changes in Indian life leading to her own fragmentation, however, Hale can still imagine a dream of possibility for regenerating the Turtle Clan. But the dream shows that "the power of the family" is unavailable outside it, and she is only "one of its broken-off pieces" (xxxiii). From fragments of a familial past in which "dysfunction begets dysfunction," she sees the dilemma of her position as a descendant transmitting only rage and illness. Narrative becomes a search for ways to reactivate, through telling family stories, the energy of a genealogical line that was dispersed with the family's departure from their Coeur d'Alene homeland.

In exploring these contradictory positionings on the meaning of her Indian identity as historical network, felt experience, and willed connection, Hale asks how to remake her lineage into a willed blood-tie that can become a foundation for recovery of community identity. Her beginning fragments acknowledge that her own family was always displaced. Her birthplace was in California, not what her memory suggests as the family's first home in northern Idaho on the Coeur d'Alene reservation. The family's migrant life in small cities of the Northwest belies her quest for the sacred homeland of the bloodline. Her recollection is of continuing migrancy—"Such a common, simple question: Where did you grow up?" (36); "I attended twenty-one schools in three states before I dropped out of school in eighth grade. No, I went a month or two in tenth" (34)—that casts about for a fixed point of origin.

But origin can only be asserted rhetorically as a marker of identity, given the facts of her childhood. She invents a different childhood to tell stories about to her daughter, one that emphasizes the continuity of tradition. Similarly, visiting a tribal school, she narrates the difference of indigenous people as a story of origin and destiny: "If Irish or Italian culture dies in America it really isn't that big a deal. They still exist in Italy and Ireland. Not so with us. There is no other place. North America *is* our old country" (xx). Blood and land are interwoven, inseparable in cultural memory, even as her personal memory contradicts this experience. This telling of identity is performative; in Sidonie Smith's phrase, "narrative performativity constitutes interiority" as an effect of the storytelling it seems to generate ("Performativity" 109). Hale's professions of authentic Indianness are asserted for specific occasions and audiences within her narrative, while other parts of her text trace divergent identities. For example, she tells a group of students in an eastern school: "I am as Coeur d'Alene in New York as I am in Idaho . . . . It . . . is an integral part of me" (xix). But this claim is extravagantly essentialist not only because of centuries of struggle, dispossession, and intermarriage that disrupted tribal identifications in her family, but because she left the reservation at age ten. The narrator's assertion of kinship and roots is an act of voluntary re-membering to clan that knowingly contradicts the facts of family history in *Bloodlines.* The tension between an identity of transhistorical connection to a primal land as blood that she performs for a younger generation and her personal memory of being alienated in her family admits of no simple narrative resolution. Rather, her storytelling attempts to negotiate this gap in the face of loss of homeland and identity.

Initially, Hale poses her autobiographical dilemma as the need to tell the truth about a familial legacy of dysfunction, to tell on others and take back her own life and, contrarily, to connect her history in time and space to a genealogical and psychic network. The norms of chronological autobiography cannot contain these contradictory impulses. She takes up diverse modes of telling in the eight chapters, remaking genres of American life-representation to reclaim ethnic identity. In telling of and telling on generations of her family and embedding their stories in her own through technologies of the real, Hale offers readers a hybrid model for using personal history to forge new stories of legacy and possibility wrested from bitter history.

The third chapter, "Autobiography in Fiction," attempts a different strategy of telling by rewriting details of Hale's life in the third person, as the narrative of a fictional protagonist, Julia (entitled "The More or Less Autobiographical Story I Will Write from My Sickbed at St. Luke's"). At that distance she can read herself as a budding writer, recalling her mother's and sisters' stories of her learning to write at age four by filling up tablets with scrolled *es* as if they were books she had written full of sincerity and intensity. But for the first-person narrator, by contrast, the past is buried in the debris of childhood and no longer accessible to her; she can only speculate that writing gave some order to "the chaos my life had become" (4). Recalling this story of coming to writing, making a story, evokes the child whom she both is and isn't: "I can see her, and she is not me" (10). The story resists her, and she is ambivalent about autobiography's "rearrangement" of fact in personal writing because of its bald "light of day" (15). Her life, obliquely tellable as a fiction in the story of a forty-year-old woman unlike herself in many ways, resists straightforward presentation. Told in the past as a patently untrue Carmen Miranda narrative, she cannot tell it as her *own* story and expose her ambivalence about the project of telling and telling on in autobiography. At an impasse in her desire to make a story of her life, the narrator turns to technologies of the real—photos, snatches of dialogue, places, and objects tied to her memories of family—to confront the trauma of her actual rather than fictionalized early life.

"Telling" and "Telling On" Family Secrets

The longest chapter in *Bloodlines*, "Daughter of Winter," represents Hale's childhood as the story of a scapegoated outsider in a family with an alcoholic father, a verbally abusive mother, and several contemptuous older sisters. In its exposure of raw nerves, this story has struck some students as more an act of vindictive "telling on" than telling, one that shames Indian heritage. But "Daughter of Winter" is, I would argue, a trauma narrative critiquing family dysfunction that makes a case for the need to undo others' powerful stories in order to claim one's own.[10]

As the chapter takes up the obsessive telling of painful moments of a traumatic past, we might first consider the associative and nonchronological operations of memory it foregrounds. Cognitive psychologists typically distinguish among three kinds of memory: semantic, episodic, and traumatic. The psychologist Daniel L. Schachter defines traumatic memory as a kind of obsessive emotional memory, clusters of recollected events whose retrieval is governed by an association or congruency of mood (211). This insistent repetitiveness may occur as flashback memory, which intrudes upon the narrative present in the form of scraps of words or images that remain charged with the original feelings of shame or pain. A flashback memory of this sort is often resistant to forgetting because the scene was so vivid and emotionally charged that its visual, auditory, and spatial particulars remain embedded as verbal fragments of memory (211). In these forms of emotional memory, a narrator's attempt to retain present-tense control of her or his story is at times swept away as the past is forcefully made present.

How does traumatic memory enter into autobiography? Cathy Caruth discusses trauma as a category of narrative that asks us to rethink notions of experience and community by noting how the teller is belatedly possessed by the event; for Caruth, the truth of a traumatic event is its crisis. Trauma narrative attempts to say what could not be said, refusing silence (8–9). In Hale's narrative of growing up, a thematics of being silenced and the recurring compulsion to tell underlies her recounting of the events of "then" that still have the force of "now." In reciting flashback memories she condemns her family's cruelty, but at the cost of losing her own temporal distance from them: "Here I am—going on forty now—but in my soul's darkest corner I am ever the motherless child, the psychologically tortured girl I used to be, the scapegoat of my troubled, troubled family" (55). Gradually, however, the process of telling the traumatic past becomes for Hale a means of writing back to memories of her mother and neutralizing their force.

In this process she relies on a technology of the real, the imagined video montage, to mobilize her memory and cast up frozen moments on a private "screen." In 1985, she writes, she can recall 1957, "seeing" herself in its incessant migration. "If I were to make a video of my early year . . . I would show . . . A montage of my mother and myself on the run" (27). The verbal "video" that she makes available to readers in flashbacks and flash-forwards is marked by place names that were temporary childhood "homes"—Lewiston, Idaho; Yakima, Omak, and Wapato, Washington; towns throughout California—all held together in her memory as a sequence of chaotic frames. Unlike the family photo, the video montage captures the rapid, discontinuous movement of memory backward, forward, or in freeze-frame without imposing narrative coherence. Its incessant motion images the displacement of her own past of cultural uprooting.

Hale narrates "Daughter of Winter" as a child who experienced years of abuse from her mother's addiction to anger and her sisters' scapegoating while refusing to be their abject victim. Narrating flashbacks of that past enables her to "talk back" to memories of her mother's and sisters' words as she could not then, exacting a kind of literary revenge upon them. Recounting her mother's wounding phrase, repeated to her as an adolescent, "'You can't fool anybody. . . . People will instinctively know what an evil thing you are'" (61), she observes the double bind in which her family placed her. Characterizing her mother as "a master, an absolute master, of verbal abuse," Hale recalls her annihilating words: "'You're not pretty . . . . You're not anything'" (60). While no response was possible at the time—"confronting my mother was always out of the question" (60)—the narrative retelling of her abuse allows her to contrast her past and present identities. When the narrator is swept up in past memories that overwhelm her, only the distance of time and place imposes protection. "I've tried to believe that it wasn't as bad as I remember. But to look with compassion requires distance and a feeling of safety . . . that you've gone beyond the reach of all that" (42). But recounting these tirades also indicts her mother.

Hale uses a present-tense narration that heightens the sense of trauma when telling stories of her mother's verbal and physical abuse, dismissing the latter as "like nothing . . . . Compared to the verbal abuse . . . and the constant uprooting" (42). She turns to the second-person "you" to urge readers to "imagine" this life of constant migration and abuse. "Your mother and your sisters have been telling you how ugly are most of your life, how strange you are, and nobody has ever said that wasn't true" (39). Only her text can be a site for self-validation, with the reader as a sympathetic audience to coexperience the abuse and validate her critique of its injustice.

Writing a traumatic narrative, then, serves to authorize Hale as an authoritative narrator not because she has endured abuse but because her analysis of family behavior is a cogent antidote to it. She offers a model of family dynamics to explain her own scapegoating and its relationship to her need for narrative catharsis: "Mom aggressively turned her anger, not inward, but outward . . . with great force . . . away from herself," while her father, by contrast, turned anger inward in alcoholism (44). Her father is a more shadowy and mysterious figure in *Bloodlines*, who occasionally took her along on drinking binges, often disappeared, and died while she was young. His lineage is less culturally legible and Hale speculates that his dilemma was to be neither a "good white-man's Indian" nor one able to fully affirm an Indian identity (174).

"Daughter of Winter" resolves itself as a second obituary for Hale's mother, a contrast to the brief, decorous one she published for a newspaper. It thus sustains the fiction that this is a private disclosure of trauma to a personal audience rather than a far more public document than the local newspaper. Here she poses theories for the inexplicable cruelty of her mother by trying to explain to herself the woman who, although uneducated, loved reading and writing; who was targeted for abuse by her husband just as she targeted her youngest daughter; who loved movies and travel, but who let her daughter be housed in a shack and refused entry to the house. And yet the central question is unanswerable: "Why did they—with Mom as their leader—excommunicate me from the family?" (60).

In searching for explanations to the mystery of her own marginalization, Hale discovers the origin of her desire to be a writer (49). She began the process that her narrative explores, constructing multiple and varied identities to liberate her from her mother's pronouncement of her worthlessness: "no matter what you do or where you go, you can't get away from what you really are" (55). Reflecting on her own power to invent stories, she finds a parallel in her mother's ability to tell stories by lying and manipulating others "to be on her side against me" (64). Writing her mother's misrepresentations lets her develop the inner voice and critique to escape the abandonment and self-hatred that traumatized her childhood self. Alternating between being an outcast and a rebel "unable to openly resist my mother's dictates but not bending to her will, either, when it went against my best interests," even at six, Hale is able to close and contain the traumatic past by recalling her mother's last days when, increasingly enfeebled and confused, she was no longer formidable but pathetic (70). Looking at a photo (not shown) of herself as a happy baby, as yet untouched by the memories of childhood, she notes that there are "no resolutions. Only an end" (86). In this self-case-study of addiction and dysfunction of the sort her manual had addressed, the process of recounting the crisis, to paraphrase Caruth, is indeed its truth.

Telling Blood: Genealogy and Collective Memory

In several autobiographical essays Hale focuses on reconstructing the history of her family and linking that history to the larger history of Indian people since the coming of whites to North America. In tracing a genealogy she is able to assert an ethnic identity but also question how dominant-culture genealogies have overwritten oral indigenous descent lines and territorial lands, using the authority of a written pedigree to revalue Indian blood quantum as a sign of inferiority.[11] Hale weaves together oral stories of her ancestors with various kinds of written documents that contextualize the bloodline, as do the photographs she describes but never shows. Her reconstruction of the early familial history of contact between Indians and whites that produced her own mixed-blood generation employs technologies of the real to validate the erasure of American Indian identity in public history and her own family and rescue both from oblivion.

The story of her Irish and Indian mixed-blood mother's family is highly "tellable"; that of her full-blood father's family is shrouded in obscurity. In the second essay in *Bloodlines,* "My Half-Brother's Mother," she sketches her father's first wife, whom she never knew. Despite tentative questions about the woman who around 1920 ran out on her father with a lover and supported her son by prostitution, Hale can call up only a remembered photograph of her half-brother and his mother, "dressed Indian style, her black hair parted in the middle" (21). The memory is a dead-end, yielding no explanatory story for understanding her own life. But the memory album without photographs of this textual bloodline has a productive site in her father's mother's story, told to her as a small child, of how that young grandmother and her family joined Chief Joseph in the long march of the Nez Percé to surrender and escape to Canada.

In tracing a genealogy in "The Only Good Indian," Hale carefully specifies dates, places, sources of information, and relationships in her mother's descent line. But unlike genealogists, she is interested in responding to and resisting its truth claims, which have authorized the exercise of white hegemony. Her chapter makes a compelling case for the meaning of origins in the quest of white settlers to lay claim to Indian lands and authorize their ownership of them. For Hale, writing genealogy is a specifying of *dis*possession and the feelings of anger and loss that it calls up. She marshalls evidence of several sorts to make her case for collective disenfranchisement, beginning with a lengthy citation from the frontier historian H. H. Bancroft in 1884 that alludes to the "degenerate posterity" produced when men of northern European descent are "debased" by marrying Indian women (109). Bancroft's example of Dr. John McLoughlin, the "father of Oregon," is a compelling one, since McLoughlin is Hale's great-great-grandfather (she asserts this on the authority of a biography owned by her mother, *The McLoughlin Empire and Its Rulers* [125],[12] and letters and documents in the Newberry Library). The chief factor of the Hudson Bay Company in the Northwest Territory, McLoughlin married a Chippewa woman a decade older with several children who had been abandoned by her husband. They went on to parent the line of McLoughlins from which her mother is descended. The genealogy in her telling is marked at each point by the pervasive racial slurs of whites toward what they call dark-skinned, inferior "half-breeds." The irony of visiting McLoughlin's house, now a state museum outside Portland, as an outsider to the white settler culture it celebrates is clear in her memory: "My mother told me the people who had built this fine house . . . were our relations. We were their descendents. Of course I didn't get it" (111). Linked to that memory is her mother's distinction between good Indians, "the kind white people approve of," and "'the bad ones, the drunken, lazy louts'" (113). And yet General Sheridan's infamous remark about the only good Indian being a dead one is, she knows even as a child, a bottom line of American cultural discourse on Indians. In that tension of opposed historical messages there is, she concludes, no way to be "good."

Hale recites her genealogy as a collection of nonchronological oral stories, with her grandmother, "Gram," as a pivotal character for understanding the contradictions of the bloodline. Gram's story uncovers a hidden history of intermarriage within what Bancroft (and for that matter the critic Frederick Hale) termed "miscegenation," since she was the daughter of McLoughlin's highly educated son David. David in turn abandoned his medical practice and, in her phrase, "went Native" (129), marrying an Indian woman, Annie Grizzly, and moving west in response to the rising tide of anti-Indian racism in the late nineteenth century that "would regard Indians as subhuman beings, as soulless savages to be done away with so that the west could be won" (130). Gram, born dark-skinned and assertive, married the Irish immigrant Sullivan in the 1880s and, to her granddaughter, seemed to see her own internalized self-hatred in the child's "darkness." Their female children, all but Hale's mother, elected to marry white men and identify as white while disparaging the Indian part of the family produced by her mother's second marriage to a full-blood Indian. Particularly in her description of her mother's sisters, who "became" white, Hale is critical: "They were rude and crude. They smoked and drank. They swore and said 'shit' a lot. They made stupid, snide remarks about Indians, too, whenever they could" (116). Clearly the sisters internalized crude stereotypes of Indians to mask their own difference. Passing on the bloodline, therefore, has meant transmitting the constructed axis of racial difference, with whiteness privileged and negotiated through marriage. For her mother's family, any quantum of Indian blood has meant contamination, and the choice to marry an Indian smacks of Bancroft's charge of degeneracy.[13] In regions such as the Northwest, where American Indians still comprise a significant part of the population, derogatory words and exclusionary practices continue to mark outsider status. In Hale's study of the line of her ancestors, only her father's grandmother Poulee escaped because she spoke no English, wore no shoes, and was "secure" (120).

But if contact implies contamination, what is a mixed-blood descendant to do? Hale alternately celebrates the bloodline's nurturance of Indian origins and ways and reads her own ancestors' ambivalence about how to negotiate their identities as a sign of the larger American crisis around racial difference. At times she essentializes across ethnicity, as when speculating on how her mother's Irish foremothers and the Kootenay women were matrilineal warriors (125). But she also acknowledges that the bloodline she has traced is a "sedimentation," indicating the overlap of intermarriage and the construction of difference in the history of western expansion (126). She expresses bitterness about the impact of the 1887 Dawes Act in forcing the indigenous to become "a white man's Indian," to be assimilated through relocation, the breakup of families, and the reeducation of Indian children. She recognizes that the mixed heritage of her ancestors to some extent protected them from governmental brutality; the bicultural daughters of David McLoughlin already spoke fluent English and were highly literate. And, she acknowledges, practices of domination were multicultural, with a male ancestor kept as a slave by another Indian nation (129). History's bitter ironies about access to the tools of dominant culture and the exploitation of the weaker speak through her bloodline: the massacre at Wounded Knee in 1890 annihilated those who had, like her ancestors, helped to open and "father" the west; and the Irish, themselves despised as outsiders, were prejudiced against Indians. In telling of and telling on the imbrication of private and public history, Hale cannot speak from a single position. Her genealogy is one of loss and the affirmation of a bloodline sedimented when, in historical struggle, Indian identity was consolidated as "different" and unique.

As in her other chapters, Hale uses her personal history to pose the question of whether she ever hated her own Indianness, as so many of her ancestors seemed to. She recalls a traumatic moment, framed in italics, in Catholic grade school when students stigmatized her for her dark skin. Recalling her responses to their refusal to touch her by trying to bleach her skin white, she reflects on how she has acted out her place in a hierarchy of whiteness (139–40). In this sense Hale's ironic narrator also "tells on" herself for having internalized difference as inferiority. Tracing the bloodline and questioning its legacy, she suggests, requires that each successive generation transvalue and revalidate its identity, in effect remaking it.

In "Transitions," the chapter preceding "The Only Good Indian," Hale again introduces her personal history to call attention to the plight of single mothers on welfare in a racist society. She negotiates this risky narrative by calling attention to the contrast between herself "then," the naive victim, and "now," an educated, accomplished writer and successful mother. As an eighteen-year-old welfare mother with a baby in San Francisco in the 1960s, she recounts how she was mocked as uneducated and abused by her husband, a white psychiatric social worker who beat her face with a heavy ashtray for running away. Although she succeeded in resisting his demands, that history remains inscribed on her as a scar. In reading her own past, Hale links the process of coming to consciousness of her own abject status as a poor, abandoned welfare mother to her desire for education and a writing career. That quest sends her to her father's reservation, the Coeur d'Alene Kootenay, for an education grant that, although it never materialized, was transformative in linking her personal circumstances to the heritage of the bloodline: "This was the first time I thought about connections to people who had come before, connections to the land—about ancestral roots that predated the white society that had superimposed itself onto North America. And this was the first time I thought about my own posterity . . . of the possibility of my own bloodline continuing down through the ages" (103). Reframing her personal story as part of a transgenerational one offers her connection to a "family" beyond her own and a historical rationale for marginalization. In rewriting her identity from solitary scapegoat in family and society to subject collectivized by blood and memory, Hale offers two conclusions to the consequences of telling her story: an imagined possibility of collective memory through the performance of narrative and a generational reflection on Indian otherness in a multicultural future.

Memory and History

> Just as memories for individual events resemble jigsaw puzzles that are assembled from many pieces, so do the stories of our lives.
> —Daniel L. Schachter

In concluding her narrative, Hale attempts to resolve, in two contradictory ways, the troubled histories of personal and collective loss and fragmentation that she has narrated. First, she reframes the linear movement of history into a circle of return that knits past and present into one story of the bloodline's ongoing fulfillment. But she also pragmatically acknowledges that her daughter will be less marked by the difference of Indian "darkness" that made her an outcast in childhood. "Return to Bear Paw" explores the first mode, insertion of personal memory into a larger, transpersonal collective whose knowledge and spirit are transmitted intergenerationally. By rhetorically reconstructing the blood tie severed from previous generations, she reinstates the continuity of the bloodline. Unabashedly essentialist in tracing lines that connect body, blood, and memory, Hale enunciates them as a virtual, future-oriented network. More than a vision, this process may be, as Hale's manual suggests, life-and-death work for Indians outside the social mainstream and caught in cycles of addiction, abuse, and despair.

"Return to Bear Paw" thus is a site of collective memory for American Indians that is transpersonal, transgenerational, and mythic. Here the landscape as well as the psyche is marked as a scene of trauma-induced forgetting to be reactivated by cultural memory as a conscious agent of healing and reidentification. The chapter recounts her trip to the site of Chief Joseph's surrender near what is now Chinook, in north-central Montana. There, after the Battle of the Bear Paw in 1877, Chief Joseph, the head of the Nez Percé, and a group of about four hundred, including her paternal grandmother, surrendered and were captured by the U.S. cavalry under Generals Sherman and

Howard, after months of pursuit through the Rockies in Montana's southwestern Big Hole area. History books have revised the encounter into a narrative of forgiveness and reconciliation. But a bronze plaque at the desolate site tells a different story than the figure of noble surrender that Chief Joseph has become for his words—"From where the sun now stands I will fight no more forever"—signaling the end of Plains Indians' autonomy.[14] Finding bullet nicks and racist words scrawled on the memorial marker, Hale reinscribes the moment as one of savage conquest. In contemplating the defaced plaque and the persistent contempt its scars speak, she is moved to make an identification with her ancestors that transcends the personal: "I was with these people, was part of them I felt . . . that part of [my grandmother] will remain forever in that place and the part of her that lives on in me, in inherited memories of her, in my blood and in my spirit" (158).

In narrating her identity as part of the past, Hale speaks momentarily through the bloodline's collective syntax and tropes. The bloodline changes from a felt lineage to a participatory myth linking individuals in an inclusionary community. In witnessing the site of conquest and slaughter, reactivated as a scene in her imagination, she links a particular defeat to the systematic destruction of Indian people that continued in smallpox-infected blankets, mission schools, and military service without citizenship rights. But in viewing and telling this narrative of loss and defacement, Hale performs a recitation of historical identification that brings her, by the chapter's end, to her own return to the Bear Paw as symbolic of her immersion in a collective Indian identification. In the imaginative operations of memory, she explores the autobiographical possibilities of an event and a site for which new stories do not seem possible. *Bloodlines*, I would argue, is in fact unromantic in recognizing the impossibility of a return to origins effaced by time. Rather, it calls for new, hybrid stories linking the collective past to personal histories that reinterpret its seeming defeats.

Stories are a primary means of making that link. Hale takes the title of her final chapter, "Dust to Dust," from the etymology of her great-grandfather's Indian name, Cole-man-née, which she was told means "dust" but has become "Campbell" in common usage (171). Meditating on the transformative power of claiming her bloodline here has different consequences. Narrating a story of her return, with her grown daughter, to the reservation as she was finishing the book, she discloses the fictions of a happy childhood with which she has raised her children, and she tells several of them. Speaking in the persona of a storyteller celebrating Indian origins—in Coyote stories and stories of the land—she takes up a storytelling voice different from the trauma-driven narrator of much of her text. And Hale acknowledges that these reconstructions of her childhood are "not the whole truth" because they have "order" and "continuity": "I think I must have made it up for myself first . . . . And tried to believe in it. . . . I had a place where I belonged, really belonged. I came from a family that valued me" (169). But while her own children hear revisionist tales, the text remains a site for confiding other, less happy, stories of lives in crisis from migrancy, poverty, and abuse.

And yet Hale discovers on returning to the reservation that the material basis of her stories is disappearing. She can no longer recognize where her family used to live; the past is obscured, in part by new construction of resorts on reservation land but in part by her own confusion about what was where. She comes to an opposite realization from that of identifying with the Indians at the Bear Paw, stating: "I can never live here, where I came from . . . . Our ancestral land is [my ancestors'] home; it can never be mine. I will remain, as I have long been, estranged from the land I belong to" (185). While writing creates a textual legacy, it cannot negotiate her social alienation from family and the Coeur d'Alene; belonging and estrangement coexist. She concludes: "I have so little to pass down to my daughter, it seems. Just the stories, the history, who we came from" (185). But unlike herself, she notes, her fair daughter can choose whether to be Indian; the ambivalent connection to "my homeland and history, my roots" through a troubled family is not an issue for her. Except in fictionalizing her past to her children and specifying the family genealogy to the extent it is knowable, Hale finds no way to tell her past without also telling on it.

In claiming an identification of blood and memory that is thoroughly performative and at the same time deeply felt, Hale makes her text a site for readers to refigure personal history as a network of relations across time and space. As her modes of telling revalue stories of loss, addiction, victimization, and poverty, she invites readers to reframe their own pasts by finding connections that situate their personal crises in public histories. Claiming the personal past in conflict and shame, struggle and conquest, can be a basis for making new stories of people who can no longer be "from" their original homes but want to stake native-emigré identity claims both in and against American history.[15] In the special circumstances of American Indians—"For us there is no other . . . old country" (xx)—the technologies of American culture, such as erecting monuments, writing narratives, giving speeches, and even commodifying what is Indian, have become means of regenerating an ethnic identity even though the homeland of the Turtle Clan cannot be repossessed by genealogical claim (xx). (In a final historical irony, much of that land is now the national "home" of the white separatist Aryan Nation movement and "Bo" Gritz's "Almost Heaven" Christian identity sect in northern Idaho.) Writing the "bloodline" as a rhetorical process of articulating identity names Hale's personal history as collective affiliation and uncovers a history of unequal differences within the family and the nation that mark the continuing crisis of American identity.

Notes

This essay is dedicated to the memory of Bonnie Heavy Runner Craig.

1. For example, neither Cook-Lynn, Donovan, or any of the essays in Bloom discusses it, though a case could be made for *Bloodlines* as both a nativist and a feminist text. One chapter from *Bloodlines*, "The Only Good Indian," is anthologized in Joy Harjo and Gloria Bird's *Reinventing the Enemy's Language*.

2. While my preference is to use the full name Campbell Hale, including both her family's and her married name, editorial convention does not permit this usage.

3. This controversy about autobiography as a significantly different genre from biography is at the heart of much contemporary theorizing of autobiography. Olney traces how autobiographical writing develops tropes of self-doubling; Eakin considers its fictions of self-representation; Smith (in *Subjectivity*) explores its strategies of embodiment; and the essays in *The Culture of Autobiography* (Folkenflik) consider the history and practices of constructions of self-representation.

4. The phrase "strategic essentialism" is discussed by Gayatri Chakravorty Spivak in an essay-conversation with Sarah Harasym. Noting her own observation in an earlier interview that "feminists have to be strategic essentialists" and Derrida's subsequent deployment of it in a lecture, Spivak states: "Since it is not possible not to be an essentialist, one can self-consciously use this irreducible moment of essentialism as part of one's strategy . . . . The relationship between the two kinds of representation brings in, also, the use of essentialism because no representation can take place—no *Vertretung*, representation—can take place without essentialism. What it has to take into account is that the 'essence' that is being represented is a representation of the other kind, *Darstellung*" (109).

5. Krupat distinguishes between two kinds of American Indian autobiographical narratives: 1) "Indian autobiographies," stories told by indigenous people to another person from another culture who elicited the story (often an ethnographer) and often shaped it through ethnographic conventions as a tale of exotic primitives; and 2) "autobiographies by Indians," life stories in English by persons of Native American heritage who now live in a bicultural world (Introduction 3–4).

6. For example, Michael Ondaatje's *Running in the Family*, Mary Clearman Blew's *All but the Waltz*, Norma Cantú's *Canícula*, and Mary McCarthy's *Memories of a Catholic Girlhood* are autobiographies that use family photographs prominently to tell complex stories. Timothy Dow Adams explores the varieties of autobiographical uses of photographs to tell counternarratives, disrupt or affirm particular textual moments,

and to "authenticate" a narrative location. Similarly, Marianne Hirsch has explored what is often a discrepancy between photo image and memory at several points in her own past, as well as that of such writers as Jo Spence and Valerie Walkerdine.

7. During a forum on Writing Ethnicity in Transnational Perspective at Ohio State University on 15 January 1999, Chadwick Allen persuasively argued for the primacy of "blood, land, and memory" in the identity construction of indigenous peoples in the Americas and New Zealand.

8. Frederick Hale, in his monograph, does not mention either this manual or Janet Campbell Hale's work for the Native Adult Education Resource Centre at Okanagan College in British Columbia.

9. From Stegner's "The Law of Nature and the Dream of Man."

10. See Michie and Warhol on twelve-step programs as narratives of recovery that may, problematically, recast individual stories within Alcoholic Anonymous formulas. What characterizes oral performance at AA meetings, they suggest, is the obsessive retelling of the *same* story of victimization and abuse.

11. My essay "Ordering the Family" discusses genealogical methods, including the pedigree, as a means of cultural legitimation for Euro-Americans and the implications for many Indians, among other Americans, of being excluded from access to accurate records of their pasts. The inscription of subjectivity in autobiography is in marked contrast to the emphasis on documentation and objectivity that characterizes the construction of a genealogy.

12. The subtitle of this biography is *Doctor John McLoughlin, Doctor David McLoughlin, Marie Louise (Sister St. Henry); An Account of Their Personal Lives and of Their Parents, Relatives, and Children; In Canada's Quebec Province, in Paris, France, and in the West of the Hudson's Bay Company.* Written by Burt Brown Barker and published by A. H. Clark Co. in 1959, the biography is another authenticating document for Hale.

13. See Allen's excellent discussion of blood quantum as a marker of Indian difference in "Blood (and) Memory."

14. In the contemporary Northwest, statues and icons of an abject Chief Joseph abound in souvenirs and on T-shirts. Sometimes these are in crudely debased forms, such as the rows of garish plaster busts on sale in the Clack Museum in Havre, Montana, not far from the battleground.

15. For a discussion of native-emigré issues in American literary history, see Lincoln's discussion of native poetics.

Works Cited

Adams, Timothy Dow. *Light Writing and Life Writing: Photography in Autobiography.* Chapel Hill: University of North Carolina Press, 2000.

Allen, Chadwick. "Blood (and) Memory," *American Literature* 71.1 (1999): 93–116.

———. "Blood, Land, and Memory." Paper delivered at the Writing Ethnicity in Transnational Perspective Brown Bag. Ohio State University. 15 Jan. 1999.

Bataille, Gretchen M., and Kathleen M. Sands. "Women's Autobiography." In *Dictionary of Native American Literature*. Ed. Andrew Wiget. New York: Garland, 1994. 187–92.

Blew, Mary Clearman. *All but the Waltz: Essays on a Montana Family*. New York: Penguin, 1991.

Bloom, Harold, ed. *Native American Women Writers*. Philadelphia: Main Line Book Co., 1998.

Cantú, Norma. *Canícula: Snapshots of a Girlhood en la Frontera*. Albuquerque: University of New Mexico Press, 1995.

Caruth, Cathy. Introduction to *Trauma: Explorations in Memory*, ed. Cathy Caruth. Baltimore: Johns Hopkins University Press, 1995. 3–12.

Cook-Lynn, Elizabeth. *Why I Can't Read Wallace Stegner and Other Essays*. Madison: University of Wisconsin Press, 1996.

Donovan, Kathleen M. *Feminist Readings of Native American Literature: Coming to Voice*. Tucson: University of Arizona Press, 1998.

Eakin, Paul John. *Fictions in Autobiography: Studies in the Art of Self-Invention*. Princeton, N.J.: Princeton University Press, 1985.

Eller, Jack David. "Ethnicity, Culture, and 'the Past.'" *Michigan Quarterly Review* 36.4 (1997): 552–600.

Folkenflik, Robert, ed. *The Culture of Autobiography: Constructions of Self-Representation*. Stanford, Calif.: Stanford University Press, 1993.

Foucault, Michel. "Technologies of the Self." In *Technologies of the Self: A Seminar with Michel Foucault*. Ed. Luther H. Martin, Huck Gutman, and Patrick H. Hutton. Amherst: University of Massachusetts Press, 1988. 16–49.

Hale, Frederick. "In the Tradition of Native American Autobiography? Janet Campbell Hale's *Bloodlines*." *Studies in American Indian Literature* 8.1 (Spring 1996): 68–80.

———. *Janet Campbell Hale*. Western Writers Series. Boise, Idaho: Boise State University Press, 1996.

Hale, Janet Campbell. *Bloodlines: Odyssey of a Native Daughter*. New York: Random House, 1993.

———. *The Jailing of Cecelia Capture*. New York: Random House, 1985.

———. "The Only Good Indian." In *Reinventing the Enemy's Language: Contemporary Native Women's Writings of North America*. Ed. Joy Harjo and Gloria Bird. New York: W. W. Norton, 1997. 123–48.

Hale, Janet Campbell, et al. *Native Students with Problems of Addiction: A Manual for Adult Educators*. Victoria: British Columbia Ministry of Advanced Education, Training, and Technology, 1990.

Harjo, Joy, and Gloria Bird, eds. *Reinventing the Enemy's Language: Contemporary Native Women's Writings of North America*. New York: W. W. Norton, 1997.

Henderson, Mae Gwendolyn. "Speaking in Tongues: Dialogics, Dialectics, and the Black Woman Writer's Literary Tradition." In *Women, Autobiography, Theory: A Reader*. Ed. Sidonie Smith and Julia Watson. Madison: University of Wisconsin Press, 1998. 343–61.

Hirsch, Marianne. *Family Frames.* Cambridge, Mass.: Harvard University Press, 1997.

Kinkaid, M. Dale. "Native Oral Literature of the Northwest Coast and the Plateau." In *Dictionary of Native American Literature.* Ed. Andrew Wiget. New York: Garland, 1994. 33–45.

Krupat, Arnold. Introduction to *Native American Autobiography: An Anthology,* ed. Arnold Krupat. Madison: University of Wisconsin Press, 1994. 3–17.

———. "Native American Autobiography and the Synecdochic Self." In *American Autobiography: Retrospect and Prospect.* Ed. Paul John Eakin. Madison: University of Wisconsin Press, 1991. 171–94.

———. *The Voice in the Margin.* Berkeley: University of California Press, 1989.

Lincoln, Kenneth. "Native Poetics." *Modern Fiction Studies* 45.1 (1999): 146–84.

McCarthy, Mary. *Memories of a Catholic Girlhood.* New York: Harcourt Brace Jovanovich, 1957.

Michie, Helena, and Robyn Warhol. "Twelve-Step Teleology: Narratives of Recovery/Recovery as Narrative." In *Getting a Life: Everyday Uses of Autobiography.* Ed. Sidonie Smith and Julia Watson. Minneapolis: University of Minnesota Press, 1996. 327–50.

Olney, James. *Metaphors of Self.* Princeton, N.J.: Princeton University Press, 1971.

Ondaatje, Michael. *Running in the Family.* New York: Random House, 1982.

Plummer, Ken. *Telling Sexual Stories.* New York: Routledge, 1993.

Schachter, Daniel L. *Searching for Memory: The Brain, the Mind, and the Past.* New York: HarperCollins, 1996.

Silko, Leslie Marmon. *Ceremony.* New York: Viking, 1977.

———. *Storyteller.* New York: Seaver Books, 1981.

Smith, Sidonie. "Performativity, Autobiographical Practice, Resistance." In *Women, Autobiography, Theory: A Reader.* Ed. Sidonie Smith and Julia Watson. Madison: University of Wisconsin Press, 1998. 108–15.

———. *Subjectivity, Identity, and the Body.* Bloomington: Indiana University Press, 1993.

Spivak, Gayatri Chakravorty. "Practical Politics of the Open End: An Interview with Sarah Harasym." In *The Post-Colonial Critic.* Ed. Sarah Harasym. New York: Routledge, 1990. 95–112.

Stegner, Wallace. "The Law of Nature and the Dream of Man." In *When the Bluebird Sings to the Lemonade Springs: Living and Writing in the West.* New York: Random House, 1992. 214–22.

Watson, Julia. "Ordering the Family: Genealogy as Autobiographical Pedigree." In *Getting a Life: Everyday Uses of Autobiography.* Ed. Sidonie Smith and Julia Watson. Minneapolis: University of Minnesota Press, 1996. 297–326.

Wong, Hertha D. Sweet. "First-Person Plural: Subjectivity and Community in Native American Women's Autobiography." In *Women, Autobiography, Theory: A Reader.* Ed. Sidonie Smith and Julia Watson. Madison: University of Wisconsin Press, 1998. 168–78.

5

Mississippi Masala, South Asian Activism, and Agency

Purnima Bose and Linta Varghese

Since its release in February 1992, Mira Nair's *Mississippi Masala* has figured large in debates about representation and activism in the South Asian diasporic context. After the initial outcry by South Asian feminists in such progressive journals as *Ms.* and *Z Magazine*—charging the film with exoticizing South Asian womanhood for the visual consumption of a white, male audience—critiques of the film surfaced in anthologies on contemporary Asian American activism such as *The State of Asian America: Activism and Resistance in the 1990s* (Aguilar–San Juan) and in edited volumes on South Asian American identity such as *Our Feet Walk the Sky: Women of the South Asian Diaspora* (Women of South Asian Descent Collective) and *Between the Lines: South Asians and Postcoloniality* (Bahri and Vasudeva). Nair's critics and partisans have enlisted discourses of the "real" to legitimize their readings of the film. Soon after its release, the feminist collective Manavi published an article that charges that even Nair's South Asian background does not exempt her from criticism, claiming it "does not immune *Mississippi Masala* from unrealistic, exotic, or even anti-feminist representations of South Asian–American womanhood" (1). According to one of Nair's advocates, however, the film "attempts to address the changes in the South Asian American community as well as bring to the surface realities that, however submerged, have always been present" (Rasiah 273). Nair herself uses the category of "realness" to authenticate her films discursively. In an interview with Gita Mehta, Nair declares that she derives her films from "life," explaining, "'I find that *real* life, the liveliness of *real* people, brings energy to my work'" (qtd. in Mehta, "Movies" 113). The centrality accorded to this cultural artifact in discussions of South Asian activism illustrates the extent to which the "real," as a category of experience for diasporic South Asians, has become a site of contestation over identity. At stake in these invocations of the discourses of the "real" in the ongoing though disparate and intermittent debates triggered by *Mississippi Masala,* we argue, are controversies over what constitutes "authentic" South Asian diasporic identity. These debates have been particularly charged because the film has been one of the very few cultural artifacts depicting the South Asian diaspora to circulate through mainstream media channels. As such, South Asian feminist responses to the film have been overdetermined by anxiety that it will be read as "representative" of the diasporic experience. Propelled in part by a burgeoning movement of South Asian feminist and electoral activism, these critical responses to the film signal a deliberate and strategic conflation of cultural and political activism through recourse to essentialist constructions of identity that seek to insert issues of South Asian gender and agency in discourses of progressive activism in the United States.

In this chapter, we will examine how the film has become a site of contestation over "real" and "authentic" media representations of South Asians; we limit ourselves here to a discussion of readings of the film that are critical of it.[1] Our reading of *Mississippi Masala* will analyze how the film problematizes the very terms of the essentialist identity critiques leveled against it insofar as it exposes immigrant identity as being a product of multiple national formations in order to challenge the gender and racial conservatism of the U.S. South Asian diaspora. Our analysis of the critical responses to the film—particularly the ways in which they draw on the category of "real experience" in monolithic terms—and our reading of *Mississippi Masala* rely on the critical strategy of invoking other South Asian experiences and realities. We are not arguing for some alternative to the "real" so much as a redefinition of the term that expands its definition. Since "all identity is constructed across difference," as Stuart Hall maintains, the "narrative status of identity in relation to the world also require[s] as a necessity, its opposite—the moment of arbitrary closure" (45). Hall reminds us that the constitution of new subjectivities and social movements "have had to accept the necessarily fictional, but also the fictional necessity, of the arbitrary closure which is not the end, but which makes both politics and identity possible" (45). New subjectivities and their articulations in political praxis—that is, social agency—begin, for Hall, with the adoption of provisional identities. Our counterreading of the film is not meant as a corrective to other feminist responses to it; rather, our analysis of Nair's work represents a contingent closure of articulation whose construction of the "real" broadens its frame of reference by drawing upon observations of contemporary South Asian social practices, empirical evidence, and the contextualization of specific events such as Idi Amin's 1972 expulsion of Asians from Uganda. While we consider some of the limitations of such a critical practice in our conclusion, reading feminist criticism of *Mississippi Masala* through these sociohistorical categories and as supplements to our own experiences allows us to interrogate the ways in which discourses of the "real," as deployed by South Asian feminists, occlude a diversity of class and regional experiences in the South Asian diaspora.

Plotting *Mississippi Masala*

Mira Nair derived the idea for *Mississippi Masala* from a *New Yorker* article about Asian Ugandan exiles, many of whom ran family-owned hotels, living in Mississippi. After numerous trips to the South, extended visits with these families, and reading interviews with Asians forced to leave Uganda, she and Sooni Taraporevala developed and produced the movie. Set in Greenwood, Mississippi, and Kampala, Uganda, *Mississippi Masala* focuses on the Loha family, Jay (Roshan Seth), his wife Kinnu (Sharmila Tagore), and their twenty-four-year-old daughter Mina (Sarita Chaudhury). Forced to leave Uganda because of Idi Amin's expulsion order, the Lohas have resettled in Greenwood, Mississippi. The movie weaves two narrative threads: one is spun around Jay and his relation to his former homeland, Uganda; the other is spun around the illicit romance that develops between Mina and Demetrius (Denzel Washington), an African American small-business owner who counts several Indian motel proprietors as customers of his modest carpet cleaning business.

The film opens in Kampala, Uganda, in the early hours of 7 November 1972, which was the official deadline for the Asian departure. The car carrying Jay and his childhood friend Okelo is stopped by soldiers. After a brief but nerve-wracking inspection at this checkpoint, Jay and Okelo are released. In the ensuing conversation between the two men, we learn that Jay was jailed for criticizing Amin during a BBC interview. In the midst of Jay's emphatic declarations of his positioning as "Ugandan first, Indian second" and that Uganda is his home, Okelo informs Jay that now "Africa is for Africans, black Africans." The harshness of Okelo's formulation of a racialized African identity is softened by our knowledge that he has intervened at great personal risk and expense to secure Jay's release from prison. Okelo's willingness to endanger himself on behalf of Jay suggests that his articulation of African identity is motivated by concern for Jay's safety and bodily integrity.

Eighteen years later, after a sojourn in England, the Lohas now reside in Greenwood, Mississippi. Jay, a lawyer by training, spends his time petitioning the government of Uganda for restitution of his property; Kinnu owns and runs a liquor store in the African American section of the town; and Mina works as a maid and desk clerk at the Monte Cristo Motel. Owned by a relative of Jay, the Monte Cristo is home to the Lohas and their extended family. With the change in setting from Uganda to Mississippi, the film shifts its focus from Jay's to Mina's perspective. Unlike Jay's narrative, which centers on his subjectivity as an Asian Ugandan in the national and racial context of Amin's regime, Mina's story line emphasizes her relationships to her immediate family and her beloved, Demetrius.

We first glimpse Mina purchasing groceries for the wedding of her cousin brother Anil, the son of the owner of the Monte Cristo. Driving back to the motel and distracted by her aunt's exhortations to drive slower, she rear-ends the car of an Anglo man, who in turn hits the back bumper of Demetrius's van. The scene establishes at a literal level the collision between the three cultures in Greenwood: African American, Anglo, and South Asian. Later that evening, Mina and Demetrius meet by chance at the Leopard Lounge, a dance club that Mina has gone to with the highly eligible South Asian bachelor, Harry Patel. After attending a birthday party for Demetrius's father several days later, Mina and Demetrius arrange to meet in Biloxi. Mina secures permission for this rendezvous by telling her parents that she is going to the beach with an Indian girlfriend. The lovers are caught in bed in Biloxi by Mina's cousin brother and his cohorts. A brawl between Demetrius, Anil, and Mina results; Jay must post bail for Mina who, presumably, has been charged with disorderly conduct for her part in the fracas.

Scandalized at the sexual transgression of one of its own, the Indian community conspires to keep the two lovers apart. Mina manages to abscond and tracks down Demetrius, who has spent a frustrating afternoon attempting to rebuild his business clientele, which has been dramatically reduced through the machinations of the Indian community. Earlier in the film, members of this community had vociferously declared racial solidarity with Demetrius out of fear that he would sue them over the car accident. After a confrontation in which Mina accuses Demetrius of using her to make his ex-lover jealous and in which Demetrius admonishes Mina for not telling him that her family "has a problem with black people," Demetrius and Mina admit their love to one another. Because they have found little support and only hostility from the three major communities in Greenwood—the Anglo capitalist classes, the South Asian business community, and the African American wage laborers—they decide to leave Greenwood, stay together romantically, and become business partners. While the young lovers come together by the end of the film, this union occurs at the expense of the Indian community's destruction of Demetrius's business and its expulsion of Mina from the diasporic fold.

Throughout the film, Nair conveys Jay's last days in Kampala through a series of flashbacks. Jay finally receives a reply from the Ugandan government regarding his petition; a court date for the hearing of his case has been set. He returns to Uganda to attend the hearing and finds that Okelo, who spent a considerable sum of money to bribe Jay's jailers to gain his release, was brutally killed following Jay's departure. The narrative logic of the film implies that Okelo's friendship with Jay and the assistance he rendered have cost him his life. *Mississippi Masala* ends like it began, in Uganda, with Jay speaking of home. Unlike the opening of the film, in which Jay's stated conception of home is located within a national formation, in the end he concludes that "home is where the heart is," in his case, with Kinnu. As the final credits scroll up the screen, the camera shows Mina and Demetrius, clothed in South Asian and African garb respectively, dancing in a cotton field.

The "Real" Conflict Zone

The ongoing skirmishes over *Mississippi Masala* among South Asian activists and critics are waged over the battleground of representation. Armed with a weaponry that includes discourses of "realness" and "authenticity," both sides in this conflict over representation, the defenders of Nair and her critics, lobby readings and counterreadings of the film in a discursive barrage against one another. As an adjective, "real" signifies multiple meanings denoting that which is actually existing or "genuine," on the one hand, and the law of immovable property (as in real estate) and the appraised purchasing power (as in real value), on the other hand. The combined senses of the word encapsulate, albeit in a convoluted way, some of the complexities of the debates around *Mississippi Masala* and South Asian identity: Nair's critics fault the film for its failure to represent "genuine" South Asian experience realistically, singling out the film's commodification of South Asian womanhood as its most egregious shortcoming.

Yet the category of the "real," as even some of the film's critics acknowledge, is not a fixed and stable one. As bell hooks and Anuradha Dingwaney urge in their scathing review of *Mississippi Masala*, the very notion of the "real" must be interrogated: "Since the informed spectator knows that the 'real' is always already a selection, then we must think critically about the choices a director makes when she seeks to represent the 'real'" (41). According to these critics, stereotypes are often a convenient means by which "to embody the concept of the 'real' or the everyday," because of their easy familiarity with a general mainstream audience (41). Access to "real" experiences is always already mediated through cultural representations that subject experiences to ideological and aesthetic processes. Louise Spence and Robert Stam emphasize this point, noting that "While posing legitimate questions concerning narrative plausibility and mimetic accuracy, negative stereotypes and positive images, the emphasis on realism has often betrayed an exaggerated faith in the possibilities of verisimilitude in art in general and the cinema in particular, avoiding the fact that films are inevitably constructs, fabrications, representations" (3). The "real" is a constructed category within the cinematic frame itself that can be utilized as a weapon of cultural criticism; its efficacy depends upon the extent to which the constructed nature of the category of the "real" is obscured.

In the war over "accurate" representations among South Asians, the "authority of experience" has been enlisted and deployed with great power. Most of the film's critics and defenders are South Asian American women who have sought to legitimate their claims for the movie by drawing on their own narratives of individual experience. The production of a diasporic community involves the identification of some characteristics that simultaneously serve to exclude outsiders and to primordialize insiders. In their reactions to *Mississippi Masala,* South Asian critics and activists mark themselves as cultural insiders, in effect presenting themselves as native informants through four major rhetorical strategies, which are sometimes overlapping. We have glancingly alluded to the first of these strategies already, what Ana Alonso terms the process of "departicularization," which is manifest in the critic's or activist's unself-conscious appropriation and valuation of his or her own experience as an index of a unitary and common South Asian diasporic cultural norm (qtd. in Foster 242). The second of these strategies entails the use of Hindi words, particularly kinship terms, to designate the critic's or activist's membership within a South Asian linguistic community. In the third strategy, the critic or activist utilizes the tropological operation of synecdoche whereby one African country, generally Uganda, is made representative of all African nations. The fourth strategy—which is closely aligned with the process of departicularization—consists of offering a visual epistemology of the film's representation of Mina that is grounded in a knowledge of South Asian social practices governing grooming and appearance.

Some of the earliest and most caustic critiques of the film originated with South Asian feminists who denounced the representation of Mina as a character purposely exoticized and "molded for the viewing pleasure of the white male audience" (Manavi 1). To counter the exoticized celluloid images of Mina presented on the screen, the reviewers reveal their perceptions of what constitutes the "real" life experiences of South Asian women. For example, Yasmin Ladha's open letter to Mira Nair is significantly titled "Dear Didi" (dear older sister) and appeared in the Canadian South Asian quarterly *Rungh.* By addressing Nair by an honorific kinship term, "didi," which recognizes age hierarchy within the extended family unit, Ladha rhetorically positions Nair and herself within a common South Asian cultural tradition. Such a positioning softens the harshness of the criticism leveled against the film through the assertion of a familial connection with Nair while it simultaneously authorizes that same criticism by implicitly locating its origins from within a broader South Asian family nexus. Throughout her review, Ladha departicularizes her own diasporic experiences as an Indian from Kenya who has settled in Canada and projects them onto the fictional representation of Mina, an Indian from Uganda who has settled in Mississippi. The conflation of distinct diasporic contexts in Africa and North America obscures important differences between immigration in these sites that have been shaped by social-class-inflected factors such as state sanctioned violence targeted at particular ethnic groups, the disparate regulation of these groups through immigration policy, and the historically dissimilar formations of racism in Canada, Kenya, Uganda, and the southern United States. For Ladha, this conflation of African contexts functions to challenge Nair's knowledge of social practices, particularly those that are rooted in kinship terminology and the aesthetics of home furnishings, among South Asians in Uganda. Ladha feels assured that the proper title for mother is "Mummy" for Indian Africans and informs Nair that "Your Mina calls her mum 'maa.' It sits on the character you try to flesh out: in Kampala, Uganda, their drawing room . . . is lampy western, African carvings and rugs (a child in such a family would call her mother 'Mummy' . . .)" (36). Here, the aesthetics of the domestic space are used to read linguistic practices within the family vis à vis their fidelity to a cultural norm based on Ladha's personal experiences as a South Asian in Kenya. If one were to adopt Ladha's reading strategy of judging Nair's representation of South Asian life in Uganda based on its verisimilitude to a "real" referent, one could note that the Ugandan domestic scenes are shot in Nair's own Ugandan home that she shares with her husband, the social scientist Mahmood Mamdani. In other words, Nair's representation of Mina's home is "realistic" insofar as it resembles at least one South Asian home in Uganda.

Ladha's tropological strategy of universalizing her Kenyan experience as representative of all African nations is echoed at a more sophisticated level by bell hooks and Anuradha Dingwaney in their review of the film. Rather than use Kenya as a benchmark by which to gauge the accuracy of Nair's representation of Uganda, hooks and Dingwaney render Uganda under Idi Amin's regime into a synecdoche for all African countries. Even more curious, given the academic backgrounds of both authors, is their failure to distinguish between different though continuous historical periods, namely, the British colonial period and the rise of African national liberation movements and the postindependence, neocolonial era of Idi Amin. Commenting on the relationship between Okelo and Jay, they note:

viewers are well into the film before we are told that Okelo is a teacher and not Jay's servant. Why does Mira Nair make the relationship between the two men so ambiguous when they are in Uganda, making it appear that Jay offers a social equality and brotherhood that Okelo rejects? In fact, Okelo's declaration that "Africa is for Africans, black Africans" is depicted as narrow nationalism and racism. The film deliberately distorts the progressive aspects of anti-colonial nationalist struggles making it appear that they are always reactionary and rooted in the same racism and xenophobia that is at the heart of white imperialistic domination . . . . Given how ignorant most Americans are about African politics and liberation struggles, this film does a grave disservice when it makes those movements synonymous with Idi Amin's dictatorship. (42)

This passage suggests that hooks and Dingwaney read Amin's regime as being part of an "anti-colonial nationalist struggle." Yet since the film's Ugandan scenes are set in 1972, a full decade after Uganda achieved independence from Britain in 1962 under the leadership of Milton Obete—whom Amin overthrew in 1971—and the Uganda People's Congress, the events that it represents are clearly after the end of formal or official colonialism. Indeed, Idi Amin's background as one of only two native officers in Uganda's military forces during the colonial period points to his status as a native collaborator rather than an ardent nationalist engaged in the anticolonial struggle against the British.

Mira Nair herself, through the titles in the film and in several interviews, insists on the specificity of the film's Ugandan postindependence context. The Ugandan scene that opens the film locates the action historically, both temporally and geographically; the title reads: "Kampala Uganda. November, 1972." Nair describes her inspiration for the film as originating in Jane Kramer's *New Yorker* article on Amin's expulsion of Asians and on articles in the Indian press that treated their experiences settling in the American South. "'They were called Potels in the article,'" she explains. "'I was so fascinated that I got in a car and started driving through Mississippi, staying in those motels. Sooni and I worked on a script, going back again and again to Mississippi'" (qtd. in G. Mehta 116). Nair contends that the script is based on "real" life experiences. In a *Mother Jones* interview published prior to the film's release, she describes a scene that captures the violence of Idi Amin's expulsion of some eighty thousand Asians in 1972:

"there is an African band in a bar playing an Indian song on the last day the Indians are in Uganda. And the Indians are drinking, just throwing their money away. . . . And the State Research Bureau boys, who were like Amin's secret police, come in their flowered shirts and their bell-bottoms and haul one of the Indians out and put him in the trunk of a car. That was drawn from reality, from people who told me these things. Some of the people in the scene really were the last Asians in Kampala, and it moved them very much. It was shockingly real for them." (qtd. in Orenstein 61)

In her invocation of the "real," Nair discloses an understanding of the category of history that anchors it in lived experience. Her representation of the Asian expulsion utilizes the narratives of the subjects who lived through this experience as the raw material that the film processes and attempts to analyze. Nair is quite explicit about the film's historical specificity and makes no claims for it as being representative of other African liberation movements. Rather, it is hooks and Dingwaney who make Amin's dictatorship synonymous with African politics and liberation struggles through their reading of the film.

Ironically, several of the film's South Asian critics have lambasted Nair on the same grounds that she uses to defend her film as being historically accurate. Invoking the category of the "real" in relation to her characterization of Mina, they charge the film with presenting a false representation of the "reality" of South Asian diasporic gendered subjectivity; these reviewers maintain that the corporeal embodiment of Mina's character fails to correspond with the reality of actual young South Asian women. The reviews that propose this particular reading of the film paradoxically duplicate one of the shortcomings of the film that they attack: the film's failure to grant Mina's character subjectivity is reproduced in the critical focus on her physical appearance. These critics share some axiological assumptions about what constitutes "authentic" identity that are based on their sometimes limited knowledge of contemporary South Asian social practices regulating female beauty and appearance. The *Manavi Newsletter,* for instance, opines: "While a South Asian woman having thick, long hair is not in and of itself surprising, it is interesting that *Mississippi Masala* depicts Mina wearing her hair loose, sexy and tousled about her face. One wonders why her mother has not forced this unruly mass into well-oiled braids" (Manavi 2). This reviewer's assumption that the normative hairstyle for South Asian young women consists of "well-oiled braids" reveals another dynamic at work in the constitution of a diasporic culture, namely, the phenomenon of disjunctive temporality. First-generation immigrants—those who were born in South Asia and have immigrated to the United States—are not familiar with the shifts in middle-class attitudes in India that have been continuous since their departure from the subcontinent and have become steadily more permissive in terms of defining acceptable sartorial, grooming, and behavioral choices for girls and women (Das Gupta, "What is 'Indian'" 4). These immigrants have rigid expectations of what constitutes appropriate behavior for their children that are grounded in a fossilized and antiquated understanding of culture. Appropriate behavior—in other words, that which is "authentically Indian"—is often anachronistic for first-generation immigrants; it is predicated on the social mores that were prevalent when the immigrants lived in South Asia and is consequently often outdated by several decades. As one young second-generation South Asian immigrant commented to an Indian woman studying in the United States, "'The difference between you and me is that you can do many more things in India than I can do here. My father's nephews and nieces in India do things he would still say "no" to. They wear their hair short, go out with friends, hold hands'" (qtd. in Das Gupta, "What is 'Indian'" 4). For South Asian women at the time of the film's release, well-oiled braids would have been only one hairstyle choice among many other possibilities. Indeed, *Mississippi Masala* does represent one hair scene that will resonate with familiarity for many South Asians, though not all, insofar as it depicts Kinnu lovingly massaging oil into her daughter's dark tresses, thus reenacting a scene of mother-daughter bonding that is common in India.

The anonymous *Manavi Newsletter* reviewer and Sayantani Das Gupta, in her *Ms.* article "Glass Shawls and Long Hair: A South Asian Woman Talks Sexual Politics," voice almost identical concerns about the costuming decisions made with Mina's character. Both authors articulate their disbelief with the representational appropriateness of Mina wearing traditional Indian clothes in the beach scene; in both cases, discourses of the "real" are mobilized to legitimize their readings. The *Manavi* review, for example, argues,

> While Meena usually wears Western outfits, she chooses to don salwaar-kameez and a glass embroidered shawl during her romantic rendezvous at the beach. This costuming choice is perhaps as absurd as the belly-dancer veils of South Asian women in James Bond films. *It must be recognized that Meena's reality is not that of an upper-middle class college-educated urbanite, who can fling about a glass embroidered shawl as she drinks cappuccino and smokes endless cigarettes. Rather, she is a twenty-four year old, high-school educated, working class woman who lives in a Mississippi small town motel and cleans toilets for a living.* In the harsh struggles of assimilation, it is preposterous to think that this woman would wear Indian garb on a Mississippi beach. (2; emphasis added)

Das Gupta similarly echoes the anonymous reviewer's reservations (and even vocabulary) about Mina's ethnic garb, declaring,

> [Mina] tosses her long hair about, and in one scene dresses and behaves like a cosmopolitan sophisticate. She tosses her long hair about, and in one scene dresses in

traditional *salwaar kameez* and a glass-embroidered Indian shawl. It is highly un-likely that a real-life woman of Indian descent would wear Indian clothing outside of community functions, particularly during a rendezvous with her boyfriend on a Mississippi beach. Real South Asian women know that ethnic garb may be de rigueur in cities and on liberal college campuses, but it is an invitation to racist insult and assault in most areas of the United States. ("Glass Shawls" 77)

At issue in these two responses to Mina's clothing are regional and class as-sumptions regarding the representational appropriateness of Nair's costum-ing decisions. Both reviews sanction college-educated urbanites to wear *kur-ta pajamas* and *dupattas* with mirror work, but not so for working-class rural women. If anything, however, the film demonstrates that class identities can be fluid: raised in upper-middle-class privilege in Uganda, Mina is working-class in Mississippi and poised to rejoin the bourgeoisie either through college, as her father wishes, or as a small-business owner with Demetrius. Moreover, a common perception of the South underwrites both authors' constructions of Mississippi as a site that is more saturated with gendered racialism and the threat of violence against people of color than other more metropolitan spaces, such as college campuses, in the United States. Yet this construction of Mis-sissippi, at least in terms of hate crimes against South Asians, does not reflect the empirical reality of violence against South Asian immigrants, which has tended to be concentrated in northeastern urban areas such as Jersey City and directed against South Asian men.[2]

Das Gupta's and the *Manavi* reviewer's complaints about *Mississippi Masala* ultimately center on their belief that the film "exoticizes" South Asian wom-en for the visual consumption of a white, male spectator. Das Gupta even gives exotification a new name; according to her, "masala-itis" is a "disease where-by the complexities of racism, sexism, and homophobia disappear, and one feels the sudden urge to exotify oneself" (76). While her reading of the film implicitly acknowledges the ways in which cultural texts produce ideological meanings, insofar as Mina's appearance seemingly participates in the Holly-wood cinematic tradition of commodifying women, we would argue that these meanings are unstable and changing. Das Gupta's formulation of the catego-ry of the "exotic," with its reliance on the notion of the male gaze, does not account for the reception of the film among diverse audiences. The spectator, in her account, is restricted to a generalized white male, thus failing to con-sider the cinematic experience of spectators with other social identities. The "exotic," like the "real," is not a stable unchanging category but is constantly in a flux that is dependent for its definition on the subject position and his-torical location of the viewer. The perception of the exotic is constituted by that which is not culturally normative for the spectator. It is precisely those elements that strike the spectator as unfamiliar, which are outside his or her cultural experience, that grant a particular object or subject mysteriousness and allure, conferring on it the status of the "exotic." While the donning of a *kurta pajama* and a mirror-work *dupatta* for a romantic evening on the beach might seem "exotic" for a non–South Asian, such a choice of clothing for a South Asian woman occurs within the range of acceptable, even predictable, sartorial options.

The discussions of the "exotic" seem to conflate it as a site of commodified identity, in terms of appropriate regional and class markers and the actual physical features of the actress Sarita Chaudhury, who plays Mina's character. The *Manavi Newsletter* maintains that "the exotification of Meena in the film is unmistakable. Her dark skin, sultry lips, almond-shaped eyes and curly black hair are used to their utmost advantage" (2). The review rather disingenuously continues with the disclaimer that "the fact that Sarita Chaudhury looks this way is not the issue at hand"; instead "the issue is how her body is utilized to conform to the stereotype of 'the exotic Easterner'" (2). Yet some South Asians do wear traditional clothing on a regular basis in the United States and do have dark skin, sultry lips, almond-shaped eyes, and curly hair. Whether their appearance marks them as being of South Asian ethnicity or as being a "stereotype of 'the exotic Easterner'" depends on the spectator's familiarity with South Asian cultural icons and social practices. As Jasbir K. Puar notes, diasporic experience problematizes categories such as the "exotic" by calling into question fixed and static understandings of "home" and "travel," "self" and "other" (76). She writes: "Diaspora may also function as a threat to certain homes while becoming the construct of home for certain Others. Bringing the home into the 'abroad' and vice versa, diaspora 'makes the exotic an everyday affair': the 'universe over here and over there,' therefore can no longer be 'named and accounted for' as distinct, separate, distant Other worlds" (76).

In assuming that Chaudhury's appearance necessarily renders her character into an exotic stereotype, the reviewer articulates a debilitating version of double consciousness that enables her to cede the power of the objectifying gaze to an idealized, male viewer in what is finally an act of cultural alienation. Theories of the male gaze, as a reading of these reviews suggests, runs the risk of too simply construing a viewing community in culturally homogenous terms and overlooking the ways in which diverse viewing communities produce meanings that might challenge dominant patriarchal values. *Mississippi Masala*'s appropriation of the generic conventions of Hollywood masala productions anticipates a culturally diverse audience for the film, a segment of which is familiar with such filmic paradigms.

The Politics of Representing Diasporic Identity

Most of the South Asian criticism of *Mississippi Masala* is based on the epistemological presupposition that a common, unified South Asian culture exists. But a common, unified South Asian culture has never existed on the subcontinent insofar as South Asia is comprised of a number of different countries— Bangladesh, India, Nepal, Pakistan, and Sri Lanka—each of which has its own distinct cultures and is internally stratified by a myriad of differences, including those of ethnicity, region, language, caste, class, gender, and religion. India alone has seventeen official languages, each with its own script and considerable body of literature. In addition to these official languages there are over a thousand regional dialects. In terms of religious identity, the diversity of the subcontinent ranges from Hinduism, Islam, Christianity, Buddhism, Jainism, Judaism, to Zoroastrianism, to name only a few of the major religions. Even the idea imaginatively unifying India to the non-Indian world, Hinduism, varies greatly from region to region.

Similarly, a common, unified South Asian diasporic culture does not exist in the United States, insofar as the South Asian immigrant population is comprised of regional, age, linguistic, caste, class, gender, and age diversity that has been exported from the subcontinent and has mingled with local U.S. contexts to produce multiple dynamic, hybrid, diasporic subcultures.[3] Unfortunately, the range of representations of these subcultures circulating in mainstream media has remained very narrow and has been restricted to stereotypes of socially awkward and studious South Asian males in films such as *Animal House* or televisual animated male figures such as Haji on the *Classic Jonny Quest* and the *Real Adventures of Jonny Quest* series and Apu on *The Simpsons*.[4] The lack of screen and televisual representations of South Asians has invested each cultural production that manages to attract attention from the culture industry with a huge "representational" burden in the political (*vertreten*) and portrait (*darstellen*) senses of the term, as delineated by Gayatri Chakravorty Spivak ("Can the Subaltern Speak?" 276). As Spivak notes, the two senses of representation include

> representation as "speaking for," as in politics, and representation as "re-presentation," as in art or philosophy. Since theory is also only "action," the theoretician does not represent (speak for) the oppressed group. Indeed, the subject is not seen as a representative consciousness (one re-presenting reality adequately). These two senses of representation—within state formation and the law, on the one hand, and in subject-predication, on the other—are related but irreducibly discontinuous. (275)

The critical responses to *Mississippi Masala* are overdetermined by its singular status as a mainstream Hollywood film that treats the South Asian diasporic experience. Thus South Asian feminist critics ask the film to represent mimetically the "real" life experiences of South Asian immigrants in order to give those experiences visibility in the political arena, collapsing distinctions between both senses of the term "representation" delineated by Spivak in the process.

Such responses conflate cultural politics and political action as a necessary condition of activism. Referencing the protests that accompanied the release of *Basic Instinct,* Michael Bronski convincingly argues that "Politics and political organizing are about symbols . . . . One might question if such a symbolic use of cultural artifacts is a good thing, but the question is moot—the conflation of cultural products with everyday political realities is inevitable. From the folk songs praising the indomitable Joe Hill to the racist scare tactics of using Willie Horton, political organizing relies on symbols to both inspire and frighten us" (87). While this genre of criticism has been too easily dismissed as a naive "condemnation of negative images," it challenges the nexus of image and authority in the media. In its most enabling articulations, readings of the structures of stereotypes within a given media artifact recognize the power of the image, its ability to shape public opinion, to provoke acts of violence targeted at specific populations, and to be codified eventually in governmental policy toward particular communities.

The conflation of cultural politics and political activism in criticisms of *Mississippi Masala* is manifest in the construction of Nair as a spokeswoman for the community who has forsaken her duty to represent, in the political and mimetic senses of the term, the diaspora adequately. Sonia Shah's "Presenting the Blue Goddess: Toward a National Pan-Asian Feminist Agenda," which appeared in *The State of Asian America: Activism and Resistance in the 1990s,* one of the first collections of its kind on Asian American activism, argues for the necessity of moving beyond the "black/white paradigm" in analyses of race and gender.[5] Instead she urges that such a paradigm be replaced by a "bicultural feminism" capable of articulating the links between cultural discrimination and other forms of oppression such as imperialism and repressive immigration policy (154–55). Curiously, Shah ends her article by reflecting on her expectations for the film *Mississippi Masala:*

> in that South Asian American women's group, we were all looking forward to Mira Nair's film, "Mississippi Masala." We took Nair as a kind of model. . . . I don't know what Nair's intentions were, but her Indian American protagonist was little more than a standard Western-defined beauty, her biculturalism little more than occasional bare feet and a chureedar [*sic*] thrown over her shoulder. Although a refugee from Uganda living in Mississippi with Indian parents, she was phenomenally uncon-

cerned with issues of race, history, culture, and gender. Given the dearth of accessible activist commentary on biculturalism and feminism beyond the black/white divide, even a sympathetic "opinion-maker" like Nair can hurt our movement by portraying us as little more than exotic, browner versions of white women, who by virtue of a little color can bridge the gap between black and white (not through activism, of course, just romantic love). If Asian American women's movements can effectively unite within bicultural feminist agendas, we can snatch that power away from those willing to trivialize us, and "Masala" and our less sympathetic foes beware. (156–57)

The turn to cultural politics at the end of an article devoted to periodizing South Asian women's activism and inserting it within the discourses of progressive, domestic, activist movements more generally attests to the ongoing power to shape social perceptions granted to *Mississippi Masala* by South Asian activists. Shah identifies "the dearth of accessible activist commentary on biculturalism and feminism" as placing a special representational burden on Nair to offer a progressive social analysis of race and gender. She seems disappointed that Mina's character is granted so little subjectivity and agency outside the realm of romantic love. Similar sentiments are voiced by bell hooks and Anuradha Dingwaney in their claim that "the film reinscribes sexism—making sexuality and romantic love the only sites where women can exercise political agency" (43). They charge that "Mina seems to care little about the racism rampant in the south. She is no civil rights activist in the making" (43). The construction of Nair as a failed spokesperson for the community is linked to the indictment of Mina's character as being wholly superficial and highly sexualized and for not being a political activist and, hence, points to the ways in which the film uncritically rehearses heteronormative Hollywood narratives as the basis of social identities.

In spite of the representational expectations placed on the film, Nair makes no pretense about being a community spokesperson. When asked about the pressures of representation exerted on "minority" filmmakers, she responds that as "'a minority filmmaker . . . you're expected to put the best foot forward, present the noble face. But I'm not one for being the ambassador of a community. The challenge is how to present the idea—if it's done well, it's not just "airing dirty laundry"'" (qtd. in Orenstein 61). Nair set out to make a film specifically about the diasporic experiences of Indians expelled from Uganda who had settled in Mississippi. The critical reception of the film, however, has willfully ignored the historical and regional specificity of *Mississippi Masala*'s subject matter.

As we have suggested, the film's singular status as a diasporic cultural artifact with widespread distribution explains in part the critical responses to

Nair's work. As Coco Fusco observes, "cultural identity and values are politically and historically charged issues for peoples in this country [the United States] whose access to exercising political power and controlling their symbolic representations has been limited within mainstream culture" (27). Wielding the particular brand of authority prominent in the critiques of *Mississippi Masala*—that of personal experience—usually leaves no space for a countercritical maneuver; it narrows the parameters of the debates on the film so that they center on the claims of the authenticity of the critic. In the face of hegemonic and anti-immigrant notions of "American-ness," R. Radhakrishnan explains, "ethnicity is often forced to take on the discourse of authenticity just to protect and maintain its space and history" (228). He cautions that it becomes hard to ascertain whether discourses of authenticity are acts of spontaneous self-affirmation or "a paranoid reaction to the 'naturalness' of dominant groups" (229). The readings of the film that will command the most authority in the mainstream will be those whose authors have most convincingly established their right to speak on behalf of the community. For instance, the subtitle of Sayantani Das Gupta's *Ms.* article, "A South Asian Woman Talks Sexual Politics," directly identifies her as a member of the diaspora. In addition to the great lengths that the author takes to establish her South Asian feminist credentials, the subtitle of her review of *Mississippi Masala* attempts to authenticate her ability to speak for the South Asian community.

Furthermore, the term "community" in discourses about *Mississippi Masala* and South Asian activism functions analogously to the discursive operations of the term "nation" as defined by Benedict Anderson. Yet while Anderson defines the "nation" as "an imagined political community—and imagined as both inherently limited and sovereign" (16), a reading of the criticisms of the film discloses the concept of "community" as having more fluid conceptual boundaries. Community can be theorized as being an imagined political formation that is imagined as simultaneously limited and elastic. All of the film's detractors speak from a position of privilege vis à vis the subject of Nair's film, which is southern, working-class South Asian immigrants. Most of the critics, significantly, are writing from the relative privilege of elite private colleges or research universities located in the Midwest and the east coast such as Oberlin College and Brown University. The efficacy of their criticism of the film depends upon their success in projecting local and regional identities on the national register, thus rendering the conceptual parameters of the term "community" elastic. Insofar as the national register must distinguish South Asians from other North Americans, the term "community" implicitly defines membership within finite boundaries. Invocations of "community" are intimately linked to the assertion of a specific South Asian identity in order to

certify its authenticity and its right to speak as a representative of a larger social collective. Yet by portraying the Indian community's calculated devastation of Demetrius's business as a collective response to his relationship with
Mina, *Mississippi Masala* raises questions about the nature of community, such
as the grounds on which it claims a representative status, the relationship between those claims and the constitution of its membership, and the extent to
which it is a stable formation. The relationship between membership in a community and support from that community, the film suggests, must be interrogated. Finally, the film asks how the community, especially if it is constituted on the basis of ethnicity, understands itself in terms of other communities
similarly identified on the basis of ethnicity and race.

The critical responses to *Mississippi Masala* can be contextualized and understood by assessing the current state of organizing among South Asians in
the United States. South Asian feminists have been on the forefront of the
organizing effort in the South Asian diaspora in their establishment of battered women's shelters in the Midwest and the east coast.[6] Some of the film's
critics have ties—direct and indirect—to these feminist organizing efforts. The
anonymous review lambasting Nair for the lack of representational appropriateness of Mina's character, for example, appears in the newsletter of the feminist organization Manavi, which offers material assistance to domestic abuse
survivors. Sayantani Das Gupta, the author of the *Ms.* review, is the daughter
of Shamita Das Gupta, a cofounder of Manavi (Webb 35). Sonia Shah's rant
against *Mississippi Masala* is immediately followed with a list of activist organizations, such as Asian Sisters in Action, New York Asian Women's Center,
Manavi, and Sneha, and their addresses. Such organizing efforts necessarily
have had to combat patriarchal elements within South Asian subcultures as
well as the misperceptions of the dominant culture that have often been based
in racism toward South Asians.

The gendered nature of South Asian activism explains in part the gendered
criticism of the film's representation of Mina as having too little subjectivity
and agency. Gayatri Chakravorty Spivak's formulation of the "strategic use of
essentialism" helps illuminate such South Asian feminist criticism of *Mississippi Masala*. Commenting on the debates around essentialism and anti-
essentialism, she notes:

> since it is not possible not to be an essentialist, one can self-consciously use this ir-
> reducible moment of essentialism as part of one's strategy. This can be used as part
> of a "good" strategy as well as a "bad" strategy and this can be used self-conscious-
> ly as well as unself-consciously. . . . The relationship between the two kinds of rep-
> resentation brings in, also, the use of essentialism because no representation can take
> place—no *Vertretung*, representation—can take place without essentialism. What

it has to take into account is that the "essence" that is being represented is a representation of the other kind, *Darstellung.* ("Practical Politics" 109)

In order to insert a South Asian feminist agenda within the discourses of progressive activism in the United States, South Asian feminist critics have had to enlist essentialist identities as a strategic response to the marginalization of their agendas. Prior to the publication of Das Gupta's review in *Ms.*, for example, the only other representation of the South Asian diaspora to appear in the pages of this journal was the largely ornamental cover photograph of a mother and daughter—ironically, Sayantani Das Gupta herself with her mother—in the November/December 1992 issue. The accompanying article featured two brief paragraphs on the photogenic duo, suggesting that their function was largely decorative and meant to bestow an aura of international cosmopolitanism on the journal. In the face of such tokenizing gestures, the criticisms of *Mississippi Masala* in the public arena have focused attention on the South Asian diaspora and have provided what Susan Stanford Friedman calls "relational narratives" that "capture the liminality of contradictory subject positions or the fluid, nomadic, and migratory subjectivities of . . . the 'new geography of identity'" (7). According to Friedman, such narratives supplement the binary categories of racialized discourse organized around the black and white axes (3). Criticisms of the film, in other words, have enabled South Asian feminists to foreground questions of female agency and diasporic identity in mainstream discussions of race that historically have privileged African American experience as the site of racialized identity. The stridency of the South Asian attacks on Nair's work, grounded in the authority of personal experience and claims to the "real," have required the assertion of an essentialist articulation of identity that insists on the possibility of its own social agency.

Recognizing that the assumption of essentialist identities is, in Stuart Hall's words, "contingent, qualified, [and] perspectival" enables us to see that they are an indispensable aspect of activism without which subjects would be unable to imagine themselves as political agents (44–46). Rather than presuppose that the South Asian feminist critics' invocations of personal experience provide the basis for an "authentic" reading of *Mississippi Masala*, we have tried to argue, as Joan Scott urges, for the necessity of interrogating how and to what ends the claims of experience and authenticity have been used.

National Identity, Race, and Class

We turn now to our reading of *Mississippi Masala.* The film challenges the more reactionary structuring discourses of the popular masala genre—which consists of formulaic films that combine romantic comedy, melodrama, and action sequences and are generally produced in Bombay—in order to confront the cultural conservatism of the U.S. South Asian diaspora, particularly in terms of its attitudes toward female sexuality and race. While the film problematizes singular constructions of national identity, however, it privileges race as a key component of identity over that of class. Spanning two generations of a family, Jay's and Mina's, the film follows one of the masala genre's standard boy-meets-girl formulas. At the same time, *Mississippi Masala* contains several subplots which establish parallel narratives that contrast with that of the main story. The lack of sexual energy between the newlyweds Anil and Chanda significantly differs from the sensuous chemistry between Demetrius and Mina. Both Jay and Mina have relationships with black men, Jay with Okelo and Mina with Demetrius. For both characters, this relationship becomes overdetermined with questions of individual and national identity. Finally, the two women gossips—one of whom is played by Nair—and Anil's male companions are the stock character types of the masala genre.

Masala films, according to Rosie Thomas, have traditionally been organized along binary oppositions, whose structuring discourses include kinship, duty, social obligation, solidarity, destiny, and human impotence in the face of fate (125–26). Within the universe of the masala genre, the characters exist in an ideal order where their respect for social obligations and familial and friendship ties maintains social equilibrium. Disruptions to the social order—in the form of excessive greed, human meddling in fate, and uncurbed heterosexual desire—typically advance the plots of masala films. At the allegorical level, plots involve conflicts between two constructions, considered, in the logic of the genre, as antithetical to one another. Goodness, morality, and tradition are identified as "Indian," while evil, decadence (generally represented as uncontrolled sexuality), and "nontradition" are associated with the "West." Though, as Thomas points out, "the West is not so much a place, or even a culture, as an emblem of exotic, decadent otherness, signified by whiskey, bikinis, an uncontrolled sexuality and what is seen as lack of 'respect' for elders and betters, and (from men) towards womanhood" (126). Seeking to reestablish the social order by the narrative's conclusion, masala films often valorize marriage and the patriarchal family.

Mira Nair complicates the binary terms of the masala genre throughout *Mississippi Masala* insofar as she problematizes the very concept of "Indian" identity by focusing on members of the Indian diaspora who have never been to India but who continue to identify culturally with the subcontinent. Two of the main characters, Mina and Jay, explicitly contest unitary constructions of national identity. Describing herself as a "masala," a pan-Indian term for a mixture of spices, Mina seems equally at home in African American and Indian settings. The cultural icons associated with her throughout the film—such as the postcard of John Lennon, her numerous *langa cholis,* and a Bob Marley T-shirt—derive from multiple cultural traditions. Jay, who is born and raised in Uganda, considers himself "Ugandan first, Indian second"; geographical location seems to be the primary component of his identity. From the African clothes that he wears, to his drunken phone calls to his Ugandan home, to the numerous letters he writes the Ugandan government petitioning for the return of his property, Jay reasserts his claims to an African identity throughout most of the film.

More importantly, Mina exposes an implicit fallacy underwriting the notion of a unitary "Indian" identity. Unitary identities can only be formulated by ignoring difference and various forms of stratification within a particular group. Describing "the progressive metaphor of social cohesion" as "the many as one," Homi Bhabha reminds us, "The 'locality' of national culture is neither unified nor unitary in relation to itself, nor must it be seen simply as 'other' in relation to what is outside or beyond it" ("Introduction" 4). By recognizing color prejudice among South Asians, Mina names one form of stratification that exists in diasporic communities. "Face it Ma," she tells her mother, "you have a darky daughter." Nair herself employs the term "hierarchy of color" to describe a central theme of the film, explaining that "'People think of racism as black versus white, but there's a different kind of consciousness of color within minority groups as we equate beauty with fairness and ugliness with darkness'" (qtd. in Orenstein 60). Contextualizing these types of racialized sentiments among Indian immigrants, Sucheta Mazumdar states that "South Asians, regardless of national origin on the subcontinent, cling to a mythography which holds that the elite (upper caste/class) are 'Aryan' and by extension 'Caucasian.' They are themselves color-conscious; they see shades of brown in skin color which to any casual observer is black" (47). The gossips in the film most overtly express these racialized views. One disparages Mina's dark complexion and Kinnu's aspirations for her daughter to marry the wealthy Harry Patel by commenting: "Arré, you can be dark and have money, or you can be fair and have no money, but you can't be *dark* and have *no* money and expect to get Harry Patel."

Mississippi Masala also addresses South Asian racism toward peoples of African descent. During a flashback to Uganda, a furious Idi Amin is shown on television explaining the reasons for his 1972 expulsion of Asians from Uganda. After emphasizing the economic disparities between Asians and Africans, he angrily points out that Asians "refuse to allow their daughters to marry Africans." The Indian fear of miscegenation is rooted in racialist ideas of contamination and "purity of blood" (Mazumdar 51). Nair structurally positions Demetrius as an equivalent of Amin insofar as it is his character who articulates a criticism of South Asian racism by confronting Jay with the charge that "you and your folks can come here from God knows where and be as black as the ace of spades and soon as you get here you start acting white." Demetrius's charge that Indian immigrants "act white" hinges on Jay's refusal to allow interracial sex, thus echoing Amin's earlier indictment of South Asians. The structural equivalence between Demetrius and Amin highlights the ways in which their different contexts, Mississippi and Uganda, shape the ideological reception of their articulations of race.

Because Jay considers Amin a "madman," naming him as such on the BBC, Amin's expulsion of Asians does not unsettle his sense of Ugandan identity. What does rattle him, however, is the fact that, as he states, "after thirty-four years, my brother Okelo told me 'Africa is for Africans, Black Africans.'" "After thirty-four years," he continues, "that's what it all came down to, the color of my skin. That's why we left, not because of Idi Amin or anything like that." The harshness of Okelo's formulation of a racialized African identity is rendered more palatable by our knowledge that he has intervened at great personal risk and expense to secure Jay's release from prison. Okelo's willingness to endanger himself on behalf of Jay suggests that his articulation of African identity is motivated by concern for Jay's safety. Shortly following Jay's departure from Uganda, Okelo is brutally murdered, implying that his friendship with Jay has cost him his life.

Jay's understanding of the causes and consequences of the Asian expulsion—which center on the primacy of a racial explanation—is somewhat simplistic. To the extent that the racism of the Indian minority in Uganda was problematic, it was not only because of the marriage prejudice per se but because the Indian domination of the small-business environment was economically problematic as well. Jay's belief that "it all came down to the color of my skin" may be a perpetuation of the notion that race is all, a notion about which *Mississippi Masala* is quite ambivalent. By presenting Amin's expulsion of Asians solely in terms of race, Mira Nair glosses over the complex social formation of Ugandan Indians and their status as a comprador class during the colonial era, a class position that would earn them the antagonism of the black Ugandan petit-bourgeoisie in the post-independence period. After the 1920–22 world economic recession, peasant farms produced most of the economic surplus in Uganda. With the growth of the peasant economy, South Asians functioned as an intermediary class that integrated the small commodity producer into the global market (Mamdani 30). Becoming part of a comprador class, South Asians exported the commodities produced by Ugandan peasants and imported metropolitan goods needed by the peasant producers. The British promoted Indian commercial interests by granting them trading licenses over those of black Africans because Indians were already trading British manufactured goods; the British viewed Indians as an "alien community that could easily be segregated from the masses and be rendered politically safe," and Indians had the reputation of being politically passive and primarily concerned with their commercial interests (31).

After Ugandan independence in 1962, animosity between the Indian commercial class and the black petit-bourgeoisie periodically flared. In an effort to create a black commercial bourgeoisie, the government began issuing trade licenses for control of commodities to members of its governing bureaucracy. Asian commercial traders responded with economic sabotage by buying goods in bulk from wholesale traders, storing these items for long periods and creating market scarcity, and then selling the products at substantially marked up prices (Mamdani 47). General Amin used such incidents to solidify his base among black Ugandans and to justify his expulsion of Asians in 1972. He could mobilize black support by appealing to racial and class sentiments. Because the Indians were "racially different" than the black majority, Amin could make the term "Ugandan" synonymous with "black." Ugandan Indian citizens and noncitizens alike were covered under the expulsion order. At the same time, Amin could point to the Indians' intense race consciousness and their attempts to remain aloof—both professionally and socially—from black Ugandans.

Mississippi Masala glosses over the economic complexities of Amin's expulsion of Asians in part by not contextualizing Jay's relationship with other Ugandans, particularly Okelo. Jay nostalgically remembers collecting water from a stream as a child with a woman who is presumably Okelo's mother. Yet Nair does not reveal the power dynamics in their relationship. Since the only other black Ugandans who Jay and Kinnu interact with are their servants, we are left wondering whether Okelo's mother also worked for the Lohas as a domestic.

In spite of the film's failure to contextualize different class positions, it does glancingly acknowledge their existence. For instance, Jay and Kinnu's elegant Ugandan home, with its breathtaking views, is perched on a mountain, literally and figuratively over the residences of black Ugandans. And among the South Asian immigrants in the United States, as revealed in the gossips' exchange about Mina's complexion, the social stigma of being dark-skinned can be partially mitigated by an elite-class background. Moreover, Kinnu's status as an owner of a liquor store in the black section of Greenwood can be read as an implicit critique of South Asian business politics in Uganda. Indians, the film seems to imply, did not learn the lesson of the 1972 expulsion: namely, that they cannot afford to profit from the exploitation of other communities. Since Kinnu and Jay do not live in the African American neighborhood in which her business is situated, nor does she sell goods of any real value (such as groceries), nor does she employ black employees, their economic livelihood depends upon the extraction of capital from the neighborhood. In this regard, *Mississippi Masala* does represent a growing reality within the United States. A significant number of South Asians now own convenience shops and drive-through liquor-gas stations in African American and Latino/a neighborhoods, though they tend to reside in primarily white suburbs.

The last frame of the film, in which Sarita Chaudhury and Denzel Washington cavort in a cotton field as the credits scroll up the screen, also acknowledges the economic register. While this scene has raised the ire of South Asian critics for being "utterly absurd" (Manavi 2) and too picturesque, with little narrative logic to connect it to the rest of the film, the couple's positioning in the cotton field is anything but arbitrary or ridiculous. Given the role of cotton in the plantation economy of slavery and in the colonial economy of British India, Nair visually reinscribes Mina and Demetrius within the historical contexts that produced them by placing them in this setting.

Exporting Shame and the Ideology of Gender

Mississippi Masala also subverts the more reactionary structuring discourses of female agency and sexuality in the masala genre in several ways, thus contesting the importation of conservative gender ideology in the South Asian diaspora. By making Mina a primary character who makes choices and acts on them, Nair establishes young South Asian women as historical agents. While this point may be an obvious one, it is important to remember that young South Asian women often have limited options, facing great family pressure to conform to social expectations of marriage within their communities. Although more South Asian immigrants are encouraging their daughters to pursue careers, these are often in fields deemed acceptable by their parents. Mina's decision, at the end of the film, to go into the carpet cleaning business with Demetrius goes in the face of her father's professional aspirations for her to attend college. The business of manually cleaning other peoples' homes and businesses violates Hindu notions of caste and class, purity and pollution.

Moreover, whereas the masala genre generally denigrates unbridled sexuality as a socially disruptive force, the film celebrates Mina's desire for Demetrius. Nair ridicules the strict policing of female sexuality in her portrayals of the two gossips and Anil and his friends. It is these characters who police Mina's sexuality: the men catch her with Demetrius in a hotel in Biloxi, while the gossips transmit the news of her indiscretion to the Indian "community" at large. The exaggerated acting of these characters clearly plays off the stock character types of the masala genre and represents their efforts to control Mina's sexuality as ludicrous. The pan–South Asian cultural concept of shame, known as *sharam* in Hindi and Urdu, underwrites the "community's" attempts to guard Mina's chastity. Greenwood's South Asian "community" is constituted by its opposition to Mina's relationship with Demetrius. Whereas previous to the disclosure of her affair, rivalry among the women and kinship tensions characterized the social interactions among the South Asians, Mina's transgression coheres them into a "community" that conspires to keep the young lovers apart by ruining Demetrius's credibility among the Anglo-dominated power structure that has provided start-up capital for his carpet cleaning business.

Sharam is one of the ideological mechanisms that restricts women's mobility and social interactions with men who are not relatives and is very much associated with female sexuality in general and the covering of the female body in particular. Though sharam has its origins in the subcontinent, it has been transported with the South Asian diaspora and has been the most theorized by South Asian immigrants in Britain. Amrit Wilson, in *Finding a Voice: Asian Women in Britain*, cites a middle-aged Pakistani woman's explanation of South Asian attitudes toward the exposure of the female body: "'You can say religion forbids us to show our legs. You can say we are not used to it because our parents never sunbathed. But deeper than all this are the values of our society. You see we think that for a woman *Sharam* (shame or shyness) itself is honour. It can be a woman's pride because it reflects her purity and sensitiveness'" (99). Gurmeet Singh, an Indian settler in Wolverhampton, makes it clear that uncovering the body is culturally taboo for females alone: "'in our society it's the man who shows his body, not the woman; and that is what makes us different from the whites'" (qtd. in Hiro 157). Wilson indicates the pervasiveness of this concept among Indians and Pakistanis:

> It is common in one form or another to all [*sic*] Indo-Pakistani cultures. Its effects can vary from never looking a man in the eye or never arguing with a man, to wearing a *Burkha*. Few women brought up in India can truthfully say that they have never felt Sharam. For the unwary it is a feeling as infectious as embarrassment or flirtatiousness. It can be very enjoyable, amusing and romantic (because it means that a relationship with a man must deepen through glances, smiles and phrases with hidden meanings). But inevitably it robs women of their strength and power and cramps their personalities. (99)

While sharam has cultural currency among immigrants in the United States similar to that in Britain, it is nuanced slightly differently here given that attitudes toward the uncovering of the female body are not as stringent in the United States (though more than one Indian immigrant woman—while expressing general approval of *Mississippi Masala*—voiced dismay at the scene in which Demetrius and Mina make love, complaining that the narrative logic of the film does not require Sarita Chaudhury to be nude). "It used to be shameful for women to wear western clothes, because they exposed the body," one elderly immigrant informed us, "but not much weight is attached to clothing nowadays . . . . Indian women here wear western clothes, except for the ones who came before the 1970s, who still wear saris" (Bose 1993). In its U.S. manifestation, sharam is more closely tied to notions of appropriate female decorum and social practices, especially those governing sexuality. Disapproval for overly familiar interactions between young South Asian women and men, for instance, is expressed often in phrases such as: "have you no shame?" One middle-aged Malayalee woman told us: "Most of the time, the phrase is used for girls rather than boys. Boys can't bring shame to the family; it's girls who bring shame to the family" (Varghese). In the U.S. diasporic setting, however, the concept of sharam is a dynamic one that has been transformed over time. As Sudesh Bose, a Punjabi woman married to a Bengali man, elaborates: "At one time for young people to talk about marriage was not considered modest . . . it is still considered shameful for both girls and boys to have sex outside of marriage, but more shame is attached to the girl" (Bose).

Sharam is part of a pair of gendered signifiers of which *izzat*—pride, honor, or self-respect—is the male counterpart. Izzat "is essentially male but it is women's lives and actions which affect it most," Wilson states. "A woman can have *Izzat* but it is not her own—it is her husband's or father's" (5). In other words, inappropriate female behavior affects the honor and name of the family as a whole. After Mina's declaration of her love for Demetrius, her mother Kinnu retorts: "You call this love? When all you've done is bring such shame on our heads." In this respect, South Asian immigrants tend to condemn any form of sex outside of marriage as a stain on family honor.

This notion of family honor and female chastity finds expression in the masala genre as well, as Steve Derné explains, which often celebrates love while giving "voice to the dominant [Indian] notion that love is a madness that should not jeopardize family honor" (188). Emphasizing the incompatibility of romantic love and joint family living, they present "romantic love as only possible outside of society" (187). Accordingly, a number of masala films end with the young couple, whose love has been sanctified by marriage, abandoning their communities. Nair appropriates this conventional ending to challenge the ideological paradigms of romantic love in the masala genre. Mina disrupts the discourse of sharam by engaging in premarital sex. *Mississippi Masala* concludes with Mina and Demetrius abandoning their respective communities, but it leaves the marital future of the young lovers ambiguous. The film does not end with a marriage proposal but a business one, accompanied with declarations of affection.

Conclusion

The debates around *Mississippi Masala* and its prominent position within discussions of South Asian activism demonstrate the extent to which it has become a focus over highly contested notions of "authentic" and "real" South Asian diasporic identity. Grounded in the authority of personal experience, critiques of the film have posited a unitary and static conception of South Asian immigrant culture. Contrary to the claims of the reviews, many South Asian women do leave their hair loose, call their mothers "Maa," and find it necessary to leave their communities. Other aspects of *Mississippi Masala* will have cultural resonances for some—obviously, not all—South Asians: the personalized license plates, the inability of the wedding guests to remember the words to "Raga Pati Raja Ram," and the use of gossip as a means of social control. The fact that multiple and diverse experiences comprise the South Asian diaspora problematizes critiques of the film that derive their legitimacy from personal experience, pointing to the necessity of interrogating social identity.

Analyzing the recent debates on representation and canon-formation in the academy, John Guillory notes that the category of social identity has been integral to the formulation of an "'imaginary' politics" that underwrites these debates, insofar as cultural artifacts are understood "as a hypothetical *image* of social diversity, a kind of mirror in which social groups either see themselves, or do not see themselves, reflected" (7). He carefully explains that the term "'imaginary' politics" is "manifestly a politics *of the image*": "Such a politics belongs to the same political domain as the ongoing critique of minority images in the national media, to the project of correcting these images for stereotyping, or for a failure to represent minorities at all. Such a politics has real work to do, as complex and interesting as the images themselves, but it is also inherently limited by its reduction of the political to the instance of representation, and of representation to the image" (7–8). As Guillory argues, the concept of social identity has played a prominent role in contemporary criticism, and its theoretical elaboration has greatly outpaced the social diversification of democratic institutions; as a result of this lag, "the venue of representation can be displaced to new arenas of contestation," such as the analyses of filmic and televisual texts (5). Imaginary politics provides the dominant analytical paradigm for the critical reception of Mira Nair's film among South Asian activists and academics who have read *Mississippi Masala* as an inadequate reflection of their "real" life experiences. Yet that displacement, even as it reconceives cultural artifacts and their production in "political" terms, Guillory cautions, "leaves unclarified the question of the precise relation between a politics of representation" in cultural criticism "and a democratic representational politics" (5).

The critical challenge posed by South Asian responses to *Mississippi Masala* is to determine how one might gauge the social effects of a given cultural artifact. That the film espouses a given politics or has been received through particular political determinants is not at issue. Rather, as Guillory suggests, "The specificity of the political here cannot mean simply a replication of the problem of 'representation' in the sphere of democratic politics, and therefore it cannot mean simply importing . . . the same strategies of progressive politics which sometimes work at the legislative level" (8–9). He recommends, in the case of the canon debates, that critics attend to the specific institutional sites that mediate political effects in the social domain. In the case of the debates around *Mississippi Masala,* one could similarly insist on shifting the framework of these questions on gender and political representation to an alternative set of institutional sites—namely, activist organizations such as progressive groups, South Asian diaspora associations, and more mainstream alliances devoted to electoral politics. These organizations, in other words, should be subjected to a reading and be held accountable for the ways in which they have historically marginalized issues of gender, sexuality, and ethnicity within their recruitment efforts and social agendas.

Guillory's suggestion that "representation" in the democratic sphere might require different strategies of activism than in the cultural sphere echoes Spivak's injunction to distinguish between representation in its senses as *vertreten* (political) and *darstellen* (portrait). South Asian feminist activists might reorient their critical gaze from imaginary politics, the politics of particular cultural representations or darstellen, to that of the democratic sphere, representation as vertreten, as manifest in specific institutional practices. While strategic essentialism has an important role to play in the imaginary politics of challenging the racialist assumptions of dominant culture, it is equally imperative that we begin to complicate our understanding of identity and the ways in which it is inflected by other sociohistorical factors such as gender, class, region, and sexuality in order to make our communities more inclusive, egalitarian, and supportive.

Notes

We are grateful to Nandi Bhatia, Gouri Bhatt, Eva Cherniavsky, Wendy Hesford, Wendy Kozol, Laura Lyons, Janet Sorensen, and Khachig Tölölyan for their comments and suggestions on earlier drafts of this article. We are also indebted to Julius Ihonvbere for bringing Mahmood Mamdani's work to our attention and to Supriya Nair and S. Shankar for thought-provoking conversations about the film.

1. For sympathetic readings of *Mississippi Masala,* see Friedman; Mehta, "Emigrants"; and Rasiah. Of these, Friedman has the most extended analysis of how the film complicates discussions of race and ethnicity in the United States more broadly. (While offering excellent readings of *Mississippi Masala* and *The Crying Game,* however, Friedman's analysis of regional conflicts tends to primordialize race and ethnicity as a major factor in ongoing territorial disputes. For instance, she surprisingly underemphasizes the role of settler colonialism in fostering political violence in the North of Ireland and apartheid South Africa. Friedman also overlooks transnationalism as a factor in the Chiapas Uprising in Mexico.) Nair offers a fascinating case study of how one young Indian woman from East Africa interprets the film through her personal experiences growing up in Africa and the United States.

2. Most of the physical attacks against South Asians have been directed at males and have taken place in the New Jersey area. On 2 September 1987 the *Jersey Journal* published a letter from a group calling itself the "Dotbusters." The letter announced: "'Look! Let's cut the small talk. We are an organization called dotbusters. We have been around for two years. We will go to any extreme to get Indians to move out of Jersey City. If I'm walking down the street and the setting is right, I will just hit him or her'" (qtd. in Wickenhaver 10).

These threats were apparently not idle ones, since over the next several months a number of South Asians were attacked and one, Navroze Mody, was beaten to death by a gang of eleven youths. The coroner's report showed that Mody had sustained severed eyeballs and a crushed skull and feet. Earlier that September, a Bangladeshi man and his Indian friend, both students at Stevens Institute, were assaulted by two of the youths charged in Mody's murder. Other racist attacks include:

1. On 24 September 1987 Kaushal Saran was discovered with a battered skull. As a result of his injuries, he was in a coma for a week. While Saran has no recollection of the attack, an anonymous caller to the *Jersey Journal* boasted of his part in it.
2. On 5 October 1987 Nimesh Kathiari was attacked by four Anglo youths when he stopped at a traffic light.
3. On 9 October 1987 assailants, muttering racial slurs as they fled, sprayed acid on Shailesh Patel and his daughter.
4. On 12 January 1988 a letter bomb was sent to an Indian home. (Information compiled by the activist group, Indian Youth against Racism, Columbia University, New York, 1988)

3. The history of South Asian immigration to the United States dates back to 1790 with the earliest recorded mention of a Madrasi gentleman who visited Massachusetts. South Asian immigration did not become significant until the late nineteenth and early twentieth centuries, when South Asian laborers, primarily from Punjab, immigrated to the Northwest. These early laborers tended to be migrant farm workers and to be employed in lumberyards. Restrictive immigration legislation, such as the California Alien Land Act (1913), the 1917 Immigration Act, the Cable Act (1922), and the Immigration Quota Act (1924) kept the number of South Asian immigrants small. In addition, these immigrants were harassed by racist organizations such as the Asiatic Exclusion League. Immigration from the subcontinent increased dramatically with the Immigration and Naturalization Act of 1965, which abolished the national-origin quota system and replaced it with hemispheric quotas. This history is routinely outlined in the increasing body of scholarly literature on the South Asian diaspora. Some standard sources on South Asian immigration to the United States include Takaki; Jensen; and Saran. For a discussion of the South Asian diaspora and global migration more generally, see Brown and Coelho; Clark et al.; Kurian and Shrivastava; and Motwani and Barot-Motwani.

4. While the figure of Apu is often dismissed as a stereotype, such criticisms miss the parodic elements of a series that more generally satirizes consumer culture. *The Simpsons* positions ethnic, age, class, and sexuality differences within the body of its male characters as evidenced by the doctor (African American), Apu (South Asian), Abe (elderly), Mr. Burns (senior capitalist), and Smithers (gay male).

5. While Shah's desire to articulate a "pan-Asian" feminism is laudable, the reference to the "Blue Goddess" in her title, which she identifies with the Hindu concept of Shakti, reproduces the hegemonic narrative of the nationalist movement that sought to appropriate religious minorities within the dominant discourse of Hinduism and has, in the ensuing years, morphed into the pernicious ideology of Hindutva. In drawing on a feminist symbol from the Hindu tradition, Shah runs the risk of alienating South Asian feminists from other religious traditions.

6. In part, the debates between the founders of Apna Ghar (a shelter in Chicago) and Sakhi (a domestic abuse hotline in New York City) highlight the ways in which the "real," "authenticity," and "cultural authority" are differently theorized on a regional basis. See Bhattacharjee for an analysis of Sakhi, gender, and domestic abuse on the east coast. For a discussion of how these issues are differently inflected in the upper Midwest, see Lynch's response to Bhattacharjee, based on her experiences working with Apna Ghar. Though Lynch is highly critical of Bhattacharjee's argument, Bhattacharjee was one of the first to offer a thoughtful and extended analysis of the dynamics of gender in the diaspora, thus opening up a much needed conversation on this issue. Bhattacharjee continues to participate actively in progressive grassroots organizations in the metropolitan New York area and she is also a founding member of *SAMAR*, the *South Asian Magazine for Action and Reflection*. In these multiple capacities, she has been instrumental in fostering dialogue between academics and activists in numerous forums.

Works Cited

Aguilar–San Juan, Karin, ed. *The State of Asian America: Activism and Resistance in the 1990s.* Boston: South End Press, 1994.

Anderson, Benedict. *Imagined Communities: Reflections on the Origins and Spread of Nationalism.* London: Verso, 1991.

Bahri, Deepika, and Mary Vasudeva, eds. *Between the Lines: South Asians and Postcoloniality.* Philadelphia: Temple University Press, 1994.

Bhabha, Homi. "DissemiNation: Time, Narrative, and the Margins of the Modern Nation." In *Nation and Narration.* Ed. Homi Bhabha. New York: Routledge, 1990. 290–322.

———. "Introduction: Narrating the Nation." In *Nation and Narration.* Ed. Homi Bhabha. New York: Routledge, 1990. 1–7.

Bhattacharjee, Anannya. "Woman, Nation, and Identity in the Indian Immigrant Community." *SAMAR* 1 (Winter 1992): 6–10.

Bose, Sudesh. Telephone interview. 26 July 1993.

Bronski, Michael. "Reel Politick: Basic Insult." *Z Magazine,* May/June 1992, 85–88.

Brown, Richard Harvey, and George V. Coelho. *Migration and Modernization: The Indian Diaspora in Comparative Perspective.* Williamsburg, Va.: Department of Anthropology, College of Willam and Mary, 1987.

Clark, Colin, et al. *South Asians Overseas: Migration and Ethnicity.* Cambridge: Cambridge University Press, 1990.

Das Gupta, Monisha. "'What is "Indian" about You?' Asian Indian Women's Experiences of Cultural Displacement in the United States." *Désiaspora.* South Asian Women for Action, 1993. 3–4.

Das Gupta, Sayantani. "Glass Shawls and Long Hair: A South Asian Woman Talks Sexual Politics." *Ms.,* Mar./Apr. 1993, 76–77.

Derné, Steve. "Popular Culture and Emotional Experiences: Rituals of Filmgoing and the Reception of Emotion Culture." In *Social Perspectives on Emotion.* Vol. 3. Ed. Carolyn Ellis and Michael Flaherty. Greenwich, Conn.: JAI Press, 1995. 171–97.

Foster, Robert J. "Making National Cultures in the Global Ecumene." *Annual Review of Anthropology* 20 (1991): 235–60.

Friedman, Susan Stanford. "Beyond White and Other: Relationality and Narratives of Race in Feminist Discourse." *Signs* 21 (Autumn 1995): 1–49.

Fusco, Coco. *English is Broken Here.* New York: The New Press, 1995.

Guillory, John. "Canonical and Noncanonical: The Current Debate." In *Cultural Capital: The Problem of Literary Canon Formation.* Chicago: University of Chicago Press, 1993. 3–82.

Hall, Stuart. "Minimal Selves." *ICA Documents* 6: 44–46.

Hiro, Dilip. *Black British, White British.* New York: Monthly Review Press, 1971.

hooks, bell, and Anuradha Dingwaney. "Mississippi Masala." *Z Magazine,* July/Aug. 1992, 41–43.

Indian Youth against Racism. "Compilation of Racial Attacks on Indians." Flyer. New York, 1988.

Jensen, Joan. *Passage from India: Asian Indian Immigrants in North America.* New Haven, Conn.: Yale University Press, 1988.

Kurian, George, and Ram Shrivastava, eds. *Overseas Indians: A Study in Adaptation.* New Delhi: Vikas, 1983.

Ladha, Yasmin. "Dear Didi . . . A Letter to *Mississippi Masala* Director Mira Nair." *Rungh* 1 (1992): 36–37.

Lynch, Caitrin. "Nation, Woman, and the Indian Immigrant Bourgeoisie: An Alternative Formulation." *Public Culture* 6 (1994): 425–37.

Mamdani, Mahmood. "Class Struggles in Uganda." *Review of African Political Economy* 4 (Nov. 1975): 26–61.

Manavi. "Mississippi Meena: A Critique of South-Asian Womanhood in *Mississippi Masala.*" *Manavi Newsletter* 4 (1992): 1–2.

Mazumdar, Sucheta. "Racist Responses to Racism: The Aryan Myth and South Asians in the United States." *South Asian Bulletin* 9.1 (1989): 47–55.

Mehta, Binita. "Emigrants Twice Displaced: Race, Color, and Identity in Mira Nair's *Mississippi Masala.*" In *Between the Lines: South Asians and Postcoloniality.* Ed. Deepika Bahri and Mary Vasudeva. Philadelphia: Temple University Press, 1994. 185–203.

Mehta, Gita. Review of *Mississippi Masala. Vogue,* Feb. 1992, 114+.

Motwani, Jagat, and Jyoti Barot-Matwani, eds. *Global Migration of Indians: Saga of Adventure, Enterprise, Identity, and Integration.* New York: National Federation of Indian-American Associations, 1989.

Nair, Savita. "Masala in the Melting Pot: History, Identity, and the Indian Diaspora." *Sagar* 2 (Fall 1995): 24–49.

Orenstein, Peggy. "Salaam America! An Interview with Director Mira Nair." *Mother Jones,* Jan./Feb. 1992, 60–61.

Puar, Jasbir K. "Writing My Way 'Home': Traveling South Asian Bodies and Diasporic Journeys." *Socialist Review* 24.4 (1994): 75–108.

Radhakrishnan, R. "Is the Ethnic 'Authentic' in the Diaspora?" In *The State of Asian America: Activism and Resistance in the 1990s.* Ed. Karin Aguilar–San Juan. Boston: South End Press, 1994. 219–34.

Rasiah, Dharini. "*Mississippi Masala* and *Khush:* Redefining Community." In *Our Feet Walk the Sky: Women of the South Asian Diaspora.* Ed. Women of South Asian Descent Collective. San Francisco: Aunt Lute Books, 1993. 267–73.

Saran, Parmatma. *The Asian Indian Experience in the United States.* New Delhi: Vikas, 1985.

Scott, Joan. "The Evidence of Experience." In *The Lesbian and Gay Studies Reader.* Ed. Henry Abelove, Michele Aina Barale, and David Halperin. New York: Routledge, 1993. 397–415.

Shah, Sonia. "Presenting the Blue Goddess: Toward a National Pan-Asian Feminist Agenda." In *The State of Asian America: Activism and Resistance in the 1990s.* Ed. Karin Aguilar–San Juan. Boston: South End Press, 1994. 147–58.

Spence, Louise, and Robert Stam. "Colonialism, Racism, and Representation." *Screen* 24.2 (1983): 2–20.

Spivak, Gayatri Chakravorty. "Can the Subaltern Speak?" In *Marxism and the Interpretation of Culture.* Ed. Cary Nelson and Lawrence Grossberg. Urbana: University of Illinois Press, 1988. 271–313.

———. "Practical Politics of the Open End: An Interview with Sara Harasym." In *The Post-Colonial Critic.* Ed. Sarah Harasym. New York: Routledge, 1990. 95–112.

Takaki, Ronald T. *Strangers from a Different Shore: A History of Asian Americans.* Boston: Little, Brown, 1989.

Thomas, Rosie. "Indian Cinema: Pleasures and Popularity—An Introduction." *Screen* 26.3–4 (1985): 116–31.

Varghese, Mary. Telephone interview. 25 July 1993.

Webb, Marilyn. "Our Daughters, Ourselves: How Feminists Raise Feminists." *Ms.,* Nov./Dec. 1992, 30–35.

Wickenhaver, Janet. "Racial Terror on the Gold Coast." *Village Voice,* 26 Jan. 1988, 10+.

Wilson, Amrit. *Finding a Voice: Asian Women in Britain.* London: Virago Press, 1978.

Women of South Asian Descent Collective, eds. *Our Feet Walk the Sky: Women of the South Asian Diaspora.* San Francisco: Aunt Lute Books, 1993.

6

Third-World Testimony in the Era of Globalization

Vietnam, Sexual Trauma, and Le Ly Hayslip's Art of Neutrality

Leslie Bow

> "Boo-sheeit! I ain't never gettin' hit in Vietnam."
> "Oh no? Okay, mothafucker, why not?"
> "'Cause," Mayhew said, "it don't exist."
> —Michael Herr, *Dispatches*

> Tell all the Truth but tell it slant—
> —Emily Dickinson

"[L]ook into the heart of one you once called enemy," writes the Vietnamese immigrant Le Ly Hayslip. "I have witnessed, firsthand, all that you went through. I will try to tell you who your enemy was" (*When Heaven* xiv). Hayslip's 1989 autobiography, *When Heaven and Earth Changed Places: A Vietnamese Woman's Journey from War to Peace,* thus promises a glimpse into what remained opaque and incomprehensible to both a television viewing audience and the soldier in the field—the heart of "our enemy." The autobiography marks yet another first-person contribution to the discourse of a war that has been said to defy representation. The incommunicability of the Vietnam experience has been a primary theme within veterans' discourse, ironically in spite of the fact that it is dominated by experiential accounts that link notions of authenticity and authority to "being there." Michael Herr's portrayal of a soldier's belief in his invincibility reflects two conventional perspectives on the war; first, that Americans were only fighting themselves, and second, that the trauma of the experience renders it essentially untransferable, hence unreal. Le Ly Hayslip's autobiography stands out among these firsthand accounts if only because it seems to offer an alternative view—that of a Vietnamese peasant woman. And to some extent it does succeed in countering dominant American representations of the Vietnamese people as mere backdrops to a hellish landscape. Vietnam and the Vietnamese, her story testifies, *exist.*

But Hayslip's story is a commodity in the glutted American media market on the war only to the extent that her race, gender, national, and class alterity would indicate that her account does not simply replay that of the journalist or solider in the field or the "multicultural" narratives of female nurses or African American GIs. But does it serve an alternative purpose either in the domestic sphere or in the context of global restructuring? The text does diverge from many of these accounts in the overtness of its intention. Her testimony performs a more specific function than reminding a forgetful American public that its so-called dirty war has continued to impact a nation. In its invocation of a firsthand experience of the war and its structure as a narrative of conversion, Hayslip's work reflects the activist potential of autobiography where the life of the individual is intended as an allegorical commentary. The book's purpose is fairly straightforward—its goal is to "heal old wounds" by elucidating the effects of war and to call for the rebuilding of Vietnam through activism and humanitarian aid. The end of the text directs the reader to various agencies committed to this task, including her own, the East Meets West Foundation. The 1993 sequel, *Child of War, Woman of Peace,* "America's story, written with a bamboo pen" (4), details not only the process of her acculturation to American society in the years following the war but her efforts to establish the foundation's clinic. The message of healing and forgiveness embedded in both narratives and in Oliver Stone's subsequent film adaptation, *Heaven and Earth,* intervened at a strategic historical moment. In February 1994, President Clinton lifted the U.S. trade embargo in force against Vietnam since 1975.[1]

This shift in U.S. foreign policy coincides with the rhetoric of forgiveness reflected in present attitudes toward Vietnam to the extent that some vets can even overlook the irony of a former "draft dodger" "ending" the war: "'it's time to stop rooting in that rag-and-bone shop of our hearts,'" notes the veteran William Broyles Jr. "'It's time for old soldiers, old enemies and old draft dodgers to make peace together.'"[2] Even within the Vietnamese exile community in southern California, where political power remained in the hands of ardent anti-Communists, a *Los Angeles Times* poll revealed that a majority of Vietnamese Americans favored the establishment of full normal diplomatic relations with Vietnam and approved Clinton's decision to lift a trade embargo that was once a litmus test of the nationalism of Vietnamese-in-exile.[3] But Hayslip's success in reaching an audience with her life story can only be partially attributed to the fact that its tenor is consistent with changing attitudes toward Vietnam. Her texts engage and circulate in a variety of discourses not only about the war but about the Asian immigrant experience in the context of multiculturalism, the increasingly global concerns of Asian American literature, Third-World women's *testimonio,* and, most significantly, the relationship between First- and Third-World nations within a modern world system. Her narratives of life in a war zone and afterward rely upon conventions of realism that appeal particularly to her multiple and shifting positionalities as a gendered, class-specific, nationally marked subject. On the one hand, Hayslip's text performs the spectacle of collective Vietnamese suffering and provides American guilt a bodily form as part of its sentimental appeal to the war's civilian toll. On the other hand, the narrative's inscription of a self-reliant subject who refuses victimization is meant to produce an identification and likeness that furthers the text's didactic purpose, exhorting its American readers to move to a salutary and proactive acceptance of responsibility toward Vietnam similar to her own. Hayslip's position as an Asian female immigrant is intrinsic to the narrative's political message even though the text is coauthored by a white American. What are the implications of Jay Wurts's byline on a book that relies upon the "real" experience of a Vietnamese woman to authenticate its presumably alternative discourse on the war?

The text's representation of women's sexual trauma structures its persuasive appeal; *When Heaven and Earth Changed Places* foregrounds women's sexual circumscription as Le Ly[4] charts her way around not the literal minefields of war but a minefield of psychosexual choices. By the time she has been tortured by both the Republicans and the Viet Cong, sexually harassed and raped, abused by American "boyfriends," prostituted, and left an unwed mother, Le Ly realizes that her survival in Vietnam and hopes for a better life in the West are dependent upon her emerging self-consciousness of her body's use value and her ability to control her sexual commodification. The text reveals that for women political allegiance is established through the body and, specifically for Le Ly, a matter of negotiating between the sexual demands of opposing sides represented by Viet Cong, Republican, and American officials, soldiers, and employers. Hayslip's work dramatizes the specific ways in which women's relationship to the state (or other institutions of governance) is established through determinations of sexual-as-political fidelity. But on another level the text's gendered discourse is intimately tied to its covert ideological agenda in which neutrality potentially justifies American interests. Usurping tactics of masculinist nationalism by linking femininity to a nationalist imaginary, *When Heaven and Earth Changed Places* attempts to invoke a maternal space that transcends national divisions; Hayslip's use of a gendered pacifism supports her implicit commentary on Vietnam's future direction within an international economy arguably dominated by its former adversary. Thus her text offers a caveat to generalizing the political function of Third-World women's testimonio; in its portrayal of naturalized gender values that purport to be transnational, her text exemplifies the ways in which women's life stories potentially collude with neocolonialism. At heart, the issue is not about Hayslip's specific agenda, Vietnam War representation, or even about the status of the subject of autobiography but about rhetoric and the multiple political uses that experiential narratives authorized by claims of alterity can serve in their appeal to the real.

In "Third-World Literature in the Era of Multinational Capitalism," Fredric Jameson notes that the primary distinction between First- and Third-World literatures concerns their social investment. In regard to the Western realist and modernist novel, he notes that "political commitment is reconstructed and psychologized or subjectified by way of the public-private split" (71). In contrast, in the literature of the Third World individual psychic and libidinal structures are always located within and determined in part by economic and political relationships. Thus, "the story of the private individual destiny is always an allegory of the embattled situation of the public third-world culture and society" (69). While Jameson's is an admittedly sweeping generalization, what is significant is not so much the distinction he draws between First- and Third-World literatures but his emphasis on the social function of art as it is connected to the nationalist critique embedded in allegory.[5] Written by an American immigrant from Vietnam, a text such as Hayslip's clearly blurs the distinction between First- and Third-World literature but marks its function as committed art through its activist intent. Recounting the repatriation of a daughter in exile, *When Heaven and Earth Changed Places* is textual performance, a staging of the suffering undergone by a faceless and voiceless peasantry made human for an American audience. It succeeds in this most graphically by embodying women's sexual trauma in the figure of Le Ly. Following Western autobiographical convention, Hayslip's is a conversion narrative, an expiation of a "traitor's" guilt also intended to expiate the guilt of American agents of war. But however privatized and individual the origins of its form, as with ethnic autobiography in general the text is continually aware of its collective function. It self-consciously takes on the burden of representing a people through a singular life and the duty implied by Frantz Fanon's comment, "I was responsible at the same time for my body, for my race, for my ancestors" (112). Hayslip's insistence on the activist role of autobiography would seem to reflect what Jameson notes as a general characteristic of Third-World literature, its investment in a social, political world. Moreover, the narrative invites the reader to interpret its social critique through the allegorical relationship between the Vietnamese civil war and the conflicts in Le Ly's family.

Following American involvement in support of the Republican army, Hayslip reveals that the Viet Cong constructed this new American enemy, like the Chinese, French, and Moroccans before them, as a threat to a Vietnamese national family:

> Americans come to kill our people,
> Follow America, and kill your relatives!
> The smart bird flies before it's caught.
> The smart person comes home before Tet.
> Follow us, and you'll always have a family.
> Follow America, and you'll always be alone! (*When Heaven* x)

"A nation cannot have *two* governments," the Viet Cong cadremen announce, "anymore [sic] than a family can have two fathers" (x). Yet Hayslip's narrative employs this same national-familial metaphor to support its own underlying ideological purposes. As a child living in a central village, Le Ly's loyalties to the North and South take the form of her familial relationships to her brothers Bon Nghe, a member of the NVA, and Sau Ban, who joins the Viet Cong to escape the Republican draft, and to her sisters, who are aligned with the opposing side—Ba, married to a Republican policeman, and Lan, a bargirl making her living off of the U.S. military presence. The ease with which other village children switch roles in playing war games—the Viet Cong versus the Republicans—is complicated for Le Ly because whichever side she takes, the enemy is still family. As sides are drawn over Le Ly's decision to marry an American, the gulf between family members becomes metaphoric of a national division:

> Although Vietnamese are raised to respect their ancestors and love their nation, they are not above civil war. In the triangle formed by our family's sad situation—Lan's contest with me for our mother's affection, our struggle against the tide of a changing society, and our different feelings about Americans—I could almost see a fishpond version of the Viet Cong war itself. If I could not make peace with my family in such matters, how could the real fighters on both sides expect to resolve their differences? (349)

Yet what are the ideological implications of this national allegory? While the danger in reading allegorically is the reduction of complex interactions to a system of simple equivalences, *When Heaven and Earth Changed Places* suggests a more fluid set of relationships in which Le Ly and her family alternately represent the political situation in Vietnam. The gendered body operates within the context of two divisions: within a family emblematic of a North/South split, and as the site where U.S./Hanoi differences are played out. In either instance, the text deploys feminine sexuality as the conduit through which the familial-as-national conflicts are defined.

This relationship reflects the work of various international feminist scholars who note the ways in which representations of women and women's concerns become harnessed to the goals of nationalism.[6] As Cynthia Enloe points out, the connection between women and nationalism is often predicated on positioning women as needing protection from corrupting and exploitative outside influences rather than as "active creators of the nation's newly assertive politics" (54). Her comment suggests that women's relationship to nation is most often expressed in ways that deny women's agency, indicating perhaps the activist limitations to nationalist appeals based on simple conceptions of feminine national embodiment. Hayslip's text exploits a somewhat different connection: as that which does not belong to women, feminine sexuality functions as a vehicle through which allegiance is read. Generally, it could be said that the feminine libidinal exists in a dialectical relationship to the public/private split: women's sexuality and desire have always been subject to the regulation of a phallocentric commodity structure. Gayle Rubin discusses this regulation through her concept of a sex/gender system that locates women's oppression within systems of kinship that define them as objects of exchange among men. Her description of this "traffic in women" that underlies the social fabric parallels Luce Irigaray's definition of the "specularization" of the feminine body—how it is transformed into a value-bearing object whose meaning exceeds its natural properties (Irigaray 180). For women, they suggest, desire is not a matter of individual agency, of an autonomous desiring subject. In *When Heaven and Earth Changed Places,* this "public" nature of feminine sexuality is manifested on several levels, particularly in regard to the way that the body becomes a determiner of national loyalty rather than an expression of individual desire. The political division in Le Ly's family is gendered; like Le Ly herself, her sisters are aligned with the South through their sexual liaisons in contrast to her brothers' allegiance to Hanoi signified by their military induction. Lan, a bargirl in Danang, supplements her job by "earn[ing] gifts" from American soldiers "just from lying on [her] back" (190). Yet Lan's "business" signifies more than a livelihood or even a repudiation of traditional values. Her involvement with American men is perceived to establish her loyalty to lover over father and as such represents a betrayal of fatherland: "my sister . . . felt torn between honoring her father, as she had been raised to do and pleasing 'her man,' which was what the American expected. In the end, she told my father to wait and took her American into the bedroom—which was actually no more than a small area of the studio bounded by a curtain—and did what she had to do to please him . . . . There were too many differences, she said, between the ways of the city and our father's to uphold the traditions" (170). Lan's choice to "please her man" over her father becomes a means of locating her positioning as a counter to the traditional emphasis on filiation for which the Viet Cong purports to fight. The potential for being denounced as "she who sells herself to the American empire" (*Child* 123) signals a thematic thread woven throughout Hayslip's representation of her life experience: a Vietnamese woman's political loyalties in the war zone are to be determined through her sexuality rather than (or in spite of) an overt declaration of affiliation.

This equivalence between sexual and cultural allegiance carries significant costs; the price of a Third-World woman's alliance with a foreigner is often estrangement from family and banishment from nation. Unlike her brothers, Le Ly lacks the opportunity to define her politics by joining the army of either side. Initially, as with the other children and adolescents in the village, her feats of minor thievery and stints at guard duty for the Viet Cong mark her affiliation as a matter of her own choice. But after her loyalty is made suspect and rape by two cadremen is her punishment, she begins to question not the merits of either position but the circumstances of war that draw boundaries and set criteria for loyalty. Yet her rape is also paradoxically figured as a reincorporation into and alliance with a powerless and manipulated peasantry: "Both sides in this terrible, endless, *stupid* war had finally found the perfect enemy: a terrified peasant girl who would endlessly and stupidly consent to be their victim—as all Vietnam's peasants had consented to be victims, from creation to the end of time! From now on, I promised myself, I would only flow with the strongest current and drift with the steadiest wind—and not resist. To resist, you have to believe in something" (*When Heaven* 97). The rape ruptures her sense of Vietnamese nationalism. No longer a virgin, she feels disqualified from fulfilling a traditional gender role that would define her alliance; like a soldier's, this is her blood sacrifice. The pacifism reflected in Le Ly's thoughts, the condemnation not of a people, an ideology, or a nation but of the structure of war, works to further the text's statement of neutrality on which Hayslip's appeal for humanitarian aid depends. Yet the passage contains a contradiction that belies this pledge of nonallegiance: victimization, she suggests, results from the people's consent, from their choosing sides. By relinquishing their agency, the Vietnamese break free from their exploitation. Yet Le Ly's refusal to choose, her decision to "flow with the strongest current" as a free agent, is itself a choice. The passage characterizes Hayslip's dual and contradictory portrayals of Le Ly as subject; she acknowledges the influence of uncontrollable external social forces that renders moot her own agency, her choices to ally herself with either the Republicans or the Viet Cong, but ultimately claims complete responsibility for her life. Such rhetorical moves simultaneously celebrate women's strength and self-direction at the same time that they refuse to assign accountability to history, culture, or the actions of others.

Le Ly's feeling of disqualification from a traditional gender role culminates in her decision to barter that which has already been taken from her, a decision that is ironically portrayed as a moment of embodied nationalism. The metaphors Hayslip employs to describe her single act of prostitution draw a similar parallel between her body and Vietnam; like Vietnam, she "took seed from the invaders" in what was an American soldier's "final, nonlethal explosion" (260). Because her body's exploitation links her to her homeland, rather than an act of dishonor that services the desires of the invaders Le Ly's prostitution is simultaneously constituted as a moment of national allegiance and the death of her national identity. Prior to the act, she forces herself to "disregard everything I had learned from my family about honor, self-respect, VD, pregnancy, rape, [and] making love for love" (259). Just as her previous rape by the Viet Cong is described as a symbolic burial that links her to the earth, so too does her prostitution leave behind "the corpse" of her father's daughter. The act both binds her to and exiles her from Vietnam—her acceptance of the "American flags," or roll of twenty-dollar bills, becomes a symbolic as well as literal exchange. Her sexual "choice" is portrayed as both a determiner of national identity representative of Vietnamese feminine strength and a betrayal of that identity.

Hayslip's representation thus counters what for others is a decisive indication of her capitulation to the "capitalist running dogs" the war was meant to expel. Yet the exchange of her body for the safety American economic superiority can buy is constructed as the most logical way to assure her own survival. Her youth and apparent farm-girl innocence become marketing advantages among the American men looking for "sweet, attractive, local girls" as companions. As attachments to American men are seen to be "an easy way out" (295), she risks her hopes on several "boyfriends" who end up abusing her: a navy medical technician pressures her to become a topless dancer, an Amerasian helicopter mechanic ends up strangling her, and a Texan air force officer secretly ships out while living with her. Ironically, these men continue to represent her "ultimate goal of finding peace and safety" (326). After she accepts the "lifeboat of America" in the form of a marriage proposal from a civilian contractor from San Diego, Le Ly's guilt over what she experiences as her nationalist betrayal becomes externalized. As "Mrs. Ed Munro," she notes that "I was no longer completely Vietnamese, but I was not quite American either. Apparently, I was something much worse. Even people I had expected to understand me, to be sympathetic to my dreams, looked down on me and called me names—not always to my back: *Di lay My! Theo de Quoc Ve My! Gai choi boi!* Bitch! Traitor! American whore! . . . . No citizen of Danang was so poor or humble that he or she was not superior to Le Ly *Munro*—turncoat to her country" (353). The narrative initially marks the space of "peace and safety" as American, yet Hayslip's pacifist message condemning not a specific side but war itself would only be convincing if tied to a position of neutrality. Hayslip reconciles this contradiction by refiguring "peace and safety" as a transnational space above the divisions created by war, thus positing her American marriage as the fulfillment of a Vietnamese daughter's duty.

The text achieves this shift through the strategic deployment of an essential feminine pacifism. The events of *When Heaven and Earth Changed Places* are ordered within a novelistic plot that provides conflict, denouement, and resolution. The challenge in Le Ly's return to Vietnam is to restore the position she has lost in the family through a marriage that represents an abandonment of family and country in crisis. Her uncertainty generates narrative suspense—how will her family and the Hanoi government receive the "American tourist," "capitalist stranger," and traitor to both her Phung Thi ancestors and to Vietnam? The parallel between the national and the personal here is obvious: if her family has the capacity to forgive her repudiation of ancestral duty and her association with the enemy, then old political grudges and rifts can also be healed as the family united by the "blood tie of birth" and "the blood bond of battle" recognize their shared past (*Child* 32).

The narrative achieves this reconciliation through the invocation of Le Ly's father as a sort of feminist patriarch and spiritual guide. Exhorting her to "choose life," a philosophy ironically belied by his own suicide, her father tells her, "'Bay Ly, you were born to be a wife and mother, not a killer. That is your duty. . . . Go back to your little son. Raise him the best way you can. That is the battle you were born to fight. That is the victory you must win'" (*When Heaven* 201). Throughout the narrative her father's voice returns to remind her that, contrary to the ancestral myths about warrior women, her role is to nurture life. Thus even the writing of the book appears as the realization of the dictates of Vietnamese filiation: "'Your job is to stay alive—to keep an eye on things and keep the village safe. To find a husband and have babies and *tell the story of what you've seen to your children and anyone else who'll listen.* Most of all, it is to live in peace and tend the shrine of our ancestors. Do these things well, Bay Ly, and you will be worth more than any soldier who ever took up a sword'" (33; emphasis added). The role of nurturer is seen to bridge national

divisions, recasting not only her unpatriotic and unfilial choices but justifying the "mission" of the book itself and, later, that of the East Meets West
Foundation. Le Ly's sexual infractions, those that she attributes to "bad karma" with men and those that result from her own agency, are thus portrayed
as committed in the service of her ancestral duty. The jobs she takes that open
her to sexual harassment, her act of prostitution, her involvement with a series of American lovers, and her eventual willingness to become "a good oriental wife" to an older man are all choices she makes justified by her need to
provide a life for her son.

In the sequel, her father's spirit returns at strategic moments with increasingly specific advice ("'Build a center, Bay Ly'" [*Child* 261]). Hayslip's pacifist
spirituality is also gendered female: "Such atrocities as I had witnessed in both
countries could only be perpetrated by men with no awareness of the sacred
origins of life. They considered children—even their own—as no more than
weeds in a garden" (174). Hayslip's appeal to an essential woman's knowledge
located in the capacity to give birth grants her the authority to critique war as
merely an "athletic field for showing patriotic prowess" and "a factory for
building bad karma" (266). Such an argument necessarily draws upon wom-
en's relationship to the sentimental; in the context of the Vietnam War it also
evokes potent connections between civilians and innocence: the horror of My
Lai is not in the actual death toll but in the massacre of women and children.
Refashioning herself from sexual opportunist to maternally asexual nurturer,
Hayslip posits her Americanization not as oppositional to her Vietnamese duty
but paradoxically as its fulfillment. This rhetorical construction reveals the
supposedly neutral maternal positioning to have a clear investment in international politics in addition to sustaining and reproducing naturalized conceptions of feminine difference.[7] Read allegorically, both autobiographies suggest that assuming a position of feminine nurturing transcendent of political
affiliation indicates a true Vietnamese nationalism. The sequel takes this equation further by generalizing this caretaking duty as the rebuilding of Vietnam
through humanitarian aid and economic investment and representing such a
duty as a karma-building spiritual quest. In light of such a portrayal, it could
be said that Hayslip's own karmic capital was substantially increased with the
opening of a medical clinic in Vietnam called, appropriately, "Mother's Love."

The connection between this realization of the book's overt agenda, solic-
iting American financing of a clinic, and the text's ideological cast is thus fairly
uncomplicated: "Mother's Love" is evidence of forgiveness. It is perhaps more
difficult to speculate on the larger economic implications of this readjustment
in the American collective perception of Vietnam. While it may be an over-
statement to connect publicity over Hayslip's life story to the recent shift in

U.S. foreign policy directly, it clearly contributes to and benefits from the rhetoric of healing that dominates current discourse on the war. And underlying the message of forgiveness in *When Heaven and Earth Changed Places* is a validation of Western technology and a call for increased intervention in a country that was still subject to U.S. embargo.

This is clearly not a neutral position. And at the time of the text's writing, Hayslip was no longer the prodigal daughter returning to a country she seemed to have forsaken; rather, as an ambassador with a message of peace and reconciliation, her own position is decidedly maternal. As the American head of an NGO, Le Ly no longer asks for Hanoi's forgiveness, she is in a position to bestow it. This shift is marked in the differences between *When Heaven and Earth Changed Places* and *Child of War, Woman of Peace;* in contrast to the former's emphasis on the personal and its depiction of her own tenuous reintegration into family as the return of the repressed, the sequel poses direct questions about who will step in as "savior" to Vietnam within the global family. Yet for the most part her own political commentary remains on the level of extolling decent human interaction and the strength of family bonds as a means of forging alliances. Direct international political analysis is represented in the text as the dialogue between various government officials whose policies she will either approve or challenge. For example, assessment of the role of the World Bank in the economic recovery of Vietnam is conveyed through the commentary of a Soviet official who tells her that the United States "not only refuses to help, it actively stands in the way of nations who want to try. It prevents the World Bank from making loans to the Vietnamese and discourages allied nations from trading with their old enemy." " 'Perhaps you can do something as an American citizen,' he suggests, 'to get your government to reconsider its policy' " (*Child* 303). Because the appearance of impartiality is a necessary ingredient for trust in her humanitarian organization, these views are not expressed as her own; she merely validates their sincerity.[8]

Still, in addition to what in both texts are occasionally very clear signals of her belief in the superiority of the capitalist system ("How much would that old man and his teenage assistant give to trade places with me for even a day . . . to enjoy a taste of life in America?" [*When Heaven* 100]), her "caught-in-the-middle" stance is most directly belied by her thoughts upon viewing Ho Chi Minh's body preserved under glass in Hanoi. In what is the strongest passage indicating American bias in either text, she notes, "Mothers like my own willingly sacrificed their sons to secure his vision of an independent Vietnam. It made little difference that his brand of 'independence' brought a totalitarian system that could not feed and care for its own people" (*Child* 326). Like her reflections upon seeing the Vietnam Memorial in Washington, D.C., her thoughts on the unnecessary sacrifices of the dead lead her to invoke maternality as a means of authorizing her critique. Hayslip implicitly contrasts the sacrifice of Vietnamese mothers with "Uncle Ho's" failure to provide for his children. In doing so, her invocation of women as biological reproducers of nation mirrors a gender representation often exploited in nationalist causes (Yuval-Davis) but toward very different ends: her commentary is neither an anti-imperialist nor a neocolonialist indictment. Moreover, her denunciation of totalitarianism is consistent with her American-influenced rhetorical logic—the comment emphasizes the parents' responsibility to the children, a view inconsistent with Buddhist emphasis on ancestor worship.

Yet in spite of what I note as Hayslip's pro-American bias, the general reception of *When Heaven and Earth Changed Places* was divided in a way that fully substantiated one of its most salient themes, that she could please neither side. When the book was published, Hayslip's message of openness toward Vietnam was taken as a validation of its Communist government; she was not only criticized by other Vietnamese exiles but received death threats from within the community, hate mail from veterans, and visits from the FBI. While one reviewer praised her "mature forgiving perspective" (Diehl 26), another found "the absence of judgment . . . in itself almost shocking" (Hoffman).[9] While Hayslip's life story has dovetailed with and potentially influenced shifting American sentiment toward Vietnam, such a shift has not taken place without controversy. Thus throughout both texts Hayslip continually reiterates her neutral positioning. The East Meets West Foundation's publicity brochure presents its intentions straightforwardly: "The mission of East Meets West is to improve the general health, welfare, and socioeconomic condition of the people of Vietnam, and to provide a solid base for the self-sufficiency of our programs, as well as the individuals they serve . . . . Eventually, all the programs will be entirely run by Vietnamese." Beyond this indication of the desirability of self-sufficiency and her belief in the potential of improving the lives of the Vietnamese people, Hayslip's work does not speculate on the implications of the increased involvement of a capitalist core nation like the United States on Vietnam's economic future or its post–cold war commitment to a socialism purchased, as she herself shows, at such a cost. The economist Gary Gereffi reveals that Vietnam is already implicated in capitalist world-system export networks particularly through the practice of "triangular manufacturing," the farming out of First-World production orders from East Asian newly industrialized countries such as Hong Kong, Taiwan, South Korea, and Singapore to low-wage countries like Vietnam (114). Similarly, as Appelbaum, Smith, and Christerson note, "By the early 1990s, manufacturers in the garment business in the United States, Hong Kong, and South Korea made clear that such far-flung sites as Vietnam, Guatemala, Burma, North Korea, and Mongolia were either targets of planned investment in export-oriented garment factories or had already gone on-line" (190). In 1997, two year-old Nike factories in Vietnam were already being called into account for violations of workers' rights and refusal to pay a living wage.[10] In addition to viewing the Vietnamese as a low-wage labor pool, American businesses are also looking upon them as potential consumers of U.S. goods: hours after the trade embargo was lifted, PepsiCo reportedly erected a giant inflatable soda can in the middle of Ho Chi Minh City and distributed forty thousand free bottles of Pepsi. "'We wanted to make a statement,' says Ken Ross, a PepsiCo vice president. 'We wanted to tell Vietnam that we're open for business'" (qtd. in Post 33). Such indications of American "forgiveness" on its own terms lend an eerie sense of prophecy to Hayslip's general comment, "Having outlasted a faltering America in an ungodly war of attrition, the Hanoi government found itself no match for America in peace" (*Child* 244). Given the effects of 1990s economic liberalization, the *New York Times* pronounced that in reverse of 1975 expectations, in fact, "Hanoi has become Saigon."[11]

Any evaluation of the significance of this "match" on different turf centers on the question, Who benefits? Will the lifting of the trade embargo, part of Hayslip's veiled agenda, result in a higher standard of living "for the common people"? Or, if Vietnam enters a world system dominated by core nations like the United States, will economic dependency come to undermine the very sovereignty for which the war was fought? *When Heaven and Earth Changed Places* does not skirt the issue of foreign imperialism—it questions the logic of U.S. military involvement in Vietnam and counters it with an appeal for forgiveness, emphasizing the United States's *human* responsibility to Vietnam now that the war is over. However, her carefully strategic neutrality and use of the book as a charitable vehicle serve to mask another arena through which American imperial dominance is assured, not the overt control signaled by the presence of troops but the economic arena enabled by the opening of Vietnam to increased Western investment.

While Hayslip's message of forgiveness encourages U.S. involvement in Vietnam, it enacts similar ideological work within a domestic sphere. Consistent with the aims of ethnic American autobiography, her texts perform the experience of America's "Other" in order to contest, confirm, or otherwise define American national identity. Within the context of liberal multiculturalism, narratives detailing the Asian experience in the United States have served to challenge a narrow definition of America based on exclusion, while at the same time they may confirm its pluralist self-image. *When Heaven and Earth Changed Places* and *Child of War, Woman of Peace* engage this dual agenda while operating within the multiple discourses defined by Vietnam War representation, Third-World women's testimonio, and Asian American autobiography. However, Hayslip's texts ultimately further a conservative multicultural agenda by reconciling Le Ly's racial, gender, and religious alterity with American liberalism.

John Carlos Rowe has pointed out that seemingly marginal accounts of the war produced by female nurses, black soldiers, and activist veterans have been incorporated into American popular consciousness in a way that co-opts their countercultural dissent. While "war at home" narratives can appear as "invariably liberal, leftist, or otherwise minority-oriented," he notes that their potential for radical commentary is contained by their recasting a "war of imperialist aggression into one of domestic conflict" (208). As a point of evidence, Rowe cites the 1985 CBS documentary *The Vietnam War* in which no Vietnamese appear; they are replaced by exploited American soldiers of color. While Hayslip's work does not allow for this type of easy displacement, it problematizes Rowe's assumption that the presence of the Vietnamese subject is enough to ensure that a critique of American imperialism not be displaced. The ideological cast of *When Heaven and Earth Changed Places* and *Child of War, Woman of Peace* renders them more in concert with Asian American autobiographies of the previous generation than personal accounts of disenfranchised Vietnam veterans. In their representation of the individual overcoming adversity to settle in a place of refuge, both texts mirror and affirm mythic American values of opportunity, freedom, and class mobility. Le Ly is the prototypical immigrant heroine fleeing her country to seek sanctuary and a second beginning in a new land. She not only survives but, as indicated by her "painted fingernails, and hygienist-cleaned teeth and four-bedroom home in California" (*When Heaven* 193), finds financial success; in *Child of War, Woman of Peace,* she discovers that her investments have made her a millionaire on paper. The implications of such a validation in the context of minority autobiography are obvious; what is less obvious is the way in which Hayslip is able to reconcile her difference from the white, Christian, male norm with the precepts and beliefs of her adopted homeland.

Le Ly's Buddhism thus initially appears as a sharp contrast to the capitalist values she confronts upon her immigration. While her subsequent activism initially threatens the wealth she has earned, the dual missions of helping her homeland and investing her money are represented as parallel rather than oppositional aims: astrologers, gurus, and monks offer concurrent advice on her spiritual and financial well-being. Her comment on "fueling" her spiritual/ activist desire forces Buddhism and American consumerism into odd harmony: "'Souls are hungry. If the car is empty, you go for the gas'" (qtd. in Evans 39). More significantly, Hayslip's rhetorical construction of her Buddhist-

motivated activism ironically seems to adopt the terms of Christian prophecy. Le Ly's humanitarian mission takes the form of a jeremiad reflective of the
rhetoric of Puritan America. Sacvan Bercovitch notes that this Puritan "political sermon" sustains and grants cohesion to a nationalism based in the belief
of an American "errand in the wilderness."[12] She is chosen, a swami who looks
like Jesus if "Jesus had been a surfer" tells her, to fulfill the mission of an ancient spiritual healer: "He says his connection to you goes back much further
than your parents. And this is not the first time he has communicated with
you. You have been visited by him in prior lives. He says that you will discover
his identity only after you have accomplished your mission in life" (*Child* 218).
Le Ly is thus portrayed as a prophet of another American "errand" extending
back to Vietnam. Hers is a spiritual quest in which the individual struggles to
influence the birthright of the collective: she is, the gurus of southern California inform her, "to lead a crowd in a long, hard climb. [She is] to practice
the healing arts but not as a doctor, medicine man, or nun" (219). Again, this
is also a maternal jeremiad; like "a mother's hard labor," the writing of the book
is characterized as a painful delivery sustained only by her conviction that she
has "a million lost souls" behind her (209).

If Hayslip's religious alterity can be portrayed as consistent with an American belief in an individual-as-collective destiny, her use of gender alterity
authorizes this destiny. As I have suggested, gender provides the vantage point
for her denunciation of the aggressive behaviors that support the military-
industrial complex, a denunciation that would appear to be a clear counter to
the masculinist war narratives that Susan Jeffords reveals justify domination
on multiple levels: "war *is* the spectacle of the masculine bond. It is the opti-
mal display of masculine collectivity in America" (25). Hayslip's work would
seem to prove an exception, an alternative to the hypermasculine accounts of
the war. Yet at one level her texts do not disprove Jeffords's general thesis; while
they may confound the pattern of masculine bonding that Jeffords characterizes as endemic to Vietnam War representation, they merely reverse its terms,
leaving patriarchal logic intact. If war is based on a masculine belief in things
worth dying for, Hayslip counters with a peace grounded in a feminine commitment to things worth living for.[13] Her text dramatizes the way in which
realism depends upon an appeal to normative conceptions of gender, specifically those that appear to be imbued with moral value.[14]

Lynda Boose notes that Vietnam War counternarrative may be "feminized"
when juxtaposed to a "masculinist" military policy located in the "mytholo-
gy of a national self born in and valorized by a history of conquest and dominance" (585). Hayslip's gendered pacifism thus meshes with a genre of politically invested narrative already marked as feminine. Yet such a pacifism loses

its oppositional quality as imperialist critique if conjoined with a tone of absolution: Hayslip's texts refuse to assign blame to the extent that the war appears to be perpetrated by individuals who have little control over their own actions. Hence throughout both texts she characterizes men, her rapists and john included, as "sad little boys." Rather than functioning as a radically oppositional discourse, Hayslip's deployment of feminine difference ends up supporting American interests by refusing to hold either side accountable for the war. Military aggression appears as a form of masculine childishness; war and suffering occur, her texts seem to suggest, as a result of bad karma.

Signaled early in the prologue's statement to GIs, "It was not your fault," Hayslip's emphasis on American absolution is portrayed as the logical outcome of a Buddhist-inflected personal philosophy derived from a series of abusive relationships with men. After being abandoned by an American for the third time, she reflects,

> I had risked my feelings on Paul—staked my happiness on his honesty. Now that it had fallen through, who had I to blame for my disappointment but myself? . . . If I could forgive Anh for abandoning me with a baby, Red for changing me around to suit his tastes, and Jim for almost killing me, how could I be less charitable to Paul, who had left me with nothing worse than pretty memories? . . . I decided I should draw the strength of compassion, not the weakness of bitterness, from this most important lesson—from the lessons I had learned from every American that fate or luck or god had sent to be my teacher. Even at their worst, each one had given me something which, to that time, I had lacked in my life. I understood the choices I had made—and the things that resulted from them. What happened had been as much my doing as theirs. For a Vietnamese woman, realizing this was like emancipation to a slave. Hating people who had wronged me only kept me in their power. Forgiving them and thanking them for the lesson they had taught me, on the other hand, set me free to continue on my way. (*When Heaven* 325–26)

What is extraordinary about the evolution of her thinking is that it can be lauded as praiseworthy—an indication, perhaps, of what *Playboy* saw as "maturity" (Diehl 26)—as well as being dismissed as simple foolishness. Her evaluation that these sexually exploitative relationships produced positive results is based on the hindsight of her current activities: they put her on the path to the present moment. Empowerment, she suggests, lies in claiming women's agency, a recognition that is not incongruent with contemporary feminist thinking. The self-reliant attitude expressed here culminates in the narrative's final tone of triumphalism tempered by humbleness ("Do not feel sorry for me—I made it; I am okay" [366]). Nevertheless, what is most startling about this passage is not necessarily the capacity for compassion it expresses but, again, her unwillingness to assign accountability for masculine perfidy or abuse. While this refusal may well be rationalized as a purely individual and spiritual response, it also strategically authorizes the text's use of individual experience as a foundation for international diplomacy: nations, like individuals, must forgive in order to free themselves. While feminists debate whether theories of feminine difference are necessary to feminist praxis or ultimately come at the expense of women, my concern is not to locate Hayslip's work within these debates but to note how her gendered (and, following passages such as this one, what some might characterize as antifeminist) rhetoric furthers a larger agenda.[15] However, I also want to point out that the events depicted in *When Heaven and Earth Changed Places* contribute to Third-World feminism by problematizing any universal concept of feminist resistance. I have suggested that Gayle Rubin and Luce Irigaray's Marxist-influenced theories are applicable to a text such as Hayslip's, which describes women's circumscription within a sex/gender system. Yet Rubin and Irigaray speak of feminist resistance in terms of women claiming their sexual pleasure and denying patriarchal systems such as marriage and heterosexuality that encode it. In contrast, Hayslip's work makes clear that Le Ly's resistance does not depend upon the denial of these systems but on her ability to recognize and exploit them materially. As sex literally becomes a commodity bartered for survival, in controlling her sexual commodification Le Ly asserts the primacy of her own agency in her distribution. Trading on what she offers as a companion—youth, sexual service, and the allure of the Orient—is a self-conscious decision that is meant to signal her refusal to be victimized. Such an emphasis on Le Ly's agency marks a significant intervention in discourses that, in their portrayal of Asian women's bodies as simple sites of colonization, view them as nothing more than victims to Third- and First-World political economies or as national metaphors rather than agents of global intervention. While her work does not offer unequivocal evidence of feminist identity, it does indicate the necessity for developing a concept of complex agency in regard to Third-World women, one that would, as Lata Mani notes, "simultaneously engage women's systematic subordination and the ways in which women negotiate oppressive, even determining social conditions" (21). This vigilance certainly applies in cases where the biases of Western feminists might intrude upon an understanding of women's self-defined contributions to nation, particularly in the case of Hayslip, where these contributions are asserted through traditional associations between motherhood and national duty. As Cynthia Enloe writes, "Women in many communities trying to assert their sense of national identity find that coming into an emergent nationalist movement *through* the accepted feminine roles of bearer of the community's memory and children is empowering" (55).[16] *When Heaven and Earth Changed Places* centers on Le Ly's ability to use her sexuality without feeling that she has compromised either her Vietnamese or feminine sense of self. By foregrounding the Asian female subject's intervention in constructing identity within the constraints imposed by nationalisms, gender, and partisan politics, the text reveals that in the process of cultural mediation Third-World women are not simply co-opted by the gender role nor do they reveal a clear-cut repudiation of it.

When Heaven and Earth Changed Places suggests that there is something irreducible about rape, torture, and outcasting. Whatever claim one could make about the way the text functions ideologically, it succeeds in articulating the horrors of war from a peasant girl's point of view. This is why Oliver Stone's film, *Heaven and Earth,* can still be compelling as a positive contribution to a discourse that has ironically ignored Vietnamese presence in Vietnam; its initial focus on Le Ly as subject distances it from prior representations of the Vietnamese as voiceless, fleeing peasants, although it may also admittedly aestheticize and subordinate them to a lush, panoramic landscape. Such an embodiment as an appeal to realism is certainly efficacious in publicizing political causes: Rigoberta Menchú is a case in point. However, as Monique T. D. Tru'o'ng has noted, Hayslip's story has been reframed and reduced to fit an American revisionist view of the war in order to provide "the film equivalent of group therapy" (237). More significant to my discussion of rhetoric here, Stone's interpretation of Hayslip's life jettisons the autobiography's narrative structure, which centers on Le Ly's reconciliation of her supposed national betrayal, in favor of a simple chronology of events and the all-too-familiar American male savior/Asian female saved narrative of *Madame Butterfly* ("Steve, you Le Ly hero. You protect Le Ly"). In Stone's film, as likewise reflected in *The World of Suzie Wong, The Good Woman of Bangkok,* or *Miss Saigon,* what is being replayed—albeit with Japan substituted for Hong Kong, substituted for Thailand, substituted for Vietnam—is a durable narrative about the Orient that operates at the nexus of discourses on nationalism, colonialism, race, and gender. However much the film intervenes by recasting *Madame Butterfly*'s ending—the disintegration of the American vet contrasted to the triumphant Vietnamese woman's homecoming—it nonetheless reaffirms the dominant representation of Asian women in American film as noble whores finding salvation in white men who turn out to be the more angst-ridden, psychologically complex subjects. One can argue whether or not the film version of Hayslip's life refashions the fleshless allegorical figure of Madame Butterfly into an agent confronted with complex cultural choices or whether it works to confirm an Orientalist fantasy already embedded within an American popular consciousness.

The question of Stone's co-optation of Hayslip's life story raises the question of coauthorship: Is the white male American "veteran"[17] responsible for the text's pro-American bias? Students of mine have posed the question another way, no less effectively: Who the hell is Jay Wurts? At the end of the text, Wurts is identified as a former Vietnam War Air Guard pilot, but otherwise his participation as coauthor goes unremarked. As Joseph Trimmer has noted, Wurts was responsible for much of the narrative crafting of what was initially a three-hundred-page manuscript typed (and presumably partly translated and edited into English) by Hayslip's son, James. By Trimmer's account, it was an active collaboration; Hayslip never relinquished control over the text or indulged Wurts's license as a storyteller.[18] Shirley Lim has raised the question of coauthorship compromising Asian American women's writing;[19] her doubts are similar to those raised historically in regard to other writers of color who have collaborated with white editors and coauthors, most notably the abolitionist writings of former slaves suspected of being manipulated (if not actually solely authored) by white abolitionists. Lim's is a valid concern, particularly in regard to an autobiography such as *When Heaven and Earth Changed Places,* whose cultural capital is dependent upon her status as an authentic informant, in other words, upon her embodying alterity. Nevertheless, this anxiety about collaboration arises from assuming a simple equivalence between subject positioning and ideological bias. Overdetermining the mediation of a coauthor would seem to counter the evolution of the text's philosophy and the fact that Hayslip consistently takes pains to inscribe Le Ly as an active agent who refuses to give her life over to the control of others; an overdetermination of Wurts's influence positions Hayslip as merely an ethnographic dupe. Understanding the nature of textual bias seems more crucial than an attempt to ascertain the text's authentic or inauthentic parts based on their source—the "real" Asian woman or white American vet. Without definitively attributing the narrative structure to either Wurts or Hayslip, I argue that the text's political bias is nonetheless intrinsically tied to this structure; in chronicling her transformation from Viet Cong peasant girl to American "tourist," the narrative moves to reconcile Le Ly's apparent sexual transgressions by portraying them as a means of fulfilling expectations of women's nurturing. By characterizing a betrayal of country as the fulfillment of her traditionally intended role, the narrative attempts to reinscribe Americanization as that which paradoxically allows Le Ly's adherence to her duty as a daughter of Vietnam. Wurts's influence has not heretofore been a subject of great controversy, nor has Hayslip's veracity been subject to the kind of scrutiny that Rigoberta Menchú's autobiography has undergone.[20] This might be attributed to the fact that while both connect individual life stories to political change, Hayslip's narrative renders her ideological agenda much less overtly than Menchú's; her bias may not be contested precisely because the narrative positions her "above" politics. Her apparent openness and willingness to document all no doubt contributes to this positioning: on one of her return trips to Vietnam, she and her sons are accompanied by an American news crew, which asks her to show the exact spot where she was raped by Viet Cong soldiers—and she does. It is as if in promoting the agenda of her foundation she acknowledges the need for hyper-realism (and the voyeurism on which it depends) to validate her personal story.

To view Hayslip's work simply within the context of the bicultural subject's identity formation in keeping with a singular focus on Asian American immigrant literature would displace the impact of its circulation in a global context. The autobiographies do represent an intervention in a body of work dominated by second-generation Chinese and Japanese Americans; it is a Southeast Asian immigrant's reminder that American intervention in the Third World is often the impetus for such immigration. As Hayslip's life story testifies, "multiculturalism" is not only concerned with internal dynamics of racial representation but with the ways in which American beliefs and values can intersect with international interests. Analysis of this intersection provides a caution about the ways in which alterity—in this case, that of a Buddhist Vietnamese woman—can authorize American ideology while appearing to either counter or remain neutral to it. The texts reinscribe one whose difference is literally marked—she is "our" enemy—into someone who is "like us": compassionate, forgiving, and tired of war. The texts enact the work of liberal multiculturalism in their incorporation of racial and national differences into a harmonious, pluralist whole through the processes of differentiation and identification. The assertion of marginal identity is thus not a substitute for political affiliation, a point often assumed in early discussions of multiculturalism.

It may be unfair to ascribe to Hayslip's activism greater motives than she herself would claim. While I point out that her rhetoric may intersect with interests she may not have foreseen, I do not question the immediate contributions of the East Meets West Foundation to improving health care in Vietnam. The first edition of *When Heaven and Earth Changed Places* reveals that Hayslip was not a professional fundraiser; the fact that the foundation's contact number printed at the end of the book was actually her home telephone number lends an oddly embodied immediacy to the relationship between author and reader. The humanitarian work that her books underwrite suggests a limit to the efficacy of any emphasis on discursivity. In other words, even in light of the implications I draw here, why *not* build a clinic? Hayslip represents a fairly clear-cut example of the committed artist, one among many Third-

World writers who, in the words of her fellow countrywoman Trinh T. Minh-ha, speak in the name of the masses by carrying "their weight into the weight of their communities, the weight of the world" (11). Jameson's emphasis on reading Third-World literature as national allegory highlights the commitment of writers like Hayslip who use art as a medium for social critique and a call to praxis. Her investment in the social would seem to realize both theorists' conditions for the artist engagé.

Yet on one level hers is not the call to praxis that either Jameson or Trinh T. Minh-ha may have envisioned. Beneath Jameson's valorization of Third-World literature's narration of collective experience lies an implicit assumption that such a narration necessarily furthers a radical agenda. While her individual story intentionally reflects the "personal is political" dictate of identity politics, Hayslip is not the "cultural intellectual, who is also a political militant" (75) that Jameson posits as the ideal native cultural worker. Though emphatically critical of the way in which hegemony is assured through the use of force, Hayslip does not speculate on the consequences of Vietnam's reinscription in a world order hostile to its commitment to communism. As Viet Thanh Nguyen notes, "Hayslip's conclusion that 'what [the United States] wants more than anything, I think, is to forgive you and be forgiven by you in return,' implies a symmetry of power that did not and does not exist" (626). An examination of Hayslip's text provides an understanding of the purposes that personal narrative may serve as it intersects and is invested in multiple discourses. Marita Sturken has noted that the Vietnam War Memorial "stands in a precarious space between . . . opposing discourses" of nationalist imperialism and the counternarratives that would challenge it (138). As recounted in two autobiographies and a film, Hayslip's life story functions as another ambivalent memorial to the war; it ruptures the masculinist logic that justifies military domination only to replace it with persistent and open-ended questions about the other forms domination may take.

Notes

An earlier version of this chapter appeared in *Prose Studies* 17.1 (April 1994): 141–60, and is used here by permission of Frank Cass and Co., Ltd.

1. In 1994, the secretary of state, Warren Christopher, met with the Vietnamese foreign minister in an effort to normalize Vietnamese-American relations, the first meeting between the foreign policy chiefs of Vietnam and the United States since 1975 (*New York Times,* 10 July 1994). Since 1995, the United States and Vietnam have established diplomatic ties but have yet to achieve full economic and trade normalization.

2. William Broyles Jr., quoted in *Newsweek,* 14 Feb. 1994, 31–32.

3. The poll was conducted in March and April 1994 in Orange County, California, which has the largest concentration of Vietnamese outside Vietnam. Sixty-eight percent of Vietnamese American voters there were registered Republican, "many believing it takes a harsher view of Communism" than the Democratic Party (*Los Angeles Times,* 13 June 1994, A24). Fifty-four percent approved lifting the embargo, and 53 percent favored full diplomatic relations with Vietnam (*Los Angeles Times,* 12 June 1994, A32).

4. Throughout this essay I make a distinction between Hayslip, the author who constructs the narrative, and Le Ly, the representation of herself as the character who plays out the action of that narrative. The fact that these entities are often presumed to be identical testifies to the strength of realism as a genre and the illusion of unmediated access to the subject of first-person narrative.

5. Although Jameson's comments are in regard to the novel, the generic distinction between fiction and autobiography is not relevant to my argument here. Rather, I am interested in the rhetorical structures that render autobiography novelistically. It is certainly the case, however, that Hayslip's narrative would not have received attention had it not been perceived as factual, especially in a genre such as Vietnam War narrative where authority is so clearly aligned with a first-person experience of the war.

6. See, for example, Jayawardena; Kandiyoti; Peterson; Heng; West, *Feminist Nationalism;* Yuval-Davis; and Yuval-Davis and Anthias.

7. In regard to other Asian American women's texts, this construction is most notably reflected in Lee's *Still Life with Rice.* While less overtly interventionist than Hayslip's autobiography, this as-told-to testimonio recounting a woman's life during the Korean Civil War draws upon concepts of maternal bonding in its plea for Korean reunification. The text ends, "I wait, hoping, aching, for the political gate that separates my son from me to fling open. And when it does, I will run in laughing and crying and singing out his name. How do I know? I am Korean, and we Koreans have this unshakable faith, for we are a strongwilled people. History proves it to be so. For more than a millennium we have lived as one people and I am certain we will be united again. Unification is possible! I say this as a woman who has survived over eighty years of living; also, I say it as a woman who has given life" (320).

8. Reuters reports that since returning to the international financial fold in 1993, Vietnam has received $8.5 billion in development assistance (Adrian Edwards, "Rights Group Appeals to Donors over Vietnam Unrest," Reuters, 10 Dec. 1997). World Bank donors pledged $2.4 billion in aid for 1998, anticipating that Vietnam would not be significantly affected by the 1997 financial crisis in Asia as it does not allow free securities trading and does not have a stock market (Edwina Gibbs, "Donors Pledge $2.4 Billion in Aid for Vietnam," Reuters, 12 Dec. 1997). However, Vietnam's policy of economic liberalization in the 1990s may take a more conservative turn with the appointment of General Le Kha Phieu as general secretary of the Party in December 1997 (Mydans).

9. It may not be surprising that the former comment praising her forgiving perspec-

tive on the war—and by extension the sexual violence perpetrated by the men who waged it—was published in *Playboy*.

10. For a discussion of Nike's labor abuses in Vietnam and elsewhere, see the website for Global Exchange at <http://www.globalexchange.org>.

11. See Whitney. Of course, such comments in the American media may merely reflect a rescripting of the Vietnam War in which the United States, like Rambo, wins in the end.

12. Echoing the rhetoric of this "national covenant," Hayslip's *Child of War, Woman of Peace* could easily be the focus of Bercovitch's assessment of Thoreau's *Walden*, which he sees as "a conversion narrative that fuses the laws of nature, reason, and economics with the spirit of America" (185).

13. A reading of *When Heaven and Earth Changed Places* does, however, challenge Jeffords's privileging of gender over racial difference in her analysis of Asian women, a privileging she makes self-conscious in her statement, "it could be just as important to understand [Vietnamese women's] construction as 'enemy' in terms of their race" (178). Her analysis of Vietnamese women focuses on the way in which the "sexual difference between men and woman is used to defer racial differences," rendering them mere vehicles for signifying power relations among white, black, Native American, Latino, and Asian men in a war zone (178). The centrality of Le Ly's point of view in *When Heaven and Earth Changed Places* does not allow a reading in which gender trumps race; the text reveals that both are integral to her self-conception as a Vietnamese woman and influence her representation of that positioning.

14. Viet Thanh Nguyen makes a similar argument in his discussion of how Hayslip's work serves the purposes of global capitalism through its appeal to a naturalized feminine body located in the "nostalgic fiction of Viet Nam as agrarian, precapitalist, and fundamentally stable and 'natural' in its social organization" (608). He further suggests how Hayslip's self-representation might also reconcile her to a Vietnamese audience through its convergence with classical literature. He notes that Hayslip's story resonates strongly with Nguyen Du's "The Tale of Kieu," in which "ideal duty must be compromised in the face of contingency" (633) as the protagonist sacrifices bodily chastity in order to fulfill her filial duty; what redeems her as a nationalist heroine is her ability to retain a sense of spiritual chastity in the face of loss. My thanks to Sau-Ling Wong for bringing this article to my attention.

15. Elizabeth Grosz's question characterizes this distinction: "Is the concept of sexual difference a breakthrough term in contesting patriarchal conceptions of women and femininity? Or is it a reassertion of the patriarchal containment of women? Is the concept essentialist, or is it an upheaval of patriarchal knowledges?" (87).

16. West also makes this point in noting the convergence of male and feminist nationalists on the centrality of the family and pronatalist (antiabortion) stances to nationalist social movements: "Feminist nationalist criticisms of Western cultural values underlie their perception that Western feminists downplay or even undermine the importance of family and kinship relations" ("Feminist Nationalist" 574).

17. Trimmer notes that in fact Wurts merely elected to fly transport missions and

never saw combat, landing in Vietnam once on a secured airstrip (34). Ironically, one can see how such a personal history would undermine Wurts's authenticity in a discourse where authority is assigned on the basis of action seen.

18. Trimmer notes, "Eventually Wurts and Hayslip agreed on a plot, conceiving the book as two journeys—a young girl's escape from Vietnam and a mature woman's return to her homeland. But to develop this plot, Wurts needed a new strategy for gathering information. He began compiling pages of written questions, asking Hayslip to remember the specific scenes and conversations he needed to complete the story of her two journeys" (34). Certainly Wurts's influence on the text can be surmised by the use of idiomatic English, for example, "She nudged my arm and I hopped to it" (*When Heaven* 12). But this influence may also be attributed to James Hayslip; *Child of War, Woman of Peace* recounts that the first book was originally written in longhand in Vietnamese so that Dennis Hayslip, who disapproved of the book project, would think his wife was merely writing letters.

19. Personal communication, December 1992.

20. Following the controversy that David Stoll's *Rigoberta Menchú and the Story of All Poor Guatemalans* generated, Menchú herself was initially willing to attribute any inconsistencies in her text to the influence of her collaborator, Elisabeth Burgos-Debray, whom she deemed "officially the author of the book." The controversy surrounding the facticity of her autobiography only reveals the extent to which discourses of the real rely on individual embodiment as an authenticating precondition. See *New York Times*, 15 Dec. 1998, A10.

Works Cited

Appelbaum, Richard P., David Smith, and Brad Christerson. "Commodity Chains and Industrial Restructuring in the Pacific Rim: Garment Trade and Manufacturing." In *Commodity Chains and Global Capitalism.* Ed. Gary Gereffi and Miguel Korzeniewicz. Westport, Conn.: Greenwood Press, 1994. 187–204.

Bercovitch, Sacvan. *The American Jeremiad.* Madison: University of Wisconsin Press, 1978.

Boose, Lynda. "Techno-Muscularity and the 'Boy-Eternal': From the Quagmire to the Gulf." In *Cultures of United States Imperialism.* Ed. Amy Kaplan and Donald E. Pease. Durham, N.C.: Duke University Press, 1993. 581–616.

Diehl, Digby. Review of *When Heaven and Earth Changed Places*, by Le Ly Hayslip with Jay Wurts. *Playboy*, July 1989, 26.

Enloe, Cynthia. *Bananas, Beaches, and Bases: Making Feminist Sense of International Politics.* Berkeley: University of California Press, 1990.

Evans, Karen. "Epilogue: Le Ly Hayslip's American Life." *Los Angeles Times Magazine*, 5 Feb. 1989, 9+.

Fanon, Frantz. *Black Skin, White Masks.* 1952. Trans. Charles Lam Markmann. New York: Grove Weidenfeld, 1991.

Gereffi, Gary. "The Organization of Buyer-Driven Global Commodity Chains: How

U.S. Retailers Shape Overseas Production Networks." In *Commodity Chains and Global Capitalism.* Ed. Gary Gereffi and Miguel Korzeniewicz. Westport, Conn.: Greenwood Press, 1994. 95–122.

Grosz, Elizabeth. "Sexual Difference and the Problem of Essentialism." *Inscriptions* 5 (1989): 86–101.

Hayslip, Le Ly, with James Hayslip. *Child of War, Woman of Peace.* New York: Doubleday, 1993.

Hayslip, Le Ly, with Jay Wurts. *When Heaven and Earth Changed Places: A Vietnamese Woman's Journey from War to Peace.* New York: Penguin, 1989.

Heng, Geraldine. "'A Great Way to Fly': Nationalism, the State, and the Varieties of Third-World Feminism." In *Feminist Genealogies, Colonial Legacies, Democratic Futures.* Ed. M. Jacqui Alexander and Chandra Talpade Mohanty. New York: Routledge, 1997.

Herr, Michael. *Dispatches.* New York: Knopf, 1977.

Hoffman, Eva. "A Child of Vietnam Grows Up to Write of the Horror." *New York Times,* 17 May 1989.

Irigaray, Luce. *This Sex Which Is Not One.* Trans. Catherine Porter. Ithaca, N.Y.: Cornell University Press, 1985.

Jameson, Fredric. "Third-World Literature in the Era of Multinational Capitalism." *Social Text* 15 (Fall 1986): 65–87.

Jayawardena, Kumari. *Feminism and Nationalism in the Third World.* London: Zed Books, 1986.

Jeffords, Susan. *The Remasculinization of America: Gender and the Vietnam War.* Bloomington: Indiana University Press, 1989.

Kandiyoti, Deniz. "Identity and Its Discontents: Women and the Nation." In *Colonial Discourse and Post-Colonial Theory.* Ed. Patrick Williams and Laura Chrisman. New York: Columbia University Press, 1994.

Lee, Helie. *Still Life with Rice: A Young American Woman Discovers the Life and Legacy of Her Korean Grandmother.* New York: Scribner, 1996.

Mani, Lata. "Multiple Mediations: Feminist Scholarship in the Age of Multinational Reception." *Inscriptions* 5 (1989): 1–23.

Menchú, Rigoberta, with Elisabeth Burgos-Debray. *I, Rigoberta Menchú: An Indian Woman in Guatemala.* Trans. Ann Wright. London: Verso, 1984.

Mydans, Seth. "A New Leader for Vietnam Who Is Wary of Markets." *New York Times,* 31 Dec. 1997.

Nguyen, Viet Thanh. "Representing Reconciliation: Le Ly Hayslip and the Victimized Body." *Positions: East Asia Cultures Critique* 5:2 (1997): 605–42.

Peterson, V. Spike. "The Politics of Identity and Gendered Nationalism." In *Foreign Policy Analysis: Contiguity and Change in Its Second Generation.* Ed. Laura Neack, Jeanne A. K. Hey, and Patrick Haney. Englewood Cliffs, N.J.: Prentice Hall, 1995. 167–86.

Post, Tom. "The War—To Cash In." *Newsweek,* 14 Feb. 1994, 33.

Rowe, John Carlos. "'Bringing It All Back Home': American Recyclings of the Vietnam War." In *The Violence of Representation: Literature and the History of Violence.* Ed. Nancy Armstrong and Len Tennenhouse. New York: Routledge, 1989. 197–218.

Rubin, Gayle. "Traffic in Women: Notes on the 'Political Economy' of Sex." In *Toward an Anthropology of Women.* Ed. Rayna Reiter. New York: Monthly Review Press, 1975. 157–210.

Stoll, David. *Rigoberta Menchú and the Story of All Poor Guatemalans.* Boulder, Colo.: Westview Press, 1999.

Stone, Oliver, dir. *Heaven and Earth.* Warner Bros., 1993.

Sturken, Marita. "The Wall, the Screen, and the Image: The Vietnam Veterans Memorial." *Representations* 35 (Summer 1991): 118–42.

Trimmer, Joseph F. "Heaven and Earth: The Making of a Cross-Cultural Autobiography." *CultureFront* (Summer 1994): 33–36, 79.

Trinh T. Minh-ha. *Woman, Native, Other: Writing Postcoloniality and Feminism.* Bloomington: Indiana University Press, 1989.

Tru'o'ng, Monique T. D. "Vietnamese American Literature." In *An Interethnic Companion to Asian American Literature.* Ed. King-kok Cheung. Cambridge: Cambridge University Press, 1997. 219–46.

West, Lois A. "Feminist Nationalist Social Movements: Beyond Universalism and towards a Gendered Cultural Relativism." *Women's Studies International* 15.5/6 (1992): 563–79.

———, ed. *Feminist Nationalism.* New York: Routledge, 1997.

Whitney, Craig R. "Hanoi Now, Meet Saigon Then." *New York Times,* 28 Dec. 1997, 6.

Yuval-Davis, Nira. *Gender and Nation.* London: Sage Publications, 1997.

Yuval-Davis, Nira, and Floya Anthias, eds. *Woman-Nation-State.* New York: St. Martin's Press, 1989.

7

The "Language of the Organs"

The Political Purchase of Tears in
Contemporary Sri Lanka

Malathi de Alwis

Between June 1990 and May 1993 there emerged in southern Sri Lanka a significant and unprecedented political movement: the Mothers' Front. With an estimated grassroots membership of over twenty-five thousand women protesting the "disappearances" of approximately sixty thousand male affines and/
or relatives, the Mothers' Front was an extraordinary political organization.
It was not only the single largest women's protest movement of its time but
arguably one of the most effective in the modern history of Sri Lanka. As I have
suggested elsewhere (de Alwis, "Motherhood"), much of the political effectivity of the Mothers' Front stemmed from their mobilization of a particular
configuration of "motherhood"—which I define as encompassing women's
biological reproduction as well as their interpellation as moral guardians, care-
givers, and nurturers—exemplified in their claim that all they wished for was
a return to a time "where we can raise our sons to manhood, have our hus-
bands with us and lead normal women's lives" (qtd. in *Island*, 9 Feb. 1991).

Such an articulation of "motherhood" is undoubtedly undergirded by specific notions of "respectability" and "domesticity" (see de Alwis, *Maternalist
Protest*), but its emotional purchase was predominantly predicated on the
construction of these women as grieving and suffering mothers. I would like
to explore here the crucial role that was played by a particular signifier of such
suffering and grief—tears. The location of tears within the naturalized female
body, which is always already constructed as a site of the "real" and the "authentic," not only evoked popular sentiment but also legitimized protest.

Maternalizing Suffering

Emotions, according to Abu-Lughod and Lutz, are among those "taken-for-
granted objects of both specialized knowledge and everyday discourse" that are

only now entering the realm of anthropological inquiry (1). Primarily the preserve of philosophy and psychology for a long time, emotions continue to be tied to "tropes of interiority" and granted "ultimate facticity by being located in the natural body"; it is the aspect of human experience that has been "least subject to control, least constructed or learned (hence most universal), least public and therefore least amenable to sociocultural analysis" (1).[1] The location of emotions in the "natural body" also enables the frequent and easy ontological slippages that, for example, masculinize aggression and feminize suffering.

The feminization of suffering is a field of study that has been greatly enhanced by feminist research and writing during the past two decades that has deconstructed as well as historicized the rationalization and medicalization of the (primarily middle-class, Euro-American) female body during the eighteenth and nineteenth centuries.[2] Hysteria, dementia, melancholia,[3] and depression are familiar terms today that were discovered through and inscribed upon the bodies of women over the centuries; the possession of a uterus and the bodily cycles that were linked to it such as menstruation, pregnancy, lactation, and menopause were perceived to be central to a woman's pathologies.

For many early feminists, such as Mary Wollstonecraft, Simone de Beauvoir, and Shulamith Firestone, the specificities of the naturalized female body provided a unique means of access to knowledge and ways of living while simultaneously limiting women's capacity for equality (Grosz 15). These epistemological positions nevertheless stemmed from "patriarchal and misogynist assumptions about the female body as somehow more natural, less detached, more engaged with and directly related to its 'objects' than male bodies" (15). The work of many contemporary feminists too frequently falls into the trap of attributing an "indisputable authenticity to women's experience," which is then perceived as enabling the construction of individual as well as collective identities and as engendering agency, resistance against oppression, and even feminism[4] (Scott, "Experience" 31). As Joan Scott has perceptively pointed out,[5] this process of making "experience visible," of valorizing it as *the* authoritative evidence that grounds what is known, precludes its historicization and the interrogation of the structures of power that enable its production (25–26). As a matter of fact, it is precisely this "'authorized appearance of the "real"'" that serves to "'camouflage the practice which in fact determines it'" (de Certeau qtd. in Scott, "Evidence" 367). Our challenge is thus not to make experience the origin of our explanations but rather the very subject that we "seek to explain" (Scott, "Experience" 26). Such a project however, must also be cognizant of the fact that what "counts as experience" is "neither self-evident nor straightforward" but always contested and therefore always political (Scott, "Evidence" 387; see also Jeganathan 212).

In this section, I am interested in unpacking how Sinhala[6] women's quotidian experiences and material practices are frequently maternalized and articulated upon and through the body of the mother. Such maternalized embodiments are produced within a discourse of suffering that engenders a particular sentiment because of their very location in such a maternalized body. For example, the Sinhala word for suffering, *duka* (which can also mean pain, grief, misery, yearning, or sacrifice, according to the context in which it is used), when used in a semantic coupling such as *dola duka*, glossed as "pregnancy cravings," enables one to move beyond the standard equation of this term with "perverse appetite" to also understand the suffering the woman experiences during this period—"her nausea, vomiting, bodily weakness and the desire for certain objects, which is painful to the individual till satisfied" (Obeyesekere 323).

It is also from this moment of pregnancy that a woman's life is frequently equated with suffering. References to "my mother who bore me for ten months" or "who suffered tenfold and birthed me into this world" invoke the mother's ten-month pregnancy—the ten being poetic license, as it enables the alliteration *dasa* (ten) *masa* (month)—as well as her suffering during labor. Such "conceits," which are mobilized in literary representations as well as formal speech, are also accompanied by other "conceits" that delineate how one's mother fed one her bloodmilk (*le kiri*), cleaned one's bodily wastes (*katha kunu*[7]), saw to one's well-being (*sapa duk*), and nourished one (*lokumahath kala*). I want to especially draw attention to the popular "conceit" *le* (blood) *kiri* (milk)—an evocative word assemblage that concisely articulates the nurturing as well as sacrificial qualities of a mother's milk; it is her blood that is transmogrified into milk. A particularly interesting mobilization of this "conceit" was visible in a poster promoting breastfeeding that was issued by the Ministry of Women's Affairs. The poster, which was displayed during the height of one of the first major government offensives against the Tamil militants in the north, in 1986 and 1987, depicted a woman dressed in cloth and jacket—a marker of Sinhalaness—breastfeeding her baby while dreaming of a man in army fatigues. The caption below exhorted: "Give your bloodmilk [*le kiri*] to nourish our future soldiers."[8]

I would like to digress briefly to qualify my use of "conceit" as an "elaborated or exaggerated metaphor."[9] It is a form of speech that is particularly well located within another term that I invoke here: "discourse." As Abu-Lughod and Lutz point out, the term "discourse" not only marks "an approach to language that is spoken and used," but it also suggests a concern with verbal productions that are "more formal, elaborate or artistic than everyday conversation" (7). While some linguists have broadened the term to encompass the nonverbal, such as music or weeping, or the "'unsaid'" of past utterances and present imaginings (Tyler qtd. in Abu-Lughod and Lutz 7), it is Foucault's systematic theorization of the term that has defined it as being productive of as well as a product of power. Discourses, notes Foucault, are the "practices that systematically form the objects of which they speak" (*Archaeology* 49). It is these varied senses and meanings of "discourse" that I will mobilize throughout this chapter.

Thus far I have discussed the "conceits" that are associated with the labor of "motherhood," such as pregnancy, birthing, and breastfeeding. I want to turn now to a "conceit"—*unu kandulu* (warm tears)—that has a more generalized usage but is also frequently produced as the most visible and tangible embodiment of a mother's suffering; the warmth of the tears suggests that they have been wrung out of her body and still retain her body heat:

> When her son Gemunu went to battle
> The venerable queen did not shed tears
> I cannot do likewise my son
> For warm tears [*unu kandulu*] are cascading down my face
>   (*Birinda*, 25 Oct. 1993; my translation)

In this verse (excerpted from a longer poem published in a women's magazine), a mother addresses her son who is at the battlefront. She poignantly affirms her humanity as well as her despair by the warm tears that she cannot stem, unlike the legendary queen Vihara Maha Devi. However, in the second verse the mother shows that she is more than a match for the queen in her patriotism, for she goes on to exhort her son not to lay down his rifle even in death and promises to send his younger brother to take his place. The mother's fervent militarism and patriotism is subtly feminized by her tears, the sign of her sacrifice and suffering.[10]

What I found most significant, however, is how the reportage on the Mothers' Front resignified women's tears as specifically maternal through their reiteration within a previously maternalized continuum of blood and milk. For example, a Sinhala newspaper carrying a photograph of a group of weeping women at a Mothers' Front rally bears the riveting caption: "Blood . . . milk and tears" (*Lakdiva*, 28 June 1992).[11] Similarly, a two-page feature on the Mothers' Front rally, by the well-known activist and journalist Sunanda Deshapriya, begins by stressing the nurturing and sacrificial qualities of tears. Modifying a phrase by Maxim Gorky, Deshapriya asserts that "to create and sustain this world, one not only requires a mother's milk and sunshine but her tears as well" (*Yukthiya*, 5 June 1992).[12] Thus the suffering produced through labor becomes linked to suffering produced through loss.[13] The production of tears as such a complex and concatenated bodily fluid, as an essence of "motherhood," proved to be one of the most powerful forms of "body speech"[14] that was mobilized in the public(ized) practices of the Mothers' Front and the discourses they engendered.

Sentimentalizing Maternity

An exploration of how suffering is discursively maternalized also necessitates an understanding of its reception, its effect. One could make the argument that the "conceits" I have discussed merely contribute to trivializing and making clichéd the deep emotions that are meant to be conveyed. However, I propose that they can be read as engendering an even greater empathy and affect because of their very familiarity. They have become a shorthand, a concise and efficient way of expressing as well as evoking a particular sentiment among those who understand the Sinhala language. "Conceits" such as *le kiri* or *unu kandulu* enable the writer to express specific sentiments about Sinhala motherhood that immediately evoke a similar sentiment in the reader for they now share a similar language—of verbal allusions as well as of refined emotion. It is this sharing, this commonality, that lends depth and poignancy to the feelings expressed and evoked.

"Formulaic language," as Abu-Lughod has noted, "allows individuals to frame their experiences as similar to those of others and perhaps to assert the universality of their experiences" (*Veiled* 239). While Abu-Lughod reads this assertion of universality as a search for a "semblance of social conformity" in a context where the poetic sentiments that are uttered are in marked contrast to everyday discourses and in violation of the moral code of the Awlad 'Ali (239), I perceive it as an index of the hegemony of a particularly Sinhala, Buddhist, and patriarchal discourse. Unlike in the poetry of the Awlad 'Ali, the "conceits" used and consequently the sentiments expressed in and evoked through Sinhala poetry are also utilized in prose and some forms of everyday discourse such as public speeches, posters, and news reports. They are part of a broader system of emotional expression that is effectively disseminated and learned *via* a variety of Ideological State Apparatuses such as the school or the family (Althusser).[15]

I also wish to argue that "conceits" engender a certain restraint and refinement of feeling because they have been codified and made formulaic, even though the language of the "conceit" itself may be rather exaggerated and effusive. Such restraint and refinement are also hallmarks of "sentiment," as suggested in the following dictionary definitions: "3. Refined or tender emotion; manifestation of the higher or more refined feelings. 4. exhibition or manifestation of feeling or sensibility, or appeal to the tender emotions, in literature, art or music. 5. a thought influenced by or proceeding from feeling or emotion. 6. the thought or feeling intended to be conveyed by words, acts, or gestures as distinguished from the words, acts, or gestures themselves."[16] "Sentiment" not only has multiple meanings, but its meaning has been transformed over the centuries so that it is now chiefly used derisively to convey "an imputation of either insincerity or mawkishness."[17] However, I wish to reclaim the notion of sentiment as both refined and restrained, as that "delicacy of feeling" that was crucial to the progress of civilization (Elias 94, 462–64) and at the heart of the "revolution in the scientific approach to the study of man [sic]" in eighteenth-century Europe (Brissenden 37).[18] It was such "nuances of civilized conduct" (Elias 464) and "fortifications for the self" (Gay 458) that were central to the development of the modern subject, whose interiority and individualism were signaled by his or her ability to discover "the truth of their being" through the cultivation of their emotions (Foucault, *History* 5).[19]

What can these specifically located arguments about eighteenth-century Europe tell us about the production of sentiment in Sri Lanka? I would like to recall my argument (de Alwis, "Production" and *Maternalist Protest*) regarding how a particular notion of "respectability" was remade in the articulatory encounter between Protestant missionaries and Sinhala Buddhist nationalists in nineteenth-century Ceylon. The missionary encounter had a similarly profound effect upon the production of affect in Sri Lanka. The cultivation of "respectability" was inextricably tied to the cultivation of "sentiment"; to be "respectable" implied that one was in control of one's emotions, that one was restrained and refined. An exemplar of such "respectable" womanhood was the American missionary Harriet Winslow, who always sought to be "moderate in all things" (397). Interestingly, however, what could not be fully reconciled within this schema of restraint was the public display of tears and copious weeping, for they were frequently perceived to be the only visible signs of Christian conviction and feeling among the heathen, be they men or women.[20] Harriet Winslow describes a "time of feeling and of triumph" when a recently converted schoolmaster at Uduvil (in northern Sri Lanka)—who had once been "awakened" but then dissuaded by his friends—led a group of schoolmasters in prayer, his utterances "several times checked by weeping" (234).[21] Similarly, she notes with satisfaction how greatly "overcome" several native girls were to hear about their kind benefactors in America whose only recompense was their conversion (206). It was events such as these that Harriet Winslow and her husband found most "affecting to see" (357). As she noted during her youthful struggles with her faith: "'Oh that my head were waters, and mine eyes a fountain of tears,' I would weep day and night, for my sins"

(17). The female missionary's propensity for such emotional expressions was not uncommon in the age of feminized religion and sentimental (i.e., mawkish) literature (Douglas). But even such displays were rarely exhibited in public and only confessed to in diaries and letters to close friends (Winslow 15, 17). In time, even the public(ized) tears of the more elite heathens—the last vestiges of their unbridled passion—were to be carefully checked and controlled in the mission schools; emotional restraint and refinement would become one of the defining characteristics of the bourgeois Sri Lankan woman.

The production of bourgeois Sri Lankan women as the epitomes of restraint and "respectability" was also dependent upon the construction of peasant and working-class women as their antitheses; the latter group was frequently portrayed as being ignorant, "unrespectable," and given to the display of wild passions.[22] What is particularly ironic is that the excessive exhibition of sentiment—that is, sentimentality in its present usage as being "Addicted to indulgence in emotion"[23]—is nevertheless imbricated in the articulation of Sri Lankan, especially Sinhala, notions of civility, refinement, and humanity. It is the maternalization of suffering and sentimentality that effects such a dialectic epitomized in the journalist Kumaradasa Giribawa's comment in a feature article on the Mothers' Front: "Tears . . . are common to all. Yet, there is nothing more powerful on earth that can wring tears from others than a mother's tears" (*Irida Lankadeepa*, 28 June 1992). Note the dual labor of tears here—they produce and signify sentiment. The colloquial description of a civilized being— "one who has a mind and a heart" (*hithak papuvak aththek*)—also encompasses such an exhibition of sentiment within the rubric of "humanism" (*miniskama*), which insists that the heart should inform the mind and vice versa. It is this conception of sentiment, as reasonable feeling (Brissenden 54), that is also evoked in the journalist Sunanda Deshapriya's observation that tears are the best indicators of one's humanity as they show one's ability to feel love (*adaraya, snehaya*) and compassion (*dayava*) (*Yukthiya* 5 July 1992).

I have explored so far how tears—a tangible signifier of suffering—have been maternalized and sentimentalized through their discursive production as a bodily essence of motherhood. Such tears were also productive of tears in others and thus provide a tangible signifier of the reception of maternalized tears as well. Tears can thus be configured as signifying the suffering of labor and loss, on the one hand, and sentiment and humanism, on the other hand. This dual configuration of tears is premised on different readings of gendered and classed Sinhala bodies that span the "natural" and the "civilized"; the more "civilized" one is, the more apt one is to restrain and refine one's embodied expressions. What remains constant, however, is the ultimate "facticity" of the body that provides a particular authenticity to its productions, in this case tears. Such a conception is given further credence by the popular Sinhala belief that one does not shed tears if one is feigning grief.

In such a context, I have been particularly interested in understanding the discursive construction of proletarian maternity as both essence and excess, as evoking sentiment as well as exhibiting sentimentality. While much of this section has been taken up with considering the former formulation, spatial restrictions preclude an extended discussion of how working-class and peasant Sinhala women have been constructed as the practitioners of sentimentality and how these women mobilize such identities of excess to their advantage (see de Alwis, *Maternalist Protest*). However, I hope to briefly pursue this trajectory of inquiry in the next section, with reference to particular practices of the Mothers' Front and certain discourses they engendered.

Producing "Authenticity"

The Mothers' Front stated clearly from the outset that they were not a political movement and frequently stressed the fact that they were neither feminists nor antigovernment. Their central demand was for a climate in which they could return to being mothers and wives and lead "normal women's lives." The fact that such an assertion of apoliticality could retain any credibility in the face of their intimate association with the Sri Lanka Freedom Party (SLFP), the opposition political party that was the primary funder and coordinator of the group, as well as have an emotional purchase was due to the public performance of maternal(ized) suffering by the members of the Mothers' Front. In fact, I would say, this is a performance of suffering in order to retain the specificity of a form of violence such as "disappearances" and the kind of suffering it engenders. My use of "performance" is not meant to suggest that these women were calculatedly staging a show of suffering but rather that when they wept and wailed at the public rallies and conventions that were organized by the SLFP, they were performing their gender as mothers and, more particularly, as suffering mothers. As Judith Butler has argued, gender is performative in the sense that it produces, retroactively, the illusion that there is an inner gender core, essence, or disposition. Such an illusion is enabled by acts, gestures, and enactments that express essences or identities that are "*fabrications* manufactured and sustained through corporeal signs and other discursive means" (Butler 136). In short, the gendered body that is performed "has no ontological status apart from the various acts which constitute its reality" (136).

The performance of maternity and suffering by the Mothers' Front was crucially sustained through "corporeal signs" (136), which I prefer to refer to as "body speech" (Schirmer, "Claiming" 189). The "language of the body," as Bourdieu has pointed out, "whether articulated in gestures or *a fortiori,* in what psychosomatic medicine calls 'the language of the organs' is incomparably more ambiguous and more overdetermined than the most overdetermined uses of ordinary language" (120). Such an overdetermination also stems from the notion that the body, perceived to be one of nature's most supreme creations, is "above suspicion" (Daston 244);[24] it is the most persuasive site of evidence. In the same way that a body under torture is considered to possess an "'absolute credibility'" because of its operation under constraint (Aristotle qtd. in Schirmer, "Dilemma" 98), the traumatized body of the woman is perceived not only to bespeak the "real" and the "authentic" but to bear witness (Das and Nandy 193).[25]

I discussed above how public discourses produced tears as the most potent "body speech" of maternalized suffering, and how this articulation of a concatenated maternal essence, which signifies both labor and loss, was crucial to engendering popular sentiment. I want to extend that discussion now by exploring how such a dialectic between maternalized suffering and sentiment—both axes, importantly, being articulated by tears—furthered the credibility and "authenticity" of the Mothers' Front's protests. Such credibility is especially embedded in the traumatized body, and I will briefly discuss a particular aspect of such an articulation.

For members of the Front (as well as their relatives) the physical transformations of their bodies were important markers of their love and sorrow for their "disappeared." For example, Seela's husband would often show me a photograph that had been taken of her prior to her son's "disappearance" and remark on how plump and fair this now dark, wraith-like woman had been. Not only had Seela lost a great deal of weight, but she frequently suffered from blackouts. While her family fretted about her health and safety, Seela seemed to welcome these moments of amnesia because she was convinced that these were the times she was communing with her "disappeared" son, wherever he was incarcerated.[26] It seemed that in her efforts to alleviate her son's suffering, Seela believed that she must submit to pain herself: "I get these terrible headaches when I regain consciousness. I think that's when my son has given some of his pain to me. If I take on some of his pain, then his pain will get less . . . no ?" Trauma counselors who have tried to work with Seela have categorized such forms of behavior as psychosomatism—the experiencing of bodily symptoms as the result of mental conflict.[27] Many symptoms that were exhibited by other members of the Front are also included within this category—dizziness, insomnia, loss of appetite, stomach cramps, shortness of breath, and chest pains.[28]

However, women like Seela have scant regard for the medicalization of what they have now taken to be a way of life. They have their own terms for the suffering that they undergo, which once again is articulated through familiar Sinhala "conceits": *Mama kandulu bibi inne* or *Mama inne andu kandulen*. These two very evocative "conceits" defy translation—a distant approximation would be "I am existing by drinking tears" and "I am in a constant state of tears." Journalists and politicians also often mobilized these "conceits" to describe the mental and physical state of the Front's members, such as Sunanda Deshapriya's further complication of one "conceit": *Handukandulin thetha baritha sithin* (with minds soaked in the tears constantly shed) (*Yukthiya*, 5 July 1997). Unlike in a situation of death (particularly when the corpse is available to the family), where funerary rites provide order as well as closure, a situation of "disappearance" draws out the process of mourning indefinitely and makes "chronic mourners" (Schirmer, "Those Who Die" 25) of the grief-stricken.[29] It is this chronicness of grief that is so poignantly captured by these "conceits"; these women's lives have become so tightly intertwined with tears that they simultaneously produce tears while deriving sustenance from them.

These "conceits" also illuminate the complicated interplay between discursivity and materiality. They are useful and concise word assemblages that are mobilized by the members of the Front to describe a very specific and concrete reality of their lives. Yet we cannot ignore the fact that these "conceits" are drawn from a hegemonic discursive tradition that is both Sinhala Buddhist and patriarchal. Such a tradition constructs its own kind of materiality and reality. As Joan Scott has reminded us, what counts as experience is "neither self-evident nor straightforward" but always contested and thus always political ("Evidence" 387). In the following section, I will analyze the political purchase of certain discourses about the Mothers' Front that contributed to the construction of a particular kind of lived materiality that was articulated in the cadences of suffering and sentiment.

The Political Purchase of Tears

The Mothers' Front was founded, funded, and coordinated by the SLFP, which also organized the few but spectacular public conventions of the Front that were held in the capital city of Colombo during the years 1991 and 1992. These conventions became crucial sites for the shrewd exploitation of the Front's tears by the SLFP, in order to shame the ruling regime and to incite the populace. In their speeches at these conventions, members of the SLFP frequently sought to provoke the tears of the women while simultaneously admonishing them to stop crying and get on with their lives. The SLFP was thus not only funding and organizing the Mothers' Front but also controlling them emotionally; the women were produced as vulnerable, weak, and hysterical. This was an image that was readily circulated by the media as well. An extreme example of this was when a father of a "disappeared" suffered a fatal heart attack at the Front's second convention in 1992, and some news reports sought to connect his death to the tears of the women. One report suggested that the sight of "hundreds of mothers weeping and wailing, some beating their breasts in anguish, supplicating to the Gods in despair" must have been unbearable for the father, despite the fact that the man had actually died before the convention had begun or the women had commenced weeping (*Island*, 2 June 1992; *Yukthiya*, 5 July 1992).

It was also the media's somewhat overwrought but nevertheless consistently sympathetic coverage of the Mothers' Front[30] that was crucial in molding the opinions of its reading public.[31] An editorial comment in the *Island*, claiming that when "mothers emerge as a political force it means that our political institutions and society as a whole have reached a critical moment—the danger to our way of life has surely come closer home" (20 Feb. 1991), crystallized the unease that many felt with the present government.[32] The fact that one of the most sacred cows of the Sinhalese—the sentimentalized and revered mother—was at the butt end of a callous government sparked the ire of many readers who responded with poems and letters to the press. One particularly long and distraught poem that began by commenting on how woman was "feted as mother" the day she "suffered and labored and bore her children," proceeded to detail how a mother's everyday sacrifices and struggles to bring up her sons had come to naught because her "innocent boys who had not yet lost the taste of milk from their mouths" no longer had the safety and warmth of her lap. The mother finally comes to the realization that her sons have been murdered and set on fire (a common occurrence during the years of the JVP uprising); with the burning of her sons' bodies, the pedestal on which she has been placed as well as the institution of "motherhood" goes up in flames. The poem ends with the despairing cry: "Mother . . . is it she who is the only cursed woman on earth?" (Damayanthi Amerasekere, *Irida Divaina*, 5 Apr. 1992; my translation). I find this poem particularly interesting because despite the fact that it provides a critique of the valorization of "motherhood" (though such a critique is closely intertwined with a criticism of the government[33]), it cannot avoid the standard "conceits" of the Sinhala language that evoke sentiments that are central to promoting and sustaining such a valorization.

However, signs of weakness, epitomized by the women's tears, could only be gently chastised in public, for there was a common understanding that the

Front's members had suffered greatly, that "one could not impose limits on the tears that poured forth from a mother on behalf of her child" (Sunanda Deshapriya, *Yukthiya*, 5 July 1992). The Front's tears thus could be fitted into an already familiar structure of sentiment that valorized a mother's capacity for suffering while also tolerating and pitying the "sympathetic sensibility of her organism" that "condemned" her to tears (Foucault, *Madness* 153–54). In fact, what rendered such tears particularly poignant and authentic was the excessive and spectacular way they were shed. News reports and features were particularly effusive in their detailed delineation of such "body speech": the mothers' tears poured forth in torrents (*Irida Lankadeepa,* 28 June 1992), they wept and wailed and beat their breasts (*Island,* 2 June 1992), they tore their hair and struck their heads against the earth (*Divaina,* 6 July 1992), they washed the meeting hall with their tears (*Lakdiva,* 28 June 1992), and their garlands of sighs encircled the entire island (*Yukthiya,* 5 July 1992). Even more powerful and moving than all these verbal illustrations were the numerous photographs of weeping women that accompanied the articles; they most certainly gave credence to the cliché that one picture was worth a thousand words.

Such excessiveness and abandon was particularly noticeable when juxta-posed against the way that the few middle-class women who were present dis-played their emotion. When Dr. Manorani Saravanamuttu, the president of the Mothers' Front, and several SLFP politicians such as Chandrika Kumara-tunga, Hema Ratnayake, and Priyangani Abeydeera (who had lost sons, hus-bands, and/or fathers) addressed the meeting, their somber voices did falter and quiver, they constantly choked back tears and frequently dabbed at their eyes, but they always managed to retain their composure and keep their emo-tions in check; Dr. Saravanamuttu and Ms. Kumaratunga were particularly emphatic: "We have cried enough. I am not saying that we should cry no more . . . but we have to move beyond that."[34] This hierarchical configuration of emotional control was of course topped by the father of a teenaged school-boy "disappeared" from the Embilipitiya region who, as Sunanda Deshapriya was quick to note, "did not weep" when he addressed the second National Convention of the Mothers' Front (*Yukthiya* 5 July 1992).

What I find most interesting is that although the members of the Front were represented as weak and hysterical or as the puppets of the SLFP (a frequent charge by the government), their credibility as suffering mothers was un-scathed. A frequent refrain that was taken up by the general populace as well as the media was that these women should not be sullied by politics, an opin-ion exemplified in the subtitle of Giribawa's feature article on the Front: "Mothers' Tears Don't Need Politics" (*Irida Lankadeepa,* 28 June 1992). How-ever, it was the very apoliticality of a symbolic essence of maternity such as tears that proved to be most useful politically. This is particularly clear when we consider how the state responded to the Front in terms of rhetoric as well as practices.

Contesting Tears

As in the case of the Madres of Argentina or the GAM (Mutual Support Group for the Reappearance of Our Sons, Fathers, Husbands, and Brothers) of Guatemala, the rhetoric of protest used by the Mother's Front can also be read as confronting a repressive state by revealing the contradictions between the state's own rhetoric and practices. By appealing for a return to the "natural" order of family and "motherhood," these women were openly embracing patriarchal stereotypes that primarily defined them through familial/domestic subject positions such as wife and mother. However, by accepting this responsibility to nurture and preserve life, which is also valorized by the state, they revealed the ultimate transgression of the state as well, for it was denying women the opportunities for mothering through a refusal to acknowledge life by resorting to clandestine tactics of "disappearance" (Schirmer, "Those Who Die" 28).

The Sri Lankan state's major rhetorical counter to such implicit accusations is very interesting. On the day the Mothers' Front organized their first rally in Colombo, President Premadasa acknowledged that he sympathized "with the mothers whose children have been *led astray* by designing elements. Many now in custody are being *rehabilitated*" (*Daily News*, 19 Feb. 1991; emphasis added). In a similar vein, Ranjan Wijeratne, the minister of state for defense, pontificated: "Mothers are not expected to stage demonstrations. Mothers should have looked after their children. They failed to do that. They did not know what their children were doing. They did not do that and now they are crying" (*Daily News*, 15 Feb. 1991). In both statements there is an overt suggestion that these protesting women have not been "good" and "capable" mothers, but the president's statement goes one further and suggests that because of their "bad" mothering he has had to take on the responsibility of "motherhood." In other words, these women should have no reason to protest but rather should be grateful to him and to his government for rectifying the wrongs they have committed through the "rehabilitation" of their children. Through the use of euphemisms such as "rehabilitation," the president also carefully circumvented accusations of the state's complicity in "disappearances" and arbitrary killings.

What is unmistakable in the government's responses, however, is that it dared not dispute or disparage the "authenticity" and depth of the women's suffering. What the government sought to do instead was organize its own rallies of grieving women, thus contesting the Front on its own terrain. For example, when the Front organized a rally in Colombo to commemorate International Women's Day on 8 March 1991, the state, under the aegis of the first lady, Hema Premadasa, and with the support of the national women's group she headed—the Seva Vanitha Movement[35]—organized a massive women's rally on that same day in another part of the city. This rally was especially dominated by the Seva Vanitha units affiliated with the armed forces and far exceeded in numbers those present at the Front's rally. While the Mothers' Front mourned the "disappearances" of their male relatives due to state repression, the state-organized women's rally mourned the deaths of their male kin who had been killed by militants either in the south or the north and east of Sri Lanka. The state-owned *Daily News* (9 Mar. 1991) carried an entire page of photographs from the state-organized rally, while no mention was made of the Mothers' Front rally.

Conclusion

The central concern of this chapter has been to understand the emotional purchase of the Mothers' Front, which I suggest was primarily premised on the discursive construction of the Front's members as grieving and suffering mothers. Such a construction was particularly enabled through the articulation of embodied signifiers of suffering—such as tears—which are maternalized and sentimentalized within Sinhala society. This "language of the organs" was especially persuasive and credible when located within the traumatized and maternalized female body; it provided the Mothers' Front with a particular authenticity that even its critics, such as the state, could not (and maybe dared not) dispute.

The political effectivity of the Mothers' Front must be understood as being predicated on the reiteration of patriarchal and Sinhala Buddhist conceptions of maternalized suffering and sentiment. However, it is also important to realize that at a time when other, more familiar and predictable voices of dissent had been silenced, it was the maternalist politics of the Mothers' Front that proved to be most effective. It is for this reason that I have argued elsewhere (de Alwis, "Motherhood" and *Maternalist Protest*) for a contingent reading of the Mothers' Front's protests. William Connolly, in his multifaceted characterization of contingency, has called attention to the variable, uncertain, unexpected, and irregular potentiality of this concept (28). My positing of the efficacy of the Mothers' Front as contingent is premised on the variable and unexpected possibilities that are presented by this concept. However, such a political as well as theoretical position does not preclude the retention of a critical voice and vision that calls attention to the limitations of maternalist politics and understands the importance of striving for less limited formulations of political protest in the future.

Notes

I am greatly indebted to Dipesh Chakrabarty, Jean Comaroff, Wendy Hesford, Wendy Kozol, and especially Pradeep Jeganathan for their incisive comments and useful suggestions on an earlier version of this chapter.

1. For an extended discussion of emotion as a cultural category see Lutz; and for a somewhat dated overview of the literature on the anthropology of emotions, see Lutz and White.

2. For a sampling of this extensive literature see the pioneering work of Ehrenreich and English; Jordanova "Natural Facts" and *Sexual Visions;* Lloyd; Showalter; Smith; Smith-Rosenberg, "Hysterical" and "Cycle"; and Wood. See Veith for a useful historicization of hysteria. For a discussion of some of these psychological states within a broader civilizational framework, see Foucault, *Madness.*

3. Radden makes a crucial differentiation between the earlier, romanticized notion of melancholia that was predominantly associated with men and modern, medicalized discourses on melancholia that are primarily focused on women and define them as deviant and deficient.

4. Mohanty has a pithy phrase for this: the "feminist osmosis thesis." It succinctly describes a phenomenon where "females are feminists by association and identification with the experiences which constitute [them] as female" ("Feminist" 32). See also Mohanty, "Under Western Eyes," for a critique of 1970s feminists such as Robin Morgan and Mary Daly who presume "experience" to be a transcendent category that unites all women across the globe. Similar important contributions have been made by King, who questions the use of lesbianism "as a privileged signifier" (85) and Riley, who offers an extended critique of the category "woman," which is centrally premised on women's experiences.

5. Scott's article, "Experience," is an abridged version of "The Evidence of Experience." I will be referring to both versions.

6. The Sinhalese are the majority community in Sri Lanka, making up about 74 percent of the population. The largest minority, the Tamils, make up about 18 percent of the population, followed by the Muslims—Moors and Malays—who comprise 7 percent, the Burghers—descendents of the Portuguese and Dutch colonists—and other Eurasians (0.8 percent).

7. *Katha kunu* is a phrase used in the popular construction of the Buddha biography to describe the bodily wastes that had been expended by female dancers in the palace during their sleep. This was a sight that revolted Prince Siddhartha and added to his resolve to renounce his "worldly" life. (I am grateful to Pradeep Jeganathan for this reference.) Note how Siddhartha's revulsion is linked to women's bodies here; it

is a formulation that is repeated in other episodes of his biography. Similar moralistic ploys are mobilized in the narratives of other religions as well, the Christian construction of Eve being the most familiar.

8. See de Alwis, "Towards a Feminist Historiography," for a location of this image within Sinhala nationalist and militarist discourses.

9. *The American Heritage Dictionary*, second college edition, s.v. "conceit."

10. For a discussion of the production of sacrifice and suffering as the chief requirements of female citizenship, see de Alwis, "Paternal States" and *Maternalist Protest*.

11. Revolutionary slogans have frequently sought to disrupt this continuum between blood and tears, however, by relegating tears to the sphere of weakness and blood to the sphere of action. For example, when a student activist at the University of Sri Jayawardenapura was killed by state troops in 1987, the JVP (a Sinhala nationalist youth movement), which was in the process of regrouping at this time, chanted the following slogan during the funeral procession: *Epa epa kandulu bonne / Le valinma paliya ganne* (Don't, don't drink tears / Extract your revenge in blood alone). Nevertheless, there have been moments when revolutionaries have found it useful to reiterate such a continuum as well. The poetry of Parakrama Kodituvakku, for example, creates the new "conceit" of "milk droplet" (*kiri kandula*—literally translated as "milk teardrop") to symbolize the rights of the masses (Maddegama 57–58). The combination of milk and tears successfully tinges the milky promise of nurture and fecundity with a suggestion of suffering and sadness. In a poem that is a clever reworking of a familiar lullaby, Kodituvakku urges the little child to seek this "droplet of milk" contained in the milking pot (which has gotten carried away by the river) that his mother has labored to collect for him and was planning to feed to him while bouncing him upon her bosom (*lamada*): "Along the river and like the never-ending river seek / Crossing smouldering deserts scour / Dodging rifles and menacing swords speed / With the milk droplet you lost on the day of your birth return" (Kodituvakku, "Gangata Udin Yakku Giya . . . !"; my translation). The mother here represents the motherland. By not having her nursing her own child (which does not fit in with the lullaby that Kodituvakku evokes), the poet manages to accentuate the labor of the mother (who has to milk the cow) by de-linking it from the more naturalized labor of breastfeeding. However, the mother continues to be portrayed as the repository of nurture, vulnerability, and dependence and thus becomes the predictable catalyst for her child/citizen's agency.

12. Deshapriya had been the recipient of such nurturance and sacrifice himself; during his imprisonment of six and a half years (for participating in a youth uprising in 1971), his mother visited him every month without fail, "carefully concealing her despair and offering words of comfort and encouragement" (*Yukthiya* 5 July 1992).

13. I am indebted to Lauren Berlant for this evocative formulation.

14. This is a term used by Schirmer ("Claiming" 189) to describe women's resistive bodily practices within public spaces. I have mobilized it differently here to suggest the communicative potentiality of tears.

15. A similar production and dissemination of sentiment by an institution of the

state, along with the support of florists in particular, is discussed in Hausen's carefully argued essay on the creation of German Mother's Day during the 1920s in order to
stem a decline in femininity and motherliness and engender a "moral rebirth" among
the German *Volk* (387). See also Johnson for a less rigorous but nevertheless interesting analysis of the production of an American Mother's Day in 1914.

16. *Random House Dictionary of the English Language*, s.v. "sentiment." For an extremely nuanced and located discussion of "sentiment" and its related terms, "sentimental," "sense," "sensibility," "feeling," and "sympathy," see "'Sentimentalism': An
Attempt at Definition," in Brissenden. For an interesting argument that seeks to posit
a distinction between "sentiment" (as innately moral) and "sensibility" (as a psycho-
logical-physical response), see "The Moral Sentiments" in Kaplan.

17. *Oxford English Dictionary*, 1989 ed., s.v. "sentiment." The nuances of "sentiment"
(both in its earlier and later meanings) were exemplified during the lead-up to Prin-
cess Diana's funeral. The royal family, struggling to uphold court etiquette from the
seventeenth century, was roundly chastised for their restraint by an emotional British
populace who perceived it as a display of indifference. This was also a moment when
the American press could trumpet that the British were after all human (i.e., like
Americans) because they "understand in a way they never have the importance of
emotion" (*New York Times*, 7 Sept. 1997). For a discussion of a "national melancholy"
in the United States see "The Year Emotions Ruled," *Time*, 22 Dec. 1997, 46–48.

18. Brissenden is referring to the paradigmatic influence of British philosophers such
as David Hume, author of *Treatise of Human Nature* (1739), and Adam Smith, author
of *The Theory of Moral Sentiments* (1759), whose work was based on the study of sentiment. For an excellent discussion of the differences between the work of Hume and
Smith with regard to sentiment and sympathy, see "Sympathy and the Production of
Society" in Mullen. For an analysis of how such ideas were perceived and transformed
in the writings of Victorian novelists, see Kaplan.

19. Foucault is speaking specifically about desire here, but I think his insights are
useful for understanding the cultivation of emotions in general as well, a point also
made by Abu-Lughod and Lutz (6). Chakrabarty employs a similar trajectory of rea-
soning to make a different point about the production of Bengali subjectivity and sentiment (14). See also Sontag for a discussion of how sickness and suffering was perceived to make men "interesting" and was thus proclaimed as a mark of individuality
and refinement by nineteenth-century romantics.

20. The writings of European Protestants in South Africa display a similar tension
between their excitement at the sight of the Gospel melting the "'flinty hearts'" of the
heathen and their "'endeavors to preserve decorum'" when the strong feelings of the
southern Tswana (at the baptism of the first converts) gave rise "'to much weeping and
considerable confusion'"; "'Sable cheeks'" became "'bedewed with tears,'" and the
chapel turned into "'a place of weeping'" where some would "'fall down in hyster-
ics'" and others would have to be carried out in "'a state of great exhaustion'" (qtd.
in Comaroff and Comaroff 239). As Comaroff and Comaroff point out, emotional-

ism was not only regarded with great ambivalence by British Nonconformists, but the display of such vehemence and lack of control was perceived as especially troubling "in those but one step away from nature" (239).

21. See also Leitch and Leitch for a description of an emotion-filled "revival meeting" in northern Sri Lanka, where people "with tears running down their cheeks" and voices "choked with emotion" prayed that their friends "be brought to Christ" (8).

22. Note how the nineteenth-century colonial/missionary view of Ceylonese natives has been mobilized to describe only a particular segment of the population. For further discussion of this point, see de Alwis, *Maternalist Protest.*

23. *Oxford English Dictionary,* 1989 ed., s.v. "sentimentality."

24. I am referring here to the popular notion that nature (and thus the human body) is devoid of human intention. As Daston points out, what is implicit in the conventional distinction between facts and evidence is that for "facts to qualify as credible evidence they must appear innocent of human intention" (244; see also Lutz). Such a distinction between facts and evidence is strongly contested and debated among historians of science, an argument that Daston herself is not interested in pursuing, as she is more concerned with exploring and historicizing how such an assumption was produced.

25. It is important to differentiate between the kind of violence "witnessed" by the bodies of the women Das and Nandy refer to and those of the Front's members. The majority of the former group of women had been repeatedly raped and abused as well.

26. The majority of the Front members refused to accept the possibility that their son or husband was dead.

27. For an excellent discussion of the intersection of somatic pain and psychological pain that is constitutive of traumatic memory and stress disorders, see Young, *Harmony* and "Suffering."

28. I am grateful to the trauma counselor (who wishes to remain anonymous) who discussed the provenance and treatment of such symptoms with me. For a Piercian analysis of similar symptoms in survivors of torture as well as survivors of the anti-Tamil riots of 1983 in Sri Lanka, see Daniel, chaps. 5 and 7. For a consideration of "numbing" in a female survivor of anti-Sikh riots, see Das, "Our Work." For an exploration of "silencing" and the public articulation of suffering via an incurable wound as well as through "fits" among female survivors of Partition, see Das, "Composition."

29. Ironically, this is also what spurred the women's stubborn refusal to give up hope; the "absence of bodies," notes Schirmer, creates a "presence of protest" ("Those Who Die" 5).

30. Coverage of the Mothers' Front was generally sympathetic except for the newspapers that were owned by the ruling party and those that were under the authority of the state; the two major TV stations that were authorized to cover local news events during this time were also under the jurisdiction of the state.

31. The ability of the media to manipulate the sentiments of a gullible audience could not have been better "exposed" or satirized than in Barry Levinson's movie *Wag the Dog* (1997).

32. When several mass graves were discovered and excavated in various parts of the island in 1994, the ruling party's reputation for barbarism and tyranny was concretized.

33. I am grateful to Wendy Kozol and Wendy Hesford for pointing this out to me.

34. Excerpt from the speech of Ms. Kumaratunga made on 23 June 1992, author's notes.

35. It was mandatory for all wives of government officials as well as all female government officials to be members of this national social service organization, which replicated the hierarchical structures of government in that the president's wife was the leader, the cabinet ministers' wives or female cabinet ministers were her deputies, and so on.

Works Cited

Abu-Lughod, Lila. *Veiled Sentiments: Honor and Poetry in a Bedouin Society.* Berkeley: University of California Press, 1986.

Abu-Lughod, Lila, and Catherine Lutz. "Introduction: Emotion, Discourse, and the Politics of Everyday Life." In *Language and the Politics of Emotion.* Ed. Catherine Lutz and Lila Abu-Lughod. Cambridge: Cambridge University Press, 1990. 1–23.

Althusser, Louis. *Lenin and Philosophy and Other Essays.* London: New Left Books, 1971.

Bourdieu, Pierre. *Towards a Theory of Practice.* Oxford: Oxford University Press, 1977.

Brissenden, R. F. *Virtue in Distress: Studies in the Novel of Sentiment from Richardson to Sade.* London: Macmillan, 1974.

Butler, Judith. *Gender Trouble: Feminism and the Subversion of Identity.* New York: Routledge, 1990.

Chakrabarty, Dipesh. "Domestic Cruelty and the Birth of the Modern Subject: A Conceptual History of Sentiments in Colonial Bengal." Manuscript in author's possession.

Comaroff, Jean, and John L. Comaroff. *Of Revelation and Revolution: Christianity, Colonialism, and Consciousness in South Africa.* Vol. 1. Chicago: University of Chicago Press, 1991.

Connolly, William E. *Identity/Difference: Democratic Negotiations of Political Paradox.* Ithaca, N.Y.: Cornell University Press, 1991.

Daniel, E. Valentine. *Charred Lullabies: Chapters in an Anthropography of Violence.* Princeton, N.J.: Princeton University Press, 1996.

Das, Veena. "Composition and the Personal Voice: Violence and Migration." *Studies in History* 7.1 (1991): 65–77.

———. "Our Work to Cry: Your Work to Listen." In *Mirrors of Violence: Communities, Riots, and Survivors in South Asia.* Ed. Veena Das. Delhi: Oxford University Press, 1990. 345–98.

Das, Veena, and Ashis Nandy. "Violence, Victimhood, and the Language of Silence." *Contributions to Indian Sociology* 19.1 (1985): 177–95.

Daston, Lorraine. "Marvellous Facts and Miraculous Evidence in Early Modern Europe." In *Questions of Evidence: Proof, Practice, and Persuasion across the Disciplines.* Ed. James Chandler, Arnold I. Davidson, and Harry Harootunian. Chicago: University of Chicago Press, 1994. 243–74.

de Alwis, Malathi. *Maternalist Protest in Sri Lanka: A Historical Anthropology of its Conditions of Possibility.* Ph.D. dissertation, University of Chicago, 1998.

———. "Motherhood as a Space of Protest: Women's Political Participation in Contemporary Sri Lanka." In *Appropriating Gender: Women's Activism and the Politicization of Religion in South Asia.* Ed. Patricia Jeffrey and Amrita Basu. London: Routledge, 1997. 185–202.

———. "Paternal States and Baby Brigades: Violence in the Name of the Nation." Paper presented at the Conference on Children and Nationalism. Centre for Child Research. Trondheim, Norway, May 1994.

———. "The Production and Embodiment of Respectability: Gendered Demeanors in Colonial Ceylon." In *Sri Lanka: Collective Identities Revisited.* Vol. 1. Ed. Michael Roberts. Colombo: Marga Institute, 1997. 105–43.

———. "Towards a Feminist Historiography: Reading Gender in the Text of the Nation." In *Introduction to Social Theory.* Ed. Radhika Coomaraswamy and Nira Wickramasinghe. Delhi: Konark Press, 1994. 86–107.

Douglas, Ann. *The Feminization of American Culture.* New York: Avon Books, 1978.

Ehrenreich, Barbara, and Deidre English. *For Her Own Good: 150 Years of the Experts' Advice to Women.* London: Anchor/Doubleday, 1979.

Elias, Norbert. *The Civilizing Process.* 1959. Oxford: Blackwell, 1994.

Foucault, Michel. *The Archaeology of Knowledge.* Trans. Alan Sheridan. London: Tavistock, 1972.

———. *The History of Sexuality: An Introduction.* Vol. 1. Trans. Robert Hurley. New York: Penguin Books, 1981.

———. *Madness and Civilization: A History of Insanity in the Age of Reason.* Trans. Richard Howard. New York: Vintage Books, 1973.

Gay, Peter. *The Education of the Senses.* Oxford: Oxford University Press, 1984.

Grosz, Elizabeth. *Volatile Bodies: Toward a Corporeal Feminism.* Bloomington: Indiana University Press, 1994.

Hausen, Karin. "Mother, Sons, and the Sale of Symbols and Goods: The 'German Mother's Day,' 1923–33." In *Interest and Emotion: Essays on the Study of Family and Kinship.* Ed. Hans Medick and David Warren Sabean. Cambridge: Cambridge University Press, 1986. 371–413.

Jeganathan, Pradeep. *After a Riot: Anthropological Locations of Violence in an Urban Sri Lankan Community.* Ph.D. dissertation, University of Chicago, 1997.

Johnson, J. P. "How Mother Got Her Day." *American Heritage* 31 (Apr./May 1979): 15–21.

Jordanova, Ludmilla. "Natural Facts: A Historical Perspective on Science and Sexuality." In *Nature, Culture, and Gender.* Ed. Carol MacCormack and Marilyn Strathern. Cambridge: Cambridge University Press, 1980. 42–69.

———. *Sexual Visions: Images of Gender in Science and Medicine between the Eighteenth and Twentieth Centuries.* Madison: University of Wisconsin Press, 1989.

Kaplan, Fred. *Sacred Tears: Sentimentality in Victorian Literature.* Princeton, N.J.: Princeton University Press, 1987.

King, Katie. "The Situation of Lesbianism as Feminism's Magical Sign: Contests for Meaning and the U.S. Women's Movement, 1968–1972." *Communication* 9 (1986): 65–91.

Kodituvakku, Parakrama. *Podi Malliye.* Gangodawila: Deepani Shilpin, 1972.

Leitch, Mary, and Margaret Leitch. *Seven Years in Ceylon: Stories of Mission Life.* New York: American Tract Society, 1890.

Lloyd, Genevieve. *The Man of Reason: 'Male' and 'Female' in Western Philosophy.* London: Methuen, 1984.

Lutz, Catherine. "Emotion, Thought, and Estrangement: Emotion as a Cultural Category." *Cultural Anthropology* 1 (1986): 405–36.

Lutz, Catherine, and Geoffrey White. "The Anthropology of Emotions." *Annual Review of Anthropology* 15 (1986): 405–36.

Maddegama, U. P. "Revolutionary Vision in Sinhala Poetry." *Sri Lanka Journal of the Humanities* 5.1–2 (1979): 54–73.

Mohanty, Chandra Talpade. "Feminist Encounters: Locating the Politics of Experience." *Copyright* 1 (1987): 30–44.

———. "Under Western Eyes: Feminist Scholarship and Western Discourses." *Boundary* 2 (1984): 333–59.

Mullen, John. *Sentiment and Sociability: The Language of Feeling in the Eighteenth Century.* Oxford: Clarendon Press, 1988.

Obeyesekere, Gananath. "Pregnancy Cravings (Dola-Duka) in Relation to Social Structure and Personality in a Sinhalese Village." *American Ethnologist* 65.2 (1963): 323–42.

Radden, Jennifer. "Melancholy and Melancholia." In *Pathologies of the Modern Self.* Ed. David Levin. New York: New York University Press, 1987. 231–50.

Riley, Denise. *"Am I That Name?" Feminism and the Category of Women in History.* Minneapolis: University of Minnesota Press, 1988.

Schirmer, Jennifer. "The Claiming of Space and the Body Politic within Nation-Security States: The Plaza de Mayo Madres and the Greenham Common Women." In *Re-mapping Memory: The Politics of Timespace.* Ed. Jonathan Boyarin. Minneapolis: University of Minnesota Press, 1994. 185–200.

———. "The Dilemma of Cultural Diversity and Equivalency in Universal Human Rights Standards." In *Human Rights and Anthropology.* Ed. Theodore E. Downing and Gilbert Kushner. Cambridge, Mass.: Cultural Survival, 1988. 91–106.

———. "Those Who Die for Life Cannot Be Called Dead: Women and Human Rights Protest in Latin America." *Feminist Review* 32 (1989): 3–29.

Scott, Joan. "The Evidence of Experience." In *Questions of Evidence: Proof, Practice, and Persuasion across the Disciplines.* Ed. James Chandler, Arnold I. Davidson, and Harry Harootunian. Chicago: University of Chicago Press, 1994. 363–87.

———. "Experience." In *Feminists Theorize the Political.* Ed. Judith Butler and Joan W. Scott. New York: Routledge, 1992. 22–40.

Showalter, Elaine. *The Female Malady: Women, Madness, and English Culture, 1830–1980.* London: Virago, 1987.

Smith, Hilda. "Gynecology and Ideology in Seventeenth-Century England." In *Liberating Women's History: Theoretical and Critical Essays.* Ed. Berenice A. Carroll. Urbana: University of Illinois Press, 1976. 97–114.

Smith-Rosenberg, Carroll. "The Cycle of Femininity: Puberty and Menopause in Nineteenth-Century America." *Feminist Studies* 1 (1973): 58–72.

———. "The Hysterical Woman: Sex Roles and Role Conflict in Nineteenth-Century America." *Social Research* 39 (1972): 652–78.

Sontag, Susan. *Illness as Metaphor.* New York: Farrar and Straus, 1977.

Veith, Ilza. *Hysteria: The History of a Disease.* Chicago: University of Chicago Press, 1970.

Winslow, Harriet. *A Memoir.* New York: Leavitt, Lord, and Co., 1835.

Wood, Ann. "'The Fashionable Diseases': Women's Complaints and Their Treatment in Nineteenth-Century America." *Journal of Interdisciplinary History* 4 (1973): 25–52.

Young, Allan. *The Harmony of Illusions: Inventing Post-Traumatic Stress Disorder.* Princeton, N.J.: Princeton University Press, 1995.

———. "Suffering and the Origins of Traumatic Memory." *Daedalus* 125.1 (Winter 1996): 245–60.

8

Relocating Citizenship in Photographs of Japanese Americans during World War II

Wendy Kozol

> The evidence which the photographic text may be assumed to represent is already overendowed, overdetermined by other, further, often contradictory meanings, which arise within the intertextuality of all photographic representation as a social practice.
> —Stuart Hall

Stuart Hall's observation that photographic representation is a social practice overdetermined by "often contradictory meanings" exposes the problematic task of reading the fifteen thousand photographs of the forced evacuation of Japanese and Japanese Americans from the west coast during World War II. At first glance these pictures reveal themselves to be government propaganda, for they overwhelmingly depict Japanese American men, women, and children smiling for the camera as they sit in their living rooms, play sports, or perform work-related tasks. The cultural authority of the National Archive, which today houses all of these photographs, foregrounds the images' value to the government's project of historical memory.[1] It is, however, difficult for historians to simply dismiss these pictures, for they are among the only visual record we have of this traumatic event in American history. Initially, no internees were allowed to have cameras (most cameras were confiscated prior to evacuation). Some camp directors later permitted studio photographers to take portraits of weddings, graduations, and other events. There are also several instances of internees who smuggled cameras into the camps.[2] Nevertheless, the internees themselves took relatively few photographs. Thus, a reliance on the government's archive as a visual record of the "real" or "authentic" experience of Japanese Americans keeps reappearing in historical analyses of this event, even by those skeptical of claims that photography provides access to an unmediated reality.

While these images are undeniably overdetermined by government intentions, as Hall reminds us, they also record competing and often contradictory agendas about the citizenship status and social identities of the Japanese Americans. To dismiss these pictures simply as propaganda ignores the self-conscious responses by internees to media representations and political characterizations, responses that attempted to refute racist stereotypes promoted in the national press. Japanese Americans, in other words, did more than pose where they were told to pose.

Most of the essays in this volume examine women's autobiographies and other resistant texts and their attempts to secure claims of an authentic gendered self. One of the crucial contributions of these analyses lies in how they problematize feminists' often urgent desires to find the "real truth" of women's experiences. Alongside these projects, however, feminists need to explore the centrality of dominant discourses in claims of authenticity and agency. Feminist historians and cultural critics (e.g. Mohanty; Parker et al.) concerned with how gender is embedded in the practices of political, economic, and social formations of nationhood offer theoretical and historical evidence for how dominant discourses aid or limit efforts to secure "authentic" identities. As we know, acts of resistance are always caught in a troubling dialogic relationship with hegemonic forces.

In the case of the Japanese Americans, the project of making visible the lives of those silenced in dominant narratives of World War II involves problematizing triumphal national narratives. Doing so, however, necessitates going beyond a project of uninterrogated recovery. One tradition in feminist historiography has been the impulse to make visible the lives of women silenced in the historical record by recovering their texts and their voices. Such efforts, however, often rely on a presumption that experience is "an essential and boundable truth, knowable and livable prior to interpretation" (Terry 280). Feminist historians like Joan Scott and Ann-Louise Shapiro challenge this presumption of a prediscursive site of experience. Instead they propose that feminist historians examine how subjects are produced *through* the interactions of material and discursive practices. Looking at these interactions in the photographic archive exposes representational struggles over identity and agency, even as these photographs promote a positive image of this violent and traumatic action by the federal government.

This case study can teach us not only about how the agency of the disenfranchised, or those culturally marked as other, is captured and contained by dominant frames but also how this capturing is not absolute. Japanese Americans had painful disagreements about how to respond to the evacuation order. While many were eager to prove their loyalty to the United States, others were defiant, resistant, and angry. Instead of reading the photographs as reflections of a coherent community, I will argue that they visualize a hegemonic position within this fractured community.[3] The government agency that ran the camps, the War Relocation Authority (WRA), had a clear agenda to show the appropriateness of the evacuation order and the loyalty of the Japanese Americans. Complementing this objective, the photographers also visually privileged the internees' humanity over racial or cultural differences. Finally, the agendas of the Japanese Americans emerge as complex attempts to assert political positions and social ideals central to their claims of citizenship. While a small number of pictures challenge the dominant narrative, most of the archive presents people who appear to comply with or accommodate to the government policy of evacuation. Analyzing the WRA's photographic strategies enables us to see how these pictures mobilized popular concepts of race and gender in these visual claims of citizenship. Yet even as these images reinforce the power relations embedded in the government's gaze they also reveal challenges to that gaze, as Japanese Americans confronted the camera to claim their status as citizens.

Feminist critics in visual studies have moved away from arguments about the power of a monolithic (male) gaze to explore the contested dynamics of racial, sexual, and gender gazes (see for example Gaines; hooks; Lutz and Collins). As Catherine Lutz and Jane Collins argue, multiple gazes are "the source of many of the photograph's contradictions . . . . It is the root of much of the photograph's dynamism as a cultural object, and the place where the analyst can perhaps most productively begin to trace its connection to the wider social world of which it is a part" (216). While this scholarship has become increasingly nuanced and has reinvigorated visual studies, we still need to explore how multiple gazes are informed by notions of the "real." The gaze cannot be separated from realist strategies, since the very concept of the "gaze" presumes an embodiment, a body who can see. Feminists call attention to the body not only as a site upon which hegemonic power is written but also as a site of the complex and often contradictory conditions of gender, racial, sexual, and/or national identity. This chapter builds on that scholarship to explore how realist strategies specific to the war years mapped geopolitical conflicts onto visualized bodies and the consequences for a historical reading of the internees' agency that emerge from such embodiments.

The concept of visibility is central to this inquiry into historical (re)construction not only because of the nature of documentary photography but also because of how it structures discourses about nationalism, citizenship, and rights. More precisely, the wartime discursive production of racial and gender visibility and invisibility shaped how the WRA represented the evacuation and how audiences then and now have come to perceive the "experiences" of the internees. Throughout the early twentieth century most Americans remained suspicious of Japanese immigrants and Japanese Americans, imposing obstacles to their legal and cultural identities as Americans. After the bombing of Pearl Harbor on 7 December 1941, the government responded to pressure from the military, politicians, and white civilians to evacuate the west coast Japanese American population, who were perceived to be a threat to national security.[4] On 19 February 1942, Executive Order 9066 authorized the removal of all Japanese and Japanese Americans from Pacific coastal states into ten concentration camps away from the coast. Seventy thousand of the 120,000 people removed were U.S. citizens (Chan 122). Executive Order 9066 stripped this population not only of their constitutional rights but also of their homes, property, livelihood, and dignity. Equally damaging, it perpetuated public animus and racist hostilities by justifying assumptions about the enemy alien status of Japanese Americans. Such justifications were based on a refusal to "see" their legitimate claims of citizenship.

In a seemingly contradictory move, however, the WRA photographic record repeatedly visualizes their "Americanness." The archive contains no pictures of menacing or threatening Japanese, pictures that might have been used to justify the further suspension of constitutional rights to American citizens for a wartime audience. Instead, numerous pictures show Japanese Americans in activities common to 1940s audiences, such as playing baseball, posing in family portraits, or at work, often in war-related jobs (fig. 8.1). Pictures of internees doing their best for the war effort present an image of loyalty and cooperation. The photographs project an idealized image that routinely emphasizes the commonalities between the internees and other Americans. But at what price? What happens to racial and cultural differences when representations visualize the subjects' common links to a national identity? And what can this tell us about the traumatic experiences and struggles to refuse victimization and assert agency on the part of the internees?

In this chapter I use the trope of relocation to discuss agency, for it foregrounds the forced, coercive nature by which the United States government displaced this population. Whatever agency we see in these pictures is never disembodied. The smiling faces and physical presence of Japanese Americans in the camps visualize the physical, social, and ideological experiences of relocation. Analyzing the historical specificity of realist strategies can push us beyond merely exposing the invisibility of experiences of suffering and trauma in pictures of Japanese Americans playing softball or sewing the American flag. As Caren Kaplan argues, "any exclusive recourse to space, place, or position becomes utterly abstract and universalizing without historical speci-

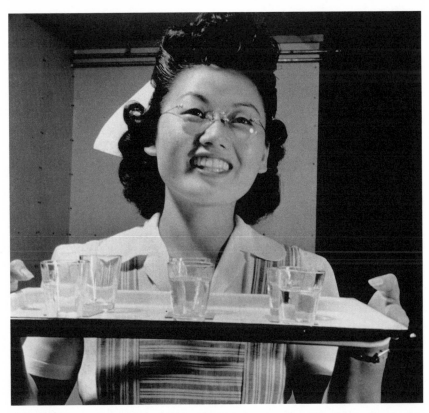

Figure 8.1. "Kiyoko Tatsukawa, former High School student from Huntington Beach, California, and a graduate of the Spring 1943 class in Nurse's Aid at the Poston Hospital. Pretty Kiyoko is shown demonstrating her most charming bed-side manner, before administrating medicine to the fortunate patient." Colorado River Relocation Center, Poston, Ariz., 3 May 1943. (No. 210-G-5B-491, Francis Stewart, Central Photographic File of the War Relocation Authority, 1942–1945 [Central File], Record Group 210 [RG 210], National Archives at College Park, College Park, Md. [NACP].)

ficity" (138).[5] Instead, the embodiment of wartime racial, gender, and national politics in these photographs demonstrates how realist strategies (re)located and (re)configured identity, experience, and agency. This chapter first examines the government's policy of evacuation and the WRA's subsequent public relations campaign to justify this action. I also discuss the photographers' objectives by focusing on the work of Dorothea Lange, the most famous of the WRA photographers. Next I consider how nationalist ideologies are embodied in the subjects of the photographs and the consequences of relocating the nation onto its "enemy alien" subjects. Exploring the consequences of visual relocation raises questions about Japanese American participation in this propaganda project. Agency then becomes a critical historical question related to Japanese Americans' apparent investment in a hegemonic discourse of nationalism. Finally, an extraordinary group of photographs of children in blackface provoke some further thoughts about the ways in which agency itself is marked by histories of power, inequality, and racism.

Publicizing Executive Order 9066

> At that age I was too young to consciously use my sexuality or to understand how an Oriental female can fascinate Caucasian men, and of course far too young to see that even this is usually just another form of invisibility. It simply happened that the attention I first gained as a majorette went hand in hand with a warm reception from the Boy Scouts and their fathers, and from that point on I knew intuitively that one resource I had to overcome the war-distorted limitations of my race would be my femininity.
>
> —Jeanne Wakatsuki Houston and James D. Houston

In her memoir, Jeanne Wakatsuki Houston explores the racial and gender politics that shaped her desire for acceptance as an American. Made self-conscious by wartime racism, she addresses the pain and trauma of invisibility. As she notes, "You cannot deport 110,000 people unless you have stopped seeing individuals" (114). Houston articulates how identity, including the legal identity of citizenship, depends upon discourses of visibility. Or, as Chandra Mohanty argues, "gender and racial regimes of contemporary liberal capitalist states operate through the ostensibly 'unmarked' discourses of citizenship and individual rights" (21). After all, as the epigraph to this section exemplifies, she became publicly visible only through the white male gaze at the "realness" of her exoticism.[6] In this way, Houston's narrative exposes how visibility and its attendant authenticity secured historically specific forms of racial and gender identity in the representational politics of Executive Order 9066.

The history of U.S. attitudes toward Asian immigration has been one of overt hostilities, ranging from individual acts of violence to institutionalized segregation.[7] Beginning in the 1880s, a series of immigration acts and antinaturalization laws prohibited legal immigration and denied Asians the rights of citizenship. Virulent anti-Asian racism on the west coast included an anti-Japanese movement that persisted throughout the 1930s. Within this context of segregation in housing, employment, and education, as well as periodic episodes of racial violence, Japanese American communities struggled to establish economic as well as social and cultural communities in the United States. In segregated communities, Issei, or first-generation immigrants, kept Japanese culture alive through local associations, immigrant press, language schools, and churches. At the same time, Nisei, or the second generation, grew up confronting the complex process of reconciling Japanese traditions and mainstream American customs (Okihiro, *Whispered* 125–26). Attending public high schools and participating in contemporary popular culture, young Japanese Americans understood themselves to be Americans. Among the reasons why the Nisei found the evacuation so devastating was this confrontation between their own knowledge of their "real" identity as American citizens and a national policy that refused to recognize that identity.[8]

The day after the bombing of Pearl Harbor, the Department of Justice imposed the first federal regulation of the war to discriminate specifically against Japanese Americans. This regulation closed land borders of the United States to all enemy aliens and "'all persons of Japanese ancestry, whether citizen or alien'" (qtd. in Daniels, *Prisoners* 27). Next, the Treasury Department froze the financial assets of the Issei while the FBI began to arrest Issei community leaders thought to be pro-Japanese. About two thousand men were taken into custody and held, often for months, prior to being reunited with their families in the camps. In addition, the FBI conducted searches of people's homes at all hours of the night looking for evidence of espionage. They removed all suspicious objects, including cameras and radios. Justifications for these constitutional violations included claims that Japanese Americans constituted a security threat because they were more loyal to Japan than to the United States. Such arguments depended for their validity on the "realness" of difference, that is, the presumption that skin color and other physiological characteristics of race determine social acts. Despite charges of espionage, however, there was never any evidence of such acts by Japanese or Japanese Americans.

In response to FBI harassment, many families destroyed anything that might provoke suspicion, including family heirlooms, books written in Japanese, and family photographs (Sone). These family archives too depended on claims of authenticity to secure identity, tradition, and family histories. Consciously or not, the FBI's confiscation of these artifacts, like people's destruction of them to avoid suspicion, rested on the assumption that it was the objects' "realness," the materiality of the artifacts, that made them so threatening. The objects, in other words, could "prove" disloyalty. Poignantly, their destruction also further removed one discourse of the real, making Japanese Americans' historical identities more invisible.

Shortly after Pearl Harbor, Lieutenant General John L. DeWitt, the commander of the Western Defense Command, pushed for mass detention because, he declared, "'the Japanese race is an enemy race and while many second and third generation Japanese born on United States soil, possessed of United States citizenship, have become "Americanized," the racial strains are undiluted'" (qtd. in Okihiro, *Margins* 170). Hysteria and racism within the War Department and military leadership provided the momentum for evacuation, especially since proponents faced only weak opposition. Support also came from politicians and white civilians whose anxieties about national security were fueled by decades-long racism. The media, especially west coast newspapers, played a critical role in sustaining this hysteria. Moreover, economic objectives propelled the increasing demands for removal from business leaders seeking to capitalize on the opportunity to limit Japanese American control of agricultural lands. In response, President Roosevelt announced Executive Order 9066 on 19 February 1942, authorizing the evacuation of anyone of Japanese descent from the Pacific coast military zone (Takaki 379–405; Chan 121–39; Daniels, *Prisoners*).

Families received one week's notice to sell or give away any assets, including houses, cars, and other personal belongings. The government limited each person to only one duffel and one suitcase, including their bedding and essential personal effects. They were not told where they were going, except to anticipate extremes of cold and heat. The army did not allow shipments of household goods to the camps, so people sold or gave away those belongings that they could not bring with them. Japanese Americans experienced extreme economic losses of household and business assets, while the personal losses are incalculable. As Kate Brown writes in her moving essay on the discarded remains of one Japanese American storage area in Seattle: "This mountain of belongings reminds one of how deprivation of citizenship and freedom is accompanied by forfeiture of concrete things—possessions, homes, jobs— which in turn leads to further losses. . . . Depriving Japanese-Americans of their possessions was a way of stripping them of the emblems that announced their citizenship, reducing them to the status of original sin: the penniless immigrant off the boat, two straw suitcases in hand" (73–74).

Stripped of their material possessions, Japanese Americans were physically dispossessed, relocated away from their communities. The army remained in charge of the internees while they went to temporary assembly centers in former race tracks, fairgrounds, and other staging areas. There they lived for months until the ten permanent camps were completed. In March 1942 the government established the WRA, a civilian agency, to oversee the camps, which were located in desolate and isolated areas away from urban populations and the coast. Relocation, the trope that the government used for both the forced movement of people and the naming of the camps, depends upon a particular realist claim of visibility—of seeing the camps as temporary and seeing the evacuation as a benign act for the security and protection of the internees rather than as concentration camps.[9] Perimeter fences, barbed wire, and armed sentries, however, refute any claims that these were not prisons and that Japanese Americans were there of their own free will.

As part of the WRA's public relations efforts, the Office of Reports and Publications developed a photographic unit whose purpose was to create a positive image of the evacuation. The office sent photographs to magazines, newspapers, public libraries, and other exhibitions. Pamphlets published by this unit include "What about Our Japanese Americans" and "New Neighbors among Us," a 1944 brochure about resettlement. One WRA memo explained the intention of these publications: "to tell what the Japanese are doing for their native land, developing land, growing food. . . . Local newspapers and local radio stations will develop . . . programs that let the people in those areas know that they are loyal Americans and are good citizens." In this way, WRA pamphlets disseminated nationalist ideologies "within and across institutional structures" (Williams 3).

By 1942, several branches of the federal government had almost ten years of experience using photography to publicize government programs (Daniel et al.; Daniels, "Dorothea Lange"). In the 1930s, Farm Security Administration (FSA) photographs established a documentary aesthetic for presenting the humanity of impoverished rural Americans, an aesthetic that depended on close-up high and low angle shots that avoided contextualization and promoted the dignity of the poor (Kozol). FSA photography used such compositional strategies to mobilize cultural ideals of family, maternity, and individualism as promotions for the programs of this New Deal agency (see Curtis; Daniel et al.; Kozol). The WRA archive bears the marks of this tradition. Most of the photographers for the WRA were neither well known nor as aesthetically capable as the photographers of the earlier project. Today, they still remain relatively unknown (Daniels, "Dorothea Lange"). Regardless, these photographers relied on documentary conventions formed in the 1930s that drew upon a faith in the capability of photographs to persuade audiences of the merits of government programs.

In addition, WRA photographers inherited aesthetic conventions and the social ideals embedded in them, namely to visualize their subjects' humanity. Dorothea Lange, the only well-known photographer to work for the WRA, was employed by the agency during 1942 and part of 1943 to photograph the evacuation process (Daniels, "Dorothea Lange"). In her work for the WRA she continued the humanitarian style that she helped to make famous with works like "Migrant Mother" (1936) and other pictures of farm workers during the Depression. For instance, in Lange's photograph of a family waiting to go the camps, a woman clutches an infant and her handbag at the center of the composition (fig. 8.2). Next to her stands a man and behind them an adolescent boy. All three stare at the camera with worried faces. Cut off at the edges of the composition are other people standing in a line, reinforcing a sense of anticipation and dread. The worried expressions, the tight hold of the infant by its mother, and the compositional focus on the tiny baby create an image of innocent victims swept along by historical forces. Roger Daniels argues that Lange's work demonstrates her strenuous objection to the evacuation, unlike most of the WRA photographers who showed little awareness that "they were recording an American tragedy" ("Dorothea Lange" 49).

Lange's photographs clearly depict injustices in the evacuation process, yet her documentary style paradoxically also sustained the public relations objec-

Figure 8.2. "As families of Japanese ancestry evacuated from farms in Contra Costa County, they gathered at Wartime Civil Control Administration Station and awaited buses for the assembly center at Turlock Fairgrounds, 65 miles away." Byron, Calif., 2 May 1942. (No. 210-G-2C-100, Dorothea Lange, Central File, RG 210, NACP.)

Figure 8.3. "Grandfather and grandson of Japanese ancestry at this War Relocation Authority center." Manzanar Relocation Center, Manzanar, Calif., 2 July 1942. (No. 210-G-10C-697, Dorothea Lange, Central File, RG 210, NACP.)

tives of the WRA. In one of the most famous pictures from the WRA archive, that of a grandfather carrying his grandson on his shoulders (fig. 8.3), Lange demonstrates her skill at capturing the humanity of her subjects. She pulls the camera in close to the subjects' faces, bringing them right up to the picture plane so the viewer comes into intimate contact with them. This beautiful portrait of familial devotion nonetheless also decontextualizes the scene, for the conditions of camp life remain invisible. There is no evidence here of the barbed wire, work stoppages, or the dangerous lack of medical supplies that led to unnecessary illnesses and deaths (Houston and Houston 86; Okihiro, *Whispered* 220–21). Lange creates a moving, indeed universal image of family but one that dehistoricizes the politics of removal. Her skill enabled her to comply with the agency's need for "documentation" while creating eloquent portraits of dignified, strong people coping with adversity. Such photographs (perhaps unwittingly) participated in the government's project of showing the internees not as enemies but as Americans. In this regard, Lange's work is emblematic of other politically self-conscious strategies of protest at the time.[10] For instance, Ansel Adams, who also photographed the camps, protested Executive Order 9066 in a 1944 exhibition titled *Born Free and Equal.* In an accompanying catalog, Adams condemns the racism of this order and states that the residents' "faith in the American life is stronger and more acute than ever before. They desire above all 'to get along with other Americans—to avoid feelings of race difference—to prove we are as good Americans as anyone else'" (109–10). This impulse to visualize the internees, to document their humanity, also depends on realist strategies to "prove" the wrongs done to people. Historians who attempt to recover histories of oppressions similarily often rely on realist strategies to prove the wrongs done to oppressed peoples. Such sincere attempts to counter dominant narratives, however, are not unequivocally positive, for they can also reproduce or perpetuate narrowly conceived historical assumptions about "real" experiences versus the ideological constraints of hegemony. For example, feminist histories have at times been trapped by revisionist moves that, in making "women's" experiences visible, leave uninterrogated differences of race, sexuality, and class (Shapiro). Thus, as other essays in this volume also argue, critical scholarship must confront the contradictory politics embedded in oppositional claims of real or authentic experiences.

Relocating American Identities

> What is being done and what has been done when it is all over should be analyzed by scholars for anything that might happen in the next generation. . . . it is important for us to have every administrative ruling, administrative notice, that goes down the line, confidential memorandum, press release, motion picture, still photographs, camp newspapers on relocation projects (issued by evacuees themselves). . . . Scholars will be able to find what they want in this material. We won't use it ourselves but it will be available for those who can use it.
> —1942 WRA Office of Reports and Publications memo

This memo[11] from the Office of Reports and Publications exemplifies the commonsense notion that memos and photographs can record history for later scholars to judge, an assumption based on a faith in documentary and a faith in history to recover the true story of "our actions." In rejecting an analytical strategy that compares images to an actual reality (i.e., how truthful are the images), we need instead to examine how the images participate in constructing the historical narrative of Executive Order 9066.

Relocation, as a trope, as an image, and as physical event, confronts the conflict between what we see and what we know in these pictures. As I noted in the introduction, what we see are images of American citizenship. A commonplace in much Western feminist theory is the critique of the binarisms of self-other, insider-outsider, and nature-culture that are presumed to be central to Western epistemologies. Yet, as Inderpal Grewal and Caren Kaplan point out, the focus on binarisms overlooks or elides the complexities of "multiply constituted identities" (10). Ignoring such complexities limits our understanding of agency as a reactive response to power rather than as a process of negotiation and contestation borne out of particular locations and relocations. The photographs, I will argue, do not reproduce simplistic binarisms because the nationalist gaze dominant in these pictures depicts the internees as part of the center, not the margin, at home, not in exile. And yet all of the surrounding intertextual practices, as Hall points out, insist that we are looking at relocation, at exile, at margins, and definitely not at home. The dominant gaze, in other words, is here more fractured and multivocal than claims of "propaganda" assume.

A 1943 photograph of women sewing a service flag at the Topaz, Utah, relocation center (fig. 8.4), for instance, features gender and patriotic symbols that emphasize the similarities between the internees and other Americans. This photograph depicts ten women seated outside around a picnic table, bent over their materials with needles in hand. Some work on individual patches and other sew stars directly onto the flag. This curiously nostalgic image of women's labor displaces industrial practices of flag production, as it harkens back to sewing bees of the nineteenth century. Realist strategies map traditional gender codes onto material bodies in a process that legitimates these Japanese American women as patriotic Americans. This in turn reinforces a message of accommodation and compliance by Japanese Americans.

Almost from the beginning, the WRA recognized that one of their primary missions would be to reintegrate Japanese Americans into mainstream society after the war (Linehan). Instead of demonizing the internees, the pictures negotiate the conflicting demands regarding Executive Order 9066, responding to hysterical racism and economic demands by whites and to the need to control the xenophobia the order itself unleashed. Such justifications took place in a home-front climate of tremendous racial hostilities. Violence erupted not only against Asians but also against African Americans in urban centers like Harlem, Detroit, and Cleveland and against Chicanos in Los Angeles (Brandt). Demands by African Americans for civil rights called attention to the hypocrisies of fighting a war for democracy in a nation divided by racial

Figure 8.4. "The sewing class teachers at Topaz making the Service Flag." Central Utah Relocation Center, Topaz, Utah, 23 April 1943. (No. 210-G-4B-716, Russell Bankson, Central File, RG 210, NACP.)

inequalities. Japanese Americans made similar arguments about civil rights in protest of the evacuation, including contesting the legality of the order through the justice system (Irons).[12]

Mediating these tensions, WRA photographs that documented the "real," the ordinary or everyday lives of the internees encode within their imagery popular midcentury ideals about race. The historian Peggy Pascoe analyzes the decline of scientific racism and the triumph of an argument of color blindness between the 1920s and the 1960s.[13] As she notes, during these years "competing ideologies [of race] were winnowed down to the single, powerfully persuasive belief that the eradication of racism depends on the deliberate nonrecognition of race" (48). Culturalists claimed that culture was more important than biology in "shaping meaningful human differences." One consequence of this position, Pascoe argues, was that "race [became] nothing more than a subdivision of the broader phenomenon of ethnicity" (67).[14] While typically the material body appears as a site of authenticity, color blindness reconfigures materiality by moving away from a simple conflation of the real with the body. This move from the "realness" of race as the primary signifier relies on the "realness" of other, historically relevant codes such as domesticity and patriotism. As Pascoe insists, however, color blindness does not mean the "nonideological end of racism" but rather is itself a racial ideology (48).

The photographs supported and, I would argue, helped to construct this racial ideology of color blindness by visualizing Japanese Americans as "Americans." Pictures of children at school, people at work, scenes of domestic life, and young couples at dances mobilize popular visual codes associated with national identity, including gender ideals, domesticity, work ethic, and leisure time.[15] Showing people engaged in daily activities, a common convention in documentary photography, naturalizes claims of sameness through an appearance of familiarity. This strategy maps national identities onto the racialized bodies of the internees. For instance, numerous photographs of men, women, and children playing sports visualize their familiarity. Unlike enemy aliens from different cultures, these Japanese Americans play baseball and volleyball and have fun. These images also convey a sense of leisure time, an important message that signals that these were not labor camps. A photograph of a group of young women playing softball shows them all smiling (fig. 8.5). In the center foreground of the composition, at the picture plane, the ball is in motion. Directly behind the ball stands the batter at midswing. The catcher, with her mitt raised, smiles as she prepares to catch the ball while several women stand behind them watching the action. The close-up shot captures the physical experience of playing this "American" sport, while the performative nature of the scene, catching the batter at midswing, underscores the spontaneity or the realness of the action. By appearing unposed, and thus real, the photograph suspends any suspicions of propaganda to ensure a reading of women playing this national sport. Onto the bodies of these smiling internees are encoded national ideals of fun, leisure, and cooperative sports.

Popular 1940s domestic ideals, likewise, visualize internees as typical nuclear families. Numerous photographs show families seated on living room sofas smiling at the camera with consumer products surrounding them. Over and over, photographers limited any visual awareness of the cramped conditions of the barracks in which the inmates lived by using camera angles that narrow the framing of the composition. Pictures of happy families with furniture, curtains, and other consumer products reinforce government claims about the positive benefits of evacuation. They also argue for the citizenship status of the internees through recognizable domestic arrangements and material objects that help to secure their identity as Americans. Yet, as Brown notes, these "trappings of Americana" used to symbolize citizenship also tell "the story of a failed American contract—work hard, save, keep out of trouble, and you too can have all the middle-class pleasures owed to every industrious Ameri-

Figure 8.5. "Maye Noma behind the plate and Tomi Nagao at bat in a practice game between members of the Chick-a-dee soft ball team, which was kept intact when the players were evacuated from Los Angeles, with a great number of other persons of Japanese descent who will remain at the War Relocation Authority center here for the duration of the war." Manzanar Relocation Center, Manzanar, Calif., May 1942. Courtesy of the Library of Congress, Box 1801091, LC-USZ62–92174.

can . . . . The Japanese-Americans had worked hard, saved and started to purchase the things of American life that brought them a measure of assimilation and normality" (75). Photographs that visualize consumer products, smiling faces, and family units emphasize that American contract even as their presence in the camps hints at its failure.

Yet intertextual discourses more than the images themselves remind us of that failure, the relocation away from home and into a prison. Dispossession and relocation placed Japanese Americans in a foreign location with an alien identity as both American and not American. This is reminiscent of Gloria Anzaldua's observation that her location in the borderland denies her any place that can be called home (Grewal 250). Likewise, these images of domesticity, which insist on their subjects' similarity to 1940s white audiences, also force viewers to confront relocation, for the subjects of these pictures remain at the margins surrounded by the perimeter fence.

This hint of failure, the traces of exile and otherness can, however, be overwhelmed by the visual privileging of one image of citizenship at the expense of other images that might show the hardships of camp life, the lack of fresh food, poor sanitation, boredom, anger, or humiliation. Most importantly, the photographs do not ever show how conditions in the camps severely altered family relations (Houston and Houston; Chan 128). Family unity deteriorated amid cramped housing where standard barracks of twenty by one hundred feet were divided into four to six rooms, one per family. Communal facilities including dining halls disrupted family rituals and made parental authority even more difficult to maintain. None of this appears in the photographs. Instead of revealing the struggles to create a life amid tremendous hardship, the mobilization of domestic codes prevalent in other media of the 1940s places the internees within the idealized image of the nuclear family. Thus domesticity becomes central to the construction of government policies and national ideals.

The impact and importance of these photographs lies not only in what they refuse to show but also in how absences themselves reproduce racial and national ideologies. This is most apparent in that which is most invisible in the pictures, the physical and emotional pain and trauma of the evacuation. Linked to the WRA's agenda of showing happy, adjusted internees, this absence demonstrates the importance of a historically located analysis. Beyond simplistic propaganda benefits, the absence of trauma in the photographs facilitates the rhetoric of color blindness and exposes the consequences of realist strategies that depict Japanese Americans as citizens. As I suggested earlier, uninterrogated representations of citizenship, including sincere acts of opposition, can erase other conditions, indeed other realities. The pain and trauma experienced by Japanese Americans were borne out of racial differences; images that emphasize their similarities to "other" Americans deny the viewer knowledge of the relationship between racial differences, traumatic dislocations, and national policies. The crucial point here is that visual strategies of color blindness constructed not simple binarisms but rather complex subjectivities framed around sameness and difference, presence and absence.

Color blindness was particularly significant in representations of resettlement because racial politics were potentially most dangerous as internees moved away from the camps. The WRA's mission was not only to run the camps but also to relocate Japanese Americans away from the west coast (Linehan). Among the stated goals of relocation was the desire to break up "Little Tokyos." President Roosevelt, for instance, said that around the country there are counties "'in [which] probably half a dozen or a dozen families could be scattered around on the farms and worked into the community. After all they are American citizens, and we all know that American citizens have certain privileges . . . 75,000 families scattered around the United States is not going to upset anyone'" (qtd. in Daniels, *Prisoners* 80).

Photographs of resettlement visualized this color-blind policy by depicting happy workers and families that, like other families, all smile for the camera. Such images present no visual evidence of racial hostilities on the part of whites or the fear and anxiety that many Japanese Americans expressed about relocation. For instance, a photograph taken in St. Louis in September 1944 of Mrs. Kim Obata shows her dressed in a white shirt and dark skirt with a contemporary haircut (fig. 8.6). She smiles while holding a telephone, standing next to a poster of white Girl Scouts raising the American flag. Although her race is not in doubt, fashion and other codes in the picture emphasize her similarities with other American women. The caption reinforces this reading: "Mrs. Kim Obata, a registrar for the Girl Scouts, answers her calls for registration. . . . She enjoys her work and is liked by everyone with whom she comes in contact." Conventional gender roles again merge with patriotic symbols to emphasize her normality, how she fits into this color-blind world that never mentions race, and the fact that she is "liked by everyone."

WRA photographs like this one also demonstrate how gender gets implicated in other regulatory discourses around race and nationalism. Another picture of resettlement shows two Japanese American young women new to the Chicago area (fig. 8.7). In order to capture their successful reintegration into American society, the photographer depicts them sitting on the shores of Lake Michigan in bathing suits, smiling at the camera. In the foreground of the picture, one woman smiles directly into the camera as she sits parallel to the picture plane, wearing a bathing suit and flowers in her hair. Directly behind her, another woman faces the camera, also smiling and wearing an almost identical outfit. The women sit in pin-up poses similar to those that appeared in *Life, Look,* and other picture magazines that were popular during the war. While the photograph visualizes the women's racial differences, other gender codes locate these women as American beauties. The caption reinforces this reading: "Another freedom of considerable importance to the young feminine mind in America is the freedom to shop for and wear pretty clothes. These two Nisei girls, evacuees from the west coast and recently relocated from the relocation center at Granada, Colorado, are again enjoying that privilege. They are shown here sporting their new swim suits." Although racial differences do not disappear, they become subordinate to the emphasis on the sameness of the "young feminine mind in America." National identity becomes

Figure 8.6. "Mrs. Kim Obata, a registrar for the Girl Scouts, answers her calls for registration. She is with her husband in St. Louis and was an evacuee from the Central Utah Relocation Center. She enjoys her work and is liked by everyone with whom she comes in contact." St. Louis, Mo., 21 September 1944. (No. 210-G-14I-519, Hiraku Iwasaki, Central File, RG 210, NACP.)

defined in terms of gender and consumption ideals, as these codes "document" the "Americanness" of these women.

The photograph thus not only envisions the geographical move of reloca-tion but also visually relocates difference by mapping national identity onto the bodies of the Other, in this case these women. Once again, however, we see that the trope of relocation is an equivocal move. These Nisei women, so re-cently stripped of their legal and social rights because of race, are here "relo-cated" through gender codes, establishing them as American women available for the camera's, the viewer's, and, presumably, the male gaze. Significantly, this also remains a racial gaze, for as much as they look like other pinups, and thus conform to those gender codes, one never loses sight of their race. By

Figure 8.7. "Another freedom of considerable importance to the young feminine mind in America is the freedom to shop for and wear pretty clothes. These two Nisei girls, evacuees from the west coast and recently relocated from the relocation center at Granada, Colorado, are again enjoying that privilege. They are shown here sporting their new swim suits on a Chicago beach." Chicago, Ill., 13 August 1943. (No. 210-G-14H-31, Chas. E. Mace, Central File, RG 210, NACP.)

foregrounding their sexuality through costume and pose, the camera makes available for the gaze an image that resonates with a history of stereotypes of Asian women's exoticism. Photographs are never read in isolation, and here realist strategies reassert the cultural assumptions that Houston experienced about Asian women's beauty, difference, and availability. Thus exoticism participates in constructing a familiar image that is still different. These women can be patriotic but never white, revealing how gender and race shape and configure each other in nationalist discourses.

While the photograph does not completely erase race, documentary strategies that appear to capture a moment of relaxation for relocated Nisei elide social inequalities by emphasizing how much the subjects are like other American women, able to do what other Americans do. In so doing, it makes power relations invisible, although not racial distinctions between different groups of Americans, so that one can be American but still be different. This also reveals how claims of color blindness are themselves fractured, demonstrating that even the most dominant discourses of race are never fixed or stable.

The WRA distributed photographs of successfully relocated Japanese Americans not only to national newspapers and magazines but also to internment camps for use in photographic exhibitions. These exhibitions were designed to convince skeptical internees of the benefits of resettlement (Linehan 59–60). Many, especially older Issei, were reluctant to leave the camps to face racial hostilities in new locations. Others chose to stay in the camps until the end of the war in order to return to their homes on the west coast. Photographic exhibitions turned the subjects of these images back upon the interned community. In such cases, documentary strategies reinforce an ideal of Japanese Americans as Americans in order to encourage reluctant internees to participate in this government project of relocation.

Gazing at Agency?

The governmental gaze embedded in these pictures suggests that Japanese Americans remain invisible even when they are the subjects of these pictures. Interrogating the history of WRA photographs in the context of the internees' struggles for recognition of their citizenship status, however, reveals a far more complex situation. It is important not to explore in isolation the ambiguities, complexities, and contradictions in these photographs. Rather, they are caught in a network of discourses—not only government public relations and the news media's replication of this ideology but Japanese American discourses as well.

Writings by Nisei at the time and later reveal painful struggles over identity, for they understood themselves to be American citizens, yet most other Americans saw them as enemies. Houston, for instance, articulates the process of negotiating national identities in the wake of the violence done to Japanese American communities: "The fact that America had accused us, or excluded us, or imprisoned us, or whatever it might be called, did not change the kind of world we wanted. Most of us were born in this country; we had no other models" (72). Japanese Americans did not stop identifying themselves as Americans but were forced to renegotiate the meanings and ideals of citizenship. All ten camps published newsletters or newspapers that, although censored, were run by the internees. The *Manzanar Free Press,* for instance, continually spoke to its readers directly about the need to counteract racist stereotypes circulating in the national press and in political arenas. A 17 February 1943 announcement in the *Free Press* explained the presence of a photographer to its readers: "The pictures taken here are to be used to supplement the written historical and documentary records now being prepared on the story of the mass Japanese evacuation from the Pacific Coast. The pictures are also to be used for publicity and public relations purposes and releases for press and other publications." This attention to the government's objectives in taking photographs indicates a self-conscious awareness of the politics of representation and perhaps helps to explain the studied look of many of the images in the archive.

This self-consciousness also points to the political importance of representing Japanese Americans as American citizens for the subjects themselves. The archive shows not only happy, compliant subjects but also self-respecting and dignified people gazing back at the camera. There are no pictures of people crying, yelling, or incapacitated. While this clearly supports government arguments about Japanese American compliance with Executive Order 9066, it also reveals subjects who refuse the status of victim. Stuart Hall writes that "there is no *one* system of realist representation, always and for ever fixed in position, from which one type of political practice, one empiricist reading of history emanates" (160). Hall's proposition that realism itself is multivocal opens up the possibility of reading these photographs in ways that expose struggles over power and resistance, agency, and victimization. For a country all too willing to see Japanese Americans as enemies, representations of dignified and proud people have political as well as cultural significance. To the many Japanese Americans who gazed at the government's cameras, their refusal to be represented as victims can be read as crucial to their political assertion of citizenship.

A reading that claims to "see" the internees' dignity and resistance, however, runs the danger of romanticizing the subjects of the photographs. Instead, the complexities of representation emerge in further explorations of Japanese Americans' participation in the picture taking, for this participation also at times appears to align them with government agendas. A series of photographs of male internees training to become camp police exposes the problematics of locating identity and agency in documentary practices. Each image shows a white man using a baton against an internee in a mock arrest, with a group of male internees watching and smiling. In one photograph, the white camp official stands in the foreground with his arm raised as if about to strike a Japanese American man who cowers beneath him to shield the blow. In the background a group of men smile at the camera as they watch the performance with the viewer. Their smiling faces reassuringly assert that this is a staged event with the internees as willing participants. Identifying internees' agency here is complicated by the potential reading of this as either a complicit act by prisoners or as a depiction of loyal Americans who uphold law and order. The photographs seem to support the government project of showing happy, integrated internees participating in national projects of security, defense, and self-regulation, themes common to Americans on the home front during the war. And yet Japanese American critics of Executive Order 9066 often pointed to these types of activities as collaborations with a corrupt government (Taylor 77–79, 133–36). Complicating questions about collaboration and loyalty even further, the Japanese American man's posture, cowering under the white man's baton, places him in a feminized position of subordination to the authority of the WRA official. The intertwined nature of race and gender further destabilizes claims of sameness in discourses of rights and citizenship.

Struggles within the camps over self-representation to the outside world also reveal a far from homogeneous response to the evacuation order. The Japanese American Citizen's League (JACL) was a Nisei organization that had been growing in popularity prior to the war. During the war the WRA relied on the organization and helped to promote the JACL's leadership and authority in various ways, including supporting them in important posts in the self-governance structure (Taylor 133–34). Photographs, too, privileged this view of the loyal Nisei. One picture of the office of the JACL visualizes the organization's patriotism through a close-up of a wall in the office that shows a photograph of a baseball team and an American flag (fig. 8.8). During the war and in subsequent debates the JACL has come under scrutiny for their position of accommodation, which argued that Japanese Americans should go willingly to the camps to prove their patriotism. Picturing camp internees engaged in policing and self-regulation thus captures other debates about loyalty, accommodation, and collaboration and participates in discursive struggles to gain ideological and/or political ascendancy in the camps.

During the war, identity was so wrapped up with questions of nationalism that to claim citizenship was to confront the politics of evacuation. Many, including younger Nisei, objected to the JACL's accommodationist approach without rejecting their own claims of loyalty or patriotism. Oppositional strategies ranged from constitutional challenges in the courts to overt refusals to sign loyalty oaths. Many who refused to sign spoke of the humiliation and betrayal embedded in such demands by their country (Chan 130; Taylor 147–53; Okihiro, *Whispered* 210–12). Conflicts also arose between internees over support for government policies and charges of collaboration, conflicts that at times led to riots and other forms of violence. Even more censored venues, such as the camp newspapers, convey something of the debates that occurred in the camps and a certain willingness to criticize the government. A review of the *Manzanar Free Press* reveals that this paper's editorial position repeat-

Figure 8.8. "Interior view of Japanese American Citizens League Headquarters." Center-ville, Calif., 7 April 1942. (No. 210-G-1A-37, Dorothea Lange, Central File, RG 210, NACP.)

edly emphasized Japanese American claims to citizenship and challenged the racism of current policies. For instance, an editorial on 1 January 1943 comments: "If the way of American life which we have been taught is to achieve fruition, we shall expect the people-at-large of America to work toward understanding the power and effects of tolerance. We shall want to know the answer to the question: Is America big enough to assimilate culture and nationalities, but not races of mankind?"

Little of this range of attitudes about the evacuation can be seen in the archive; instead what emerges is a more accomodationist position, visually dominating the archive at the expense of images of draft dodgers, No-No boys, and others who challenged the moral and constitutional violations of Executive Order 9066.[16] This raises questions about whose agency we see when we look at Japanese American internees gazing back at the camera. These pictures, I argue, provide evidence of a hegemonic position within this fractured and divided community. In this way, the trope of relocation as a material, embodied discourse exposes the discontinuous nature of agency. Agency is not in this formulation a pure act of resistance to power but historically determined by conditions and opportunities. As Grewal notes, "many immigrants or diasporic subjects, even those multiply located or with multiple voices, are not automatically oppositional" (251). Images like the ones of the police demonstration reveal that agency is a situated practice, dependent on contemporaneous conditions to shape and indeed limit the representation of subjectivity, identity, and action.

Although a hegemonic position of accommodation dominates the archive, a small number of photographs reveal instances where representation can challenge this hegemony. One picture taken at the Salinas Assembly Center in March 1942 shows a couple in their "home" (fig. 8.9). The caption notes: "Evacuees of Japanese descent enjoy a moment of relaxation before setting up housekeeping at this assembly center." The caption emphasizes the ordinary routines of domesticity, as if to normalize this traumatic experience. The photograph, however, disturbs this domestic ideal, for the center of the composition is

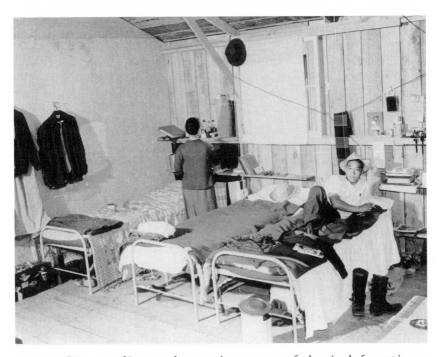

Figure 8.9. "Evacuees of Japanese descent enjoy a moment of relaxation before setting up housekeeping at this assembly center." Salinas Assembly Center, Salinas, Calif., 31 March 1942. (No. 210-G-3A-224, Clem Albers, Central File, RG 210, NACP.)

empty, while the man just off-center lies on a cot staring at the camera without emotion. Meanwhile, the woman in the far left corner has her back to the camera. The lack of a positive focal point for the viewer's gaze and the off-center nature of the composition destabilizes the picture's organization, while the woman's turned-away face further disrupts the ideal of domesticity promised in the caption. The viewer is denied the pleasure and reassurance of seeing the smiling housewife relaxing at home. This denial of her subjectivity coupled with the man's direct stare engages the viewer with the politics of incarceration. Photographs like this are not common in the archive, but their presence reminds viewers of the discursive struggles that shape historical knowledge about Japanese American experiences.

Blackface: Locating Authenticity in Masks

One last series of images further demonstrates how realist strategies mediate the interactions between the public spectacle of patriotism and contestations over racial identity and citizenship. A series of photographs of a Thanksgiving harvest festival at Gila River Relocation Center in Arizona in 1942 show children dressed as pilgrims, children carrying American flags, and a float with the Queen of the Parade (fig. 8.10). These are rather predictable images that mobilize conventional icons of 1940s American life to secure the performance of accommodation. Here there are no perimeter fences or guards with rifles to disrupt such illusions.

Among these photographs, however, are some startling images of Japanese American children dressed in blackface that disrupt a transparent reading of racial codes (fig. 8.11). The enormous complexity of these pictures confronts us immediately: what can it mean for Japanese American children—children who are incarcerated for being potential enemies of the state without any evidence of subversive activity to substantiate such charges—to blacken up? At a moment when many Japanese Americans were working hard to assert their loyalty as citizens, why take on the image of blackness, an image that is deeply steeped in a history of stereotyped caricatures? Moreover, who were they blackening up for? Who is the intended audience of this performance? Given the cultural power accorded photography to represent identity, what happens to the "real" when we look at the mask of blackface? Finally, what does agency mean for these children in burnt cork?

At the end of this series of photographs on the festival is a picture of children on a makeshift proscenium stage reenacting a slave auction (fig. 8.12). The caption states only that this was "Part of a play given by the Dramatics Department at the Harvest Festival Talent Show." Perhaps this slave reenactment

Figure 8.10. "One of the floats in the Harvest Festival Parade which was held at this center on Thanksgiving Day." Gila River Relocation Center, Rivers, Ariz., 26 November 1942. (No. 210-G-6D-629, Francis Stewart, Central File, RG 210, NACP.)

narrativizes Japanese American claims for citizenship and freedom through a blackface performance that invokes the history of slavery and African Americans' struggle for freedom. For a people claiming American citizenship against a government and a national culture that has already displayed its willingness to deny that claim, the politics of blackface could be read as associating their experiences with other American histories of racial oppression. These images of blackface, especially the photograph of the slave auction, not only connote stereotypes that marginalize but also historical struggles to claim rights of citizenship, another American tradition. At the least they expose the instabilities of racial identities as Japanese American children blacken up to critique slavery and/or incarceration.

Although this is a compelling reading of these photographs, there are dangers of appropriating white racist codes for subversive purposes because they also reproduce hierarchies of color in the United States. In other words, is this another example of asserting the privilege of not being black? The complex politics of national identity, of who belongs to the imagined community of citizens, are here played out through blackface in which histories of race, inequal-

Figure 8.11. "Harvest Festival Parade held at this center on Thanksgiving Day." Gila River Relocation Center, Rivers, Ariz., 26 November 1942. (No. 210-G-6D-632, Francis Stewart, Central File, RG 210, NACP.)

ity, and power are painted onto the faces of these Japanese American children. The political scientist Michael Rogin questions interpretations of blackface as (potentially) subversive or a radical practice of marginal groups because "it displays the peculiar feature of American nationalism, a popular expression that emerges . . . not to free oppressed folk but to constitute national identity out of their subjugation" (18). I agree with Rogin that no matter how subversive the intent, blackface depends on subordinating African Americans through caricature. Thus even resistant moments that use this particular strategy cannot escape the hegemonic structures embedded in this historically racist practice.

Even if we knew the play to be a subversive critique, the use of blackface implicates these children in discourses of racial hierarchy and marginalization. This in turn forces us to confront the dialogic nature of resistance and hegemony in which structures of domination reside in resistant acts (Mohanty).

Figure 8.12. "Part of a play given by the Dramatics Department of the Harvest Festival Talent Show." Gila River Relocation Center, Rivers, Ariz., 27 November 1943. (No. 210-G-6G-407, Francis Stewart, Central File, RG 210, NACP.)

In this context, when we return to the question of what it can mean for Japanese American children to blacken up, more clearly here perhaps than in any of the other pictures agency emerges not as a pure or unproblematic act of resistance. Instead these images demonstrate that agency is a discursive and a material struggle that is contingent on historical processes for its political and cultural significance.

Rejecting any fixed notion of agency enables us to interrogate the power of the "real" to negotiate identity. If government photographers attempt to speak for Japanese Americans by showing them as Americans, in the blackface photographs Japanese Americans speak for or at least invoke African American history. The realness of the children's blackened faces associates their experiences with other American histories of racial oppression and exploitation, yet in ways that also reproduce that exploitation. In mobilizing concepts of race, nationalism, and history, the blackface photographs force us to reconsider questions about contesting and negotiating identities and claiming agency within and not outside of dominant cultural, social, and political spaces.

Conclusion

While the government's gaze shapes our visual understanding of Executive Order 9066 and its impact on the Japanese American population, the WRA archive contains more than propaganda. In challenging a reading of the archive as simply reproducing the government's gaze, however, we need to view these pictures historically within the wartime politics of identity and (re)location. Overlapping agendas between the government and Japanese American internees resulted in representations that at times make the internees' objectives appear consonant with those of the WRA. Yet just as the notion of a totalizing governmental gaze is highly problematic so too is any presumption that the pictures show the "real" experiences of the Japanese Americans. Pictures that show proud, strong people refusing to be depicted as victims, I argue, reveal something of Japanese Americans' attitudes, even their agency. But "agency" proves often to be itself a hegemonic position, and one not ultimately representative of a unified "community."

In arguing that we cannot fully recover Japanese Americans' experiences of evacuation, however, questions such as who is looking and who is speaking for whom reveal important information about struggles over identity. Rather than see photographs as static moments, as capturing the trace of something else, the WRA photographs participate in producing claims of citizenship. While they can never hold up a mirror through which to see "real" experiences, photographs do reveal the political struggles over representation itself. In this regard, the trope of relocation foregrounds another mobility, that is, the intertextual movements of discursive and material conditions that shape visibility. Within the context of forced confinement and censorship, these photographs demonstrate how visual culture engages in the social process of contesting and negotiating identities, including citizenship. Images of domesticity rely on normative gender ideals to claim Americanness, just as those of the slave auction challenge the viewer to think about democracy. Such pictures reveal how the politics of demanding social and political legitimacy by Japanese Americans also implicated them within the government's agenda. Equally important, this points to the complex problematic of photographing citizenship.

Notes

I wish to thank Anna Agathangelou, Ann Cooper Albright, Jan Cooper, Maggi Kamitsuka, Christin Mamiya, Paula Richman, Augusta Rohrbach, Sandy Zagarell, and an anonymous reviewer for their thoughtful criticisms. Nell Farrell and Susan Pearson were superb research assistants as well as traveling companions. Steven Wojtal once again generously provided his support and editorial skills. I am deeply grateful to Wendy Hesford for her incisive readings of multiple drafts which strengthened this argument.

1. *Central Photographic File of the War Relocation Authority, 1942–1945,* Record Group 210, National Archives at College Park, College Park, Md.

2. The most notable example is Toyo Miyatake, a professional photographer prior to evacuation who smuggled in a lens and shutter to the Manzanar, California, relocation center, where he then built a camera. The camp director, Ralph Merritt, eventually allowed him to establish a portrait studio in the camp (Armor and Wright xviii–xx). At the Topaz, Arizona, relocation center, Dave Tatsuno smuggled in his 8mm home movie camera. In 1997 this home movie, "Topaz," was added to the National Film Registry, only the second home movie to be selected for the Registry (Email Network of the Association of Asian American Studies, press release, 18 Dec. 1997).

3. I am grateful to Gary Okihiro for initially suggesting this to me.

4. The following discussion of the events leading up to the evacuation is drawn from several excellent histories, including Takaki; Chan; Daniels, *Prisoners;* Taylor; Okihiro, *Whispered.*

5. In referring to this trope of relocation, I am building on Kaplan's critique of feminist arguments about the politics of location that use the term as a "reflection of authentic, primordial identities." Instead she argues that the concept is most effective when used to "destabilize unexamined or stereotypical images that are vestiges of colonial discourse and other manifestations of modernity's structural inequalities." She goes on to write that "as a practice of affiliation, a politics of location identifies the grounds for historically specific differences and similarities between women in diverse and asymmetrical relations, creating alternative histories, identities, and possibilities for alliances" (139).

6. Brown also discusses this passage (85–86).

7. For historical discussions of immigration, settlement, and legal and social discriminations, see Takaki; Chan; Okihiro, *Margins.*

8. Autobiographical accounts capture vividly these conflicts for young Nisei; see for example Sone; Houston and Houston.

9. See Daniels for a discussion of the uses and avoidance of the term "concentration camps" during and after the war (*Prisoners* 66).

10. Although there was widespread support for Executive Order 9066, there was also some notable opposition. I conducted a review of popular magazines and newspapers from 1941 to 1946 that revealed that several national journals, such as *Commonweal,* opposed this policy (see also Okihiro, *Whispered* 174). Lange's husband, Paul Taylor, an influential social scientist, was among the first critics to publish articles denouncing the evacuation in nationally circulated magazines (Daniels, "Dorothea Lange").

11. File 22.010, "Roundtable discussion between J. C. Baker, M. M. Tozier, Ray Mil-

ler, Mr. Specter, and Mr. Goode," 23 June 1942; Headquarters, entry 16, general file; Records of the War Relocation Authority, Record Group 210, National Archives Building, Washington, D.C.

12. For an excellent discussion of African American attitudes toward Japan and Japanese Americans as well as the interethnic coalitions that emerged during and after the war, see Lipsitz, 184–210.

13. See Omi and Winant for their influential analysis of racial formations that also informs Pascoe's argument.

14. Omi and Winant discuss how ethnicity theory between the 1930s and the 1960s shaped discourses of race in these years. In critiquing this theory, they argue that "the entire model for comparing and evaluating the success of ethnic groups . . . is limited by an unwillingness to consider whether there might be any special circumstances which racially defined minorities encounter in the U.S., circumstances which definitively distinguish their experiences from those of earlier European immigrants and make the injunction to 'pull yourselves up by your bootstraps' impossible to fulfill" (22).

15. Interestingly, photographers not employed by the WRA used similar iconography in their representations of the internees. Adams's photographs in the 1944 exhibition *Born Free and Equal,* like the WRA archive, depict the internees through pictures of families, baby nurseries, students in classes, and men playing baseball. The similarities between Adams's photographs and those of the WRA demonstrate how these pictures participated in larger cultural discourses about wartime nationalism and debates over race, ethnicity, and citizenship.

16. One extremely painful exception is a series of photographs of the dead body of John Yoshida, a twenty-three-year-old man who committed suicide by lying across a railroad track (Jerome Relocation Center, Arizona, January 1944. Nos. 210-9K-513 to 210-9K-518, Central File of the War Relocation Authority, 1942–1945, Record Group 210, National Archives at College Park, College Park, Md.).

Works Cited

Adams, Ansel. *Born Free and Equal: Photographs of the Loyal Japanese Americans at Manzanar Relocation Center, Inyo County, California.* New York: U.S. Camera, 1944.

Armor, John, and Peter Wright. *Manzanar.* New York: Times Books, 1988.

Brandt, Nat. *Harlem at War: The Black Experience in WW II.* Syracuse, N.Y.: Syracuse University Press, 1996.

Brown, Kate. "The Eclipse of History: Japanese America and a Treasure Chest of Forgetting." *Public Culture* 9 (1996): 69–91.

Chan, Sucheng. *Asian Americans: An Interpretive History.* Boston: Twayne Publishers, 1991.

Curtis, James. *Mind's Eye, Mind's Truth: FSA Photography Reconsidered.* Philadelphia: Temple University Press, 1989.

Daniel, Pete, Merry A. Foresta, Maren Stange, and Sally Stein. *Official Images: New Deal Photography.* Washington, D.C.: Smithsonian Press, 1987.

Daniels, Roger. "Dorothea Lange and the War Relocation Authority: Photographing Japanese Americans." In *Dorothea Lange: A Visual Life.* Ed. Elizabeth Partridge. Washington, D.C.: Smithsonian Press, 1994. 45–56.

———. *Prisoners without Trial: Japanese Americans in World War II.* New York: Hill and Wang, 1993.

Gaines, Jane. "White Privilege and Looking Relations: Race and Gender in Feminist Film Theory." *Screen* 29.4 (1988): 12–27.

Grewal, Inderpal. "Autobiographic Subjects and Diasporic Locations: Meatless Days and Borderlands." In *Scattered Hegemonies: Postmodernity and Transnational Feminist Practices.* Ed. Inderpal Grewal and Caren Kaplan. Minneapolis: University of Minnesota Press, 1994. 231–54.

Grewal, Inderpal, and Caren Kaplan. "Introduction: Transnational Feminist Practices and Questions of Postmodernity." In *Scattered Hegemonies: Postmodernity and Transnational Feminist Practices.* Ed. Inderpal Grewal and Caren Kaplan. Minneapolis: University of Minnesota Press, 1994. 1–33.

Hall, Stuart. "Reconstruction Work: Images of Post-War Black Settlement." In *Family Snaps: The Meanings of Domestic Photography.* Ed. Jo Spence and Patricia Holland. London: Virago, 1991. 152–64.

hooks, bell. "The Oppositional Gaze: Black Female Spectators." In *Black Looks: Race and Representation.* Boston: South End Press, 1992. 115–31.

Houston, Jeanne Wakatsuki, and James D. Houston. *Farewell to Manzanar.* New York: Bantam Books, 1973.

Irons, Peter, ed. *Justice Delayed: The Record of the Japanese American Internment Cases.* Middleton, Conn.: Wesleyan University Press, 1989.

Kaplan, Caren. "The Politics of Location as Transnational Feminist Critical Practice." In *Scattered Hegemonies: Postmodernity and Transnational Feminist Practices.* Ed. Inderpal Grewal and Caren Kaplan. Minneapolis: University of Minnesota Press, 1994. 137–52.

Kozol, Wendy. "Madonnas of the Fields: Photography, Gender, and 1930s Farm Relief." *Genders* 2 (1988): 1–23.

Linehan, Thomas M. "Japanese American Resettlement in Cleveland during and after World War II." *Journal of Urban History* 20.1 (1993): 54–80.

Lipsitz, George. *The Possessive Investment in Whiteness: How White People Profit from Identity Politics.* Philadelphia: Temple University Press, 1998.

Lutz, Catherine A., and Jane L. Collins. *Reading National Geographic.* Chicago: University of Chicago Press, 1993.

Mohanty, Chandra Talpade. "Cartographies of Struggle: Third World Women and the Politics of Feminism." In *Third World Women and the Politics of Feminism.* Ed. Chandra Mohanty, Ann Russo, and Lourdes Torres. Bloomington: Indiana University Press, 1991. 1–47.

Okihiro, Gary. *Margins and Mainstreams: Asians in American History and Culture.* Seattle: University of Washington Press, 1994.

———. *Whispered Silences: Japanese Americans and World War II.* Seattle: University of Washington Press, 1996.

Omi, Michael, and Howard Winant. *Racial Formation in the United States: From the 1960s to the 1990s.* 2d ed. New York: Routledge, 1994.

Parker, Andrew, Mary Russo, Doris Sommer, and Patricia Yaeger. *Nationalisms and Sexualities.* New York: Routledge, 1992.

Pascoe, Peggy. "Miscegenation Law, Court Cases, and Ideologies of 'Race' in Twentieth-Century America." *Journal of American History* 83.1 (1996): 44–69.

Rogin, Michael. *Blackface, White Noise: Jewish Immigrants in the Hollywood Melting Pot.* Berkeley: University of California Press, 1996.

Scott, Joan W. "Experience." In *Feminists Theorize the Political.* Ed. Judith Butler and Joan W. Scott. New York: Routledge, 1992. 22–40.

Shapiro, Ann-Louise, ed. *Feminists Revision History.* New Brunswick, N.J.: Rutgers University Press, 1994.

Sone, Monica. *Nisei Daughter.* Seattle: University of Washington Press, 1953.

Takaki, Ronald. *Strangers from a Different Shore: A History of Asian Americans.* New York: Penguin Books, 1989.

Taylor, Sandra. *Jewel of the Desert: Japanese American Internment at Topaz.* Berkeley: University of California Press, 1993.

Terry, Jennifer. "Theorizing Deviant Historiography." In *Feminists Revision History.* Ed. Ann-Louise Shapiro. New Brunswick, N.J.: Rutgers University Press, 1994. 276–303.

Williams, Brackette. "Introduction: Mannish Women and Gender after the Act." In *Women Out of Place: The Gender of Agency and the Race of Nationality.* Ed. Brackette Williams. New York: Routledge, 1996. 1–33.

9

The Smiles and Tears of Representation

A Cross-Talk Essay

Patrick Brantlinger

> Sunt lacrimae rerum.
> —Virgil

What can be done to counteract the violence of misrepresentation? Or is representation always, whether accurate or not, inherently violent? Although they acknowledge the force of poststructuralist interventions in cultural studies, the contributors to *Haunting Violations* all take "critical realist" approaches to questions of representation, authenticity, and traumas such as rape and genocide. These essays foreground the attempts (and are themselves such attempts) of feminist and postcolonial activist intellectuals to realistically or authentically represent or "speak for" the victims—women, children, "subalterns"—of oppression and violence, including the violence of some forms of representation.

In her essay on representations of rape, Wendy S. Hesford writes, "Cultural narratives and fantasies are not antithetical to material 'reality,'" but are instead major aspects and shapers of that reality. This is to say, reality is always mediated by and, in various complex ways, constructed through representation. There isn't any end to representation—that is an inescapable feature of the human condition—and linguistic, textual, and cultural attempts to shape and claim ultimate truths about the "real" involve endless epistemological struggles over evidence, authenticity, and meanings. In their essay on *Mississippi Masala*, Purnima Bose and Linta Varghese cite Gayatri Chakravorty Spivak on the distinction between representation as discourse and representation as political process while insisting, with Spivak, that the two categories are inseparable. The inseparability of the two types of representation, discursive and political, is a theme throughout *Haunting Violations,* as is its corollary: the regressive politics of such major forms of (mis)representation as racist stereotyping demands a progressive politics of criticism and resistance and the production of accurate, realistic representations.

The specific representation that Hesford focuses upon—Margie Strosser's autobiographical film, *Rape Stories*—raises the further issue of the nature (including the "real"-ness) of traumas. Hesford emphasizes the "traumatic paradox," whereby an experience of violence or oppression doesn't become a trauma until it is remembered and represented as such, which means that trauma is dependent on—or perhaps just *is*—its symbolic repetitions. Does *Rape Stories* resist and help to dismantle conventional, stereotypic attitudes toward women and rape (such as the assumption that rape victims must have been asking for it)? Or does it in some manner, by representing and therefore repeating it, constitute the trauma that Strosser experienced and continues to experience? Or both? This dangerous doubleness of representation—to resist violence it must give violence expression if not approval—is complicated in *Rape Stories* by its inclusion of Strosser's "revenge fantasy." Strosser imagines killing the rapist with his knife and, "at my leisure," shaving off "thin slices" of his corpse, which she mails "to all my friends who have been raped, with my condolences." Strosser's revenge fantasy turns the tables on the rapist, but by continuing the violence rather than ending it. If *Rape Stories,* or any other representation of rape such as the documentary film on Bosnian war crimes, *Calling the Ghosts,* in some sense helps to constitute the trauma it seeks to end, Strosser's revenge fantasy reinforces that paradox by putting the victim in the role of the rapist and having her commit the violence that she most feared (murder) when she was raped.

Rape is also at the traumatic center of Leela Fernandes's analysis of the fascinating story—stories, rather—of Phoolan Devi, the "Indian Bandit Queen." Having been repeatedly raped by high-caste men, the low-caste Phoolan Devi led a band of *dacoits,* or robbers, and took her revenge, like a female Robin Hood, by killing some of her violators, stealing from the rich, and giving the loot to the poor. Fernandes focuses on the differences between the autobiographical text, *I, Phoolan Devi,* and the film, *Bandit Queen,* directed by Shekhar Kapur for British television. An illiterate, non-English-speaking subaltern, Phoolan Devi told her story to the writers who produced the printed text for literate, upper-class, mainly Western readers. The film, by an Indian male director, was also produced with a mainly Western audience in mind. Fernandes points out that, for Indian viewers, the film offers a powerful critique of Indian gender politics and the caste system. At the same time, for Western viewers, especially through its multiple rape scenes, it is likely to reinforce rather than undo stereotypes of Indian barbarism and backwardness. Fernandes acknowledges the impossibility of establishing some ultimate, true version of those stories (even through Phoolan Devi's own testimony) and searches for more adequate ways of representing or "speaking for" the Third-World woman as "subaltern." She calls her approach "feminist 'critical realism,'" which, rather than claiming some direct, miraculous access to the "real," involves understanding the complex interplay of texts, contexts, and translations across boundaries of language, religion, caste, class, culture, race, nation, and gender.

Fernandes notes that the title of Phoolan Devi's autobiography echoes *I, Rigoberta Menchú*, which Susan Sánchez-Casal calls "the most widely read testimonial 'autobiography' in the U.S. academy." Like Phoolan Devi's narrative, Menchú's was transcribed by its "editor" from her oral testimony; it is perhaps partly its basis in orality that tempts readers to interpret it as the direct, unmediated voice of truth about the Quichés of Guatemala, their oppression, and their struggle against genocide. Sánchez-Casal's argument that the text is "dialogical" and conflicted or ambivalent in a variety of ways—that its "speaking subject" is "ontologically plural"—is only strengthened by the recent controversy over its truthfulness (for a summary, see Cohen). But neither that controversy nor Sánchez-Casal's critique of those "testimonial editors and critics who advance essentialist notions of subaltern subjectivities" undermines the power and importance of Menchú's account of her life, of Quiché culture and society, of "indigenous oppression," and of "indigenous resistance to genocide." On the contrary, Sánchez-Casal's insistence on "the need to read critically the discourse of the Other" is itself a way of resisting stereotypic patterns of representation and interpretation that, no matter how well-intended, reify and "exotify" the complexities of others' lives, motives, values, and struggles. To treat Menchú as the unconflicted, direct voice of truth about the Quichés is, Sánchez-Casal argues, a way of ensuring that she will never teach her readers anything very significant.

The rhetoric of Menchú's autobiography and its essentializing, noncritical commentators produces the illusion of a unified, authentic "indigenous" self. In contrast, Julia Watson points out, Janet Campbell Hale's *Bloodlines*, an account of her "dysfunctional" childhood as a "mixed-blood" Native American, represents experience as hybrid and fragmentary. Instead of the unifying literariness evident in some other narratives by Native American authors, *Bloodlines* fractures standard expectations about psychological and cultural cohesion. It does so in part by employing a variety of what Watson calls "technologies of the real": discursive practices that express personal experience and thereby validate life narratives. But such "technologies" as photographs, letters, and mementoes in *Bloodlines* seem to be fragments of the real rather than guarantors either of a more coherent reality or of a unified self beyond those fragments. Hale turns to the notion of "bloodlines" not in an essentializing way, but "as a basis for making new stories of people who can no longer be 'from' their original homes." Appealing not to sophisticated, college-educated readers but to Native Americans who cannot be "from" white America—who have been subjected to poverty, racism, violence, and, too often, alcohol and drug addiction—*Bloodlines,* Watson concludes, offers "new ways" of understanding "loss" and "dysfunctionality."

In their analysis of a very different text, Mina Nair's *Mississippi Masala,* Purnima Bose and Linta Varghese criticize the ways that "critics and partisans" of that film have sought to enlist the "real" to support their arguments. "As a category of experience for diasporic South Asians," Bose and Varghese contend, the "real" isn't something fixed and stable, but is instead "a site of contestation over identity." The film problematizes invocations of the "real" that seek to fix or stabilize South Asian identities. Partly because of the paucity of mass media representations of South Asians and partly because of its mainstream, Hollywood status, the film has carried a huge "representational burden," especially for South Asian feminists. Bose and Varghese show how criticisms of the film by such feminists often depend on falsely essentializing notions of South Asian identity. Yet they are inclined to excuse the film's feminist-activist critics on the grounds that they are employing what Spivak calls "strategic essentialism."

But the critics of *Mississippi Masala* also overlook or minimize the cultural-critical work that it performs. Bose and Varghese interpret the film as, among other things, deconstructing the binary oppositions and patriarchal gender politics that characterize Indian "masala films." Like the masala films themselves, most critics of *Mississippi Masala* overlook or minimize the great diversity of cultures, languages, religions, races, and experiences that the phrase "South Asian" encompasses. Given that *Mississippi Masala* deals with South Asian characters expelled from Uganda by Idi Amin in 1972, some of whom have never been to the subcontinent and "diasporically" wind up in Mississippi of all places, assertions that it should have been more representative of an authentic, unitary South Asianness sound more like wishful thinking than valid criticism. Bose and Varghese support the feminist and antiracist activism of many of the film's severest critics, yet they see Mina Nair as in several respects also expressing progressive social and political values. For the South Asian activists and the South Asian filmmaker (and also for Bose and Varghese), the politics of representation and especially the struggle against racist and sexist stereotypes and images is a central battleground.

The very real (but nonetheless imaginary and ideological) politics of the image is a main theme throughout *Haunting Violations.* And from the time of its invention in the 1830s, one form of the reproduction and dissemination of images that has figured prominently in debates about "realist" epistemology has been photography. "Mad or tame? Photography can be one or the other." Thus Roland Barthes concludes *Camera Lucida*, adding: "The choice is mine: to subject its spectacle to the civilized code of perfect illusions, or to confront in it the wakening of intractable reality" (119). Perhaps the same is true of all forms of representation: depending on how they are interpreted, they are either tame (converting the madness of "intractable reality" into "the civilized code of perfect illusions") or mad (allowing for or expecting "the wakening of intractable reality" to occur, so to speak, in reality). But, as Barthes well knew, the photographer with his or her photographic apparatus intervenes as a first line of interpretation, a first taming or maddening.

As Wendy Kozol shows, the photographs of interned Japanese Americans taken for the War Relocation Authority "project an idealized image that routinely emphasizes the commonalities between the internees and other Americans." While a critique of the notion of the happy prisoner may be implicit in the photographs taken by Dorothea Lange, both the WRA and the Japanese Americans, Kozol suggests, had a stake in producing images that tamed and normalized ethnic-cultural difference and the traumas of arrest, confiscation, imprisonment, and relocation. She further contends that the "photographs supported and . . . helped to construct [the] racial ideology of color blindness by visualizing Japanese Americans as 'Americans'"—playing softball, sewing American flags, and so on. But once the viewer understands the purposes for which they were made, the madness of the reality shines or smiles out from the images anyway. As Kozol demonstrates, those purposes were logically, politically mad: to normalize these supposed outsiders, to show that they are no different from anyone else, while insisting upon their difference as a dangerous element that justifies their incarceration.

In *Mythologies*, Barthes says that the "petit-bourgeois is a man unable to imagine the Other." He can do so only by treating "the Other" as something monstrous, "a scandal," or as just like himself, as more of the same (151). One way, madness; the other, tameness (or sameness, another sort of madness). Like the petit-bourgeois man, the WRA photographs are doubly mad because they cannot bring into focus a realistic, coherent version of ethnic and cultural difference. Instead they register the monstrosity of sameness or the sameness of monstrosity. American citizenship may mean being an interned Japanese American woman sewing an American flag or conversely an American photographer (presumably a color-blind one: white, middle-class, normal, no different from any other American) working for the American government by taking pictures of this dangerously different sameness, this potentially monstrous Americanness. So what is *American*, anyway?

As Kozol points out, such questions and their undecidability multiply in relation to the photographs of interned Japanese American children in black-face. To say the least, these images "disrupt a transparent reading of racial codes." Participating in the dramatization of a slave auction, the children, or rather their parents, may or may not be critiquing "slavery and/or incarceration." But even if they are engaged in "a subversive critique," Kozol argues, "the use of blackface implicates these children [and their parents] in discourses of racial hierarchy and marginalization." On the one hand, blackface reveals the social constructedness and stereotypic madness of all versions of racial difference: it is manifestly a performance, implying the performativity of race in general. On the other hand, blackface reinforces the racism that has tragically underwritten white Americanness for three centuries. The Japanese American children in blackface dramatize the madness/tameness registered in all of the WRA photographs: *we are the same as you, because these others are different from both of us.* We, interned Japanese American citizens, are just the same as other Americans, even though we are different . . . or *because* we are different: Americanness as a coerced unity of unacknowledged difference.

Given their contradictory purposes, the photographs seem extraordinarily artificial or contrived, in part because of their documentary status. Whether in photography, news reporting, or other forms, the more a representation announces that it is an unmediated and unposed rendition of reality, the more it is likely to seem posed and artificial and the more whatever is meant by the "real" seems to evade the net of representation. This leads to the suspicion, at least, that what is real is unrepresentable and its corollary, that all forms of representation are unreal. The suspicion of the unreality or inadequacy of representation emerges from what I take to be the *punctum* in all of these photographs: the smiles on the faces of these supposedly happy prisoners, much as in blackface depictions of smiling, happy slaves at the slave auction or down on the plantation.

The most disturbing photograph in *Camera Lucida* depicts a grieving mother and her family or neighbors standing over a corpse in the street of a Nicaraguan village. The corpse is covered by a sheet. The mother holds in her arms, also wrapped in a sheet, what appears to be the corpse of a child, no doubt her own. She and a woman in the background are weeping. Because of its stark, apparently spontaneous or unposed quality, the photograph registers a moment of trauma, of the "real" in one meaning of that term, in a way that the WRA photographs of happy Japanese Americans do not. Is it the mother's tears, her evident signs of grief, that constitute what Barthes calls the punctum of this photograph and others like it? Is it the sheet-draped corpses? The foot that protrudes from beneath the sheet covering the corpse lying in the street? Or is it the evident signs of poverty: the broken pavement, the boarded-up doorway, and so on? Or is the punctum made up of all of these details? "A photograph's *punctum*," Barthes writes, "is that accident which pricks me (but also bruises me, is poignant to me)" (27). The punctum, then, is a tear, a gash, or a wound in the image through which the wound and the madness, the trauma, of the real can be at least fleetingly glimpsed. In that case, it seems to me that this entire photograph, and not just a detail within it, is its punctum. And perhaps all forms of realistic representation—at least when they manage to reflect or express a "real" reality (and therefore a trauma)—are constituted by or simply are punctums? Wounds opening onto wounds, tears onto tears, slicing open the fabric of ordinariness that otherwise blinds us to what is terrifying and monstrous about the ordinary.

Despite their apparent authenticity and spontaneity (and therefore their realism), photographs are never unmediated slices of reality. But what about the tears shed by the members of the Mothers' Front in Sri Lanka? Are mothers' tears better guarantors of a "real" than either photographs or incarcerated mothers' smiles? As Virgil says, there are tears in things. Tears on the faces of prisoners or slaves would at least not register the contradiction evident in smiles. But tears can also be crocodile tears. The custom, practiced in various parts of the world, of hiring mourners to participate in funerals entails the production of counterfeit tears.

At the end of James Fenimore Cooper's novel about the decimation of Native America, Chingachgook and Natty Bumppo stand hand-in-hand in an "attitude of friendship" and bow "their heads together, while scalding tears [fall] to their feet, watering the grave of Uncas," the "last of the Mohicans" (349). Because Cooper's novel writes the future emergence of the new (white) American republic as the outcome of that decimation or, in other words, of the genocidal "vanishing" of Native Americans, the tears shed by "these two sturdy and intrepid woodsmen" might as well be stars on one of the American flags being sewn by the Japanese American women photographed by the WRA. The tears in Cooper's text are those of a "philanthropic" sentimentality that help to underwrite American national identity and patriotism at the expense of Native Americans. (Caring representation of postmodern consumerism, the tearful Indian is today a familiar icon in American advertising, a stereotype at odds with the "dysfunctional" selves depicted in *Bloodlines* and with the political activism inscribed in *I, Rigoberta Menchú*). But in Cooper's novel, the reality that the tears guarantee is not that of death, the desecration of nature, Natty's and Chingachgook's mutual grief, or even of the genocide of Native America; it is instead that of the future American republic (the tears can be readily converted to smiles by Cooper's savvy, white, all-American readers).

As Malathi de Alwis points out, however, the tears shed by the members of the Sri Lankan Mothers' Front, as "a tangible signifier of suffering," are "both maternalized and sentimentalized through their discursive production as a bodily essence of motherhood." What the tears of the Mothers' Front seem to guarantee is nothing less than the reality of motherhood itself, always seen as essentially a condition of suffering and self-sacrifice and even more so when the immediate objects of that suffering and self-sacrifice—children—have been "vanished" or "disappeared." "Body speech" of this type, de Alwis argues, constitutes an especially powerful form of propaganda, partly because it is bodily (both physical and wordless). But while this "body speech" composed of mothers' "bloodmilk" is capable of mobilizing political protest, it is also limited because it reinforces sexist, essentializing constructions of motherhood and women: "The political effectivity of the Mothers' Front [was] predicated on the reiteration of patriarchal and Sinhala Buddhist conceptions of maternalized suffering and sentiment." This limitation is similar to that which South Asian feminists see in *Mississippi Masala* (it reinforces rather than contests gender stereotypes) and in a more complex way to that which Hesford finds in *Rape Stories* as an attempt to overcome trauma by representing it and even, through Strosser's "revenge fantasy," by reversing the roles of victim and rapist.

Rather than opposing the Mothers' Front directly, the government adopted its tactics, including its rhetoric of mothers' tears, by organizing its own women's rally to mourn "the deaths of their male kin who had been killed by militants." The government was only too ready to reinforce patriarchal conceptions of motherhood and women's roles in Sri Lankan society and politics. These conceptions, de Alwis notes, are evident as well in the conceits or formulaic metaphors that serve as "a shorthand, a concise and efficient way of expressing as well as evoking a particular sentiment among those who understand the Sinhala language." Like real tears as signifiers of grief, such conceits as mothers' "bloodmilk" and "minds soaked in the tears constantly shed" "illuminate the complicated interplay between discursivity and materiality." They also serve to underscore the "universality" of mothers' suffering and self-sacrifice as well as of death and mourning.

Not only do mothers' tears work as effective protest and in support of patriarchy, they also work against specificity by universalizing grieving motherhood. That the government could so easily appropriate the tactics of the Mothers' Front is an indication of what is problematic about tears as signifiers of any particular reality. Expressing a universal condition of grief, tears, though like blood the products of wounded, traumatized bodies, cannot speak to the crimes or horrors of any specific event or moment in history. It isn't the tears of the Nicaraguans that give the photograph in *Camera Lucida* its stark, tragic specificity. It is, on the contrary, every nonuniversal detail: the woman's dress, the broken pavement, the protruding foot, the letters "FSLN" on the boarded-up doorway. The experience of tears may be a universal reality, but what is real because quite specific, immediate, and traumatic escapes that universalization or, rather, escapes because of that universalization. And perhaps the punctum of a photograph is always something so specific that it is almost wordless, almost unrepresentable (though it is always there, represented). While the image of the grieving Nicaraguan mother may in part reinforce an essentialized, universal stereotype of motherhood, the photograph includes the signs of the specific trauma—the violence, the political graffiti, the corpses—that has caused her to grieve. And yet the corpses are covered with sheets; we cannot see faces, specific identities. So this photograph both specifies a particular trauma and works to universalize the experiences of violence, death, and mourning.

Any representation of an action always involves two sorts of agency or questions about agency. The first concerns the agency of the actor(s) or the participant(s) in the action; the second concerns the agency of the representer(s). In the case of the WRA photographs, the agency of the photographers is quite distinct and opposed to that of the interned Japanese Americans. Despite having an official task to perform and despite the structural limitations of the photographic apparatus, the photographers are presumably free to act in ways their subjects are not. And yet as representers distinct from those whom they represent, the photographers are also stand-ins for ideology; for one thing, they interpellate their subjects as objects. Perhaps the photographers are free agents only in the sense that they themselves are not the immediate objects of surveillance and interpellation through others' representations. Ironically, both the photographers and their subjects have a stake in representing a normalized, cheerful, and patriotic version of American citizenship. Whatever agency the Japanese Americans may seem to exercise in or through the photographs, it appears to reside in complying with the photographers' (and the government's) aim of rendering them as docile bodies—that is, as cheerful, even grateful, patriotic prisoner-citizens.

In contrast to the WPA photographs, even in the mediated, edited texts by Phoolan Devi and Rigoberta Menchú the autobiographer is both subject and object, representer and represented. As Leslie Bow points out, the autobiographies by Le Ly Hayslip are also mediated, by her son as translator and by Jay Wurts as "coauthor." In terms of the question of agency, they are further complicated by Hayslip's gender and by her past and present ethnic, religious, and national subject positions, involving necessarily divided loyalties. As with the Mother's Front in Sri Lanka, so too for Hayslip and, Bow contends, for all women: "political allegiance is established through the body." More specifically, for Vietnamese peasant women such as the young Le Ly and her sisters, it is the commodified, sexualized body-for-sale—in one sense, the least mystified version of "the traffic in women"—that victimizes and subjugates them while making a degree of agency and choice of "political allegiance" available to them. "As sex literally becomes a commodity bartered for survival, in controlling her sexual commodification Le Ly asserts the primacy of her own agency." But the assertion of agency is not the same as having it. For Bow, there isn't any simple opposition between self-control and domination, freedom and entrapment, agency and determinism. Certainly Le Ly's multiple subject-positions—which play into the multiculturalism that, Bow contends, is all too easily co-opted by liberal ideology—give her, as Vietnamese peasant woman and as autobiographer, a certain flexibility and range of movement, though still circumscribed by gender, nationality, and the other ideological factors that construct identity.

Does Hayslip's ability (albeit through collaboration with her son and Jay Wurts) to write and market her story constitute another, higher, disembodied agency that is nevertheless analogous to prostitution? In all autobiographical discourse the main proof of achieved agency is the autobiographical act itself. The teleological goal of Hayslip's autobiographies is no different in this respect from that of, say, *The Narrative of the Life of Frederick Douglass:* the writing and dissemination of the narrative is the end, in both senses, of any autobiographer's life story. Just as Douglass escapes from slavery (and hence from the condition of being treated as a commodity) and then marks his freedom by producing and circulating the commodified narrative of his life, so Hayslip escapes from the situation of war and poverty that forced her into prostitution and marks her freedom by producing and selling her autobiographies. That these texts are commodities, circulating within a globalized system of transnational capital, in no way undercuts what their author has accomplished. Instead of being at best merely the object of others' representations, Hayslip, like Douglass, can represent herself. Even though she relies, like the Mother's Front in Sri Lanka, on "naturalized gender values," and even though her narratives are published and disseminated via transnational capitalism, Hayslip's is a self-help success story in the familiar tradition of capitalist individualism. At the same time, even though her life story "does not offer unequivocal evidence of feminist identity," like the autobiographies of Phoolan Devi and Rigoberta Menchú and also like *Mississippi Masala,* "it does indicate the necessity for developing a concept of complex agency in regard to Third-World women."

A similar conclusion about "complex agency" can be drawn from de Alwis's analysis of the Mother's Front and its "tears" and even, though much more ambiguously, from Kozol's account of the WRA photographs of interned Japanese Americans. The representational agency available to trauma victims always, perhaps, produces a type of wounded representation that can enter the psyches of the nontraumatized only through chinks in their ideological armor like the punctums of photographs. It seems unlikely, to say the least, that the man who raped Margie Strosser could be reformed by seeing *Rape Stories* or even frightened by her "revenge fantasy." Moreover, perhaps wounded representation is all that is possible through the "conventions of realism." But when the victims—Hayslip, Phoolan Devi, Menchú, Strosser, Hale, Douglass—are in charge of those conventions or, in other words, when they can represent themselves, then something more is achieved, and greater prospects of agency and freedom are opened for everyone.

The autobiographies by Hayslip, Phoolan Devi, and Menchú are moments in which Third-World women subalterns can and do speak for themselves. Even if one defines subalterns as those unable to represent themselves ("they cannot represent themselves, they must be represented," as Marx said of the French peasantry [608]), Hayslip's self-representations mark her achievement of agency. In contrast, the smiling faces of the Japanese American interns in the WRA photographs offer little if any reason to be optimistic about agency, freedom, or realistic representation as capable of undoing ideology and domination. After all, didn't Douglass, when he was a slave, have to smile and whistle Dixie when his masters were nearby? And didn't Le Ly and her sisters also have to pretend to be happy and to smile at the soldiers who bought and abused their bodies? Like photographs, autobiographies, news stories, and official documents, both smiles and tears can lie.

Works Cited

Barthes, Roland. *Camera Lucida: Reflections on Photography.* Trans. Richard Howard. New York: Farrar, Straus, and Giroux, 1981.

———. *Mythologies.* Trans. Annette Lavers. New York: Hill and Wang, 1979.

Cohen, Hal. "The Unmaking of Rigoberta Menchú." *Lingua Franca* 9.5 (July/Aug. 1999): 48–55.

Cooper, James Fenimore. *The Last of the Mohicans.* Oxford: Oxford World's Classics, 1990.

Marx, Karl. "The Eighteenth Brumaire of Louis Bonaparte." In *The Marx-Engels Reader.* 2d ed. Ed. Robert Tucker. New York: W. W. Norton, 1978. 594–617.

10

Reading Crises of the "Real"

A Cross-Talk Essay

Dion Farquhar

> What counts as experience is neither self-evident nor straightforward;
> it is always contested, always therefore political.
> —Joan W. Scott

At stake in the essays in this book is the protean question of the possibility of intervening politically in the United States and internationally. For those interested in what is not real—the not-yet and only imagined realm of possibility—the very historicity of the "real"—its mutability and contingency—gestures toward a radical openness, difference, and unpredictability that might be more inclusionary and democratic than the present. *Haunting Violations* does not incline toward closure, resolution, or the authority of final arbitration but rather complicates the process of political contestation. In fact, its contributors share Susan Sánchez-Casal's understanding that testimonial texts claiming to narrate "real" experience may present as many problems as they solve. The history of the shifting justifications that push and pull the boundaries of inclusion and exclusion track how the social world has been defined and legitimated.[1] As this volume shows, this history also mobilizes desires, resistances, and hopes for newness and future transformations.

Current academic and popular debates about the nature of power, personal agency, and political action traffic in conflicting claims, demands, and desires. Through teasing out some of the fraught relations between the "real," on the one hand, and representation, on the other hand, *Haunting Violations* enacts the opposition between centralizing, normative political projects and postmodern deconstructionist ones. Its essays attempt to reconcile different political articulations of identity or experience with a postmodern episteme's incredulity toward all metanarratives and insistence on relation, specificity, and context.

The problem of identities—who's what? what constitutes the "real"? or what really happened?—is central to any account claiming to represent particular experiences or events; in short, all of history, autobiography, and cultural criticism. If all discourse about the ontology of the "real" is also discourse about the "true," then, as Foucault has suggested, we need to dispense with the obsessive calibration of truth's ontology and "take up the problem posed by Nietzsche: how is it that, in our societies, 'the truth' has been given this value, thus placing us absolutely under its thrall?" (45).

Haunting Violations is a timely intervention into the scholarship on the ever-expanding realist genre of testimonial, confessional, autobiographical, and ethnographic literature, which represents the narratives of trauma, violence, or oppression told by survivors as more "real" or "authentic" than hegemonic "objective" accounts. These accounts of suffering retell histories of trauma or domination from the underrepresented vantage point of the oppressed or erased.[2] In addition to analyzing autobiographical accounts that grapple with the crisis of testifying or witnessing personal and historical trauma, some essays in *Haunting Violations* examine historical accounts of fissures in a dominant gaze opened by contradictory strategies employed by resistant subjects. Yet other essays in the volume explore questions of dominance and hegemonic control within oppositional practices.

Histories of alterity in general and accounts of exclusion as pained experience in particular typically rely on politicized identities as foundational to truth claims. These accounts often assume that subjects' experiences (ontology) and knowledges (epistemology) constitute a unified and unifying field. Instead we need to understand how tensions between testifying subjects' authorizing politics and assertions of the systematicity of social power inhabit the space of the political. In this case, fragmentation, mutual exclusiveness, and conflict manifested by identities and agencies competing for recognition and legitimacy become an inexorable part of the endlessly negotiated contemporary political landscape.

The strategic multiplication of micronarratives of suffering and resistance issued by minority communities of the First World and Third World peoples is itself a response to the postmodern exhaustion of arrogant metanarrative. Yet this burgeoning of theoretical and political narrative space is fraught with new contradictions as well as new pleasures, like the cataclysmic national and international contexts it responds to—intensified globalization *and* fragmentation. Writing of the complexity and contingency of contemporary political representation, Ella Shohat characterizes the contemporary historical moment as one "of both rupture and continuity, when the macronarrative of women's liberation has ebbed yet sexism and heterosexism still prevail, and when the metanarratives of anticolonial revolution have long been eclipsed yet where issues of (neo-) colonialism and racism persist" (12–13).

The historiographic fantasy that events have a proper and coherent unfold-ing, completeness, and closure masked the moral authority of traditional nar-rative history and drove its transformation "from a manner of speaking into a paradigm of the form that reality itself displays to a 'realistic' consciousness" (White 24). The relatively new first-person genre that chronicles trauma or identity formation (or trauma as identity) explicitly embraces the experience of suffering as its epistemic and moral capital, sharing the moral impulse with traditional disciplinary historiography. While it implicitly repudiates the "ob-jectivity" of disciplinary history, trauma narration that writes to establish elid-ed presence also seeks its own inclusion in or legitimation by it.

Many of this volume's contributors problematize oppositional uses of real-ist discourse. Through an examination of written, filmic, and photographic texts, *Haunting Violations* takes up the contemporary question of how to read critically the discourse of the other without romanticizing or mythologizing his or her suffering or uniqueness, critiquing rather than "exotifying" differ-ence. The philosophical principles that engage the contributors are those that concern most contemporary thinkers—how to make sense of the relation of the material *and* discursive worlds, the relationship of embodiment to dis-course. Before the contributions of French theory entered the scene, assump-tions about the self-evidence of the body's materiality and stability and dis-course's unproblematic referentiality and determinacy were axiomatic in most of Western epistemology.[3] Taking the debate beyond simplistic realism-versus-radical-social-construction positions that fail to address the anxieties each position conveys, the contributors to this volume have expanded on the dia-logue between the material real and the discursively constructed. The narra-tives in this volume represent the struggles of multiply situated agents to elab-orate their material and discursive subject positions against or in spite of sexual violence, racism, and/or colonialism at the same time that they recognize the degree to which they are also partly and provisionally constituted by them.

Generalized group identities are produced and adjudicated as agents who claim to be essentially deprived of or lacking in rights or entitlements, while the individual identities of survivors of personal or historical trauma are elab-orated by testimonial accounts. Both are part of the historical landscape of discursive struggle around cacophonous *fin-de-siècle* micropolitical identity formation that spreads like contestatory wildfire—from new understandings of the self, others, nature, and power extending even to problematic identities like alien abductees and the reincarnated.

However, historically excluded groups like white women, racial minorities, and lesbians and gays have insisted on difference and alterity from and against inclusionary homogenizing liberal state rhetoric precisely at the moment when that rhetoric gestures to include them. Likewise, the contemporary proliferation of literature that speaks about the experience of trauma is itself necessarily both a victory of politicized identities and its institutional domestication. For example, women and children (and their representatives) have organized themselves into a "population" that can now narrate and thereby confer ontological status on family or personal experiences they could not formerly name as traumatic.[4]

All identity, including traumatized identity, is inherently unstable and subject to historical and personal variation. This is apparent in Malathi de Alwis's analysis of the Sri Lankan Mothers' Front's legitimation of their protest against the "disappearance" of male relatives through the use of tears to signify both the "realness" of their grief and the authenticity of their maternal essence. The political deployment of tears guaranteed their normative femininity (as sufferers and as mothers) and their nonpolitical character. De Alwis notes: "it was the very apoliticality of a symbolic essence of maternity such as tears that proved to be most useful." De Alwis contends that the Mothers' Front's appropriation of normative maternity was relatively effective when other modes of dissent were silenced.

As this case study demonstrates, the therapeutic and political value of the burgeoning genre of testimonial literature is tied to the rise of identity politics, with its attendant contributions and problems. That the emancipatory potential for identity politics is problematic in the context of liberal universalism's accommodationist embrace of its more domesticated versions ("diversity," antidiscrimination statutes, corporate "human resources" departments, etc.) has been noted by those eager to maintain their subversive and oppositional intents.[5] For example, proponents of "gay marriage"—the rights and protections of legal marriage equally accorded to persons of the same sex—acquiesce to as well as contest the heterosexism of marriage norms. By the inclusion of same-sex couples in the marriage dyad on the grounds that they are just like opposite-sex couples, gay marriage does nothing to challenge the atomizing marriage ideology of couple formation, monogamy, and personal relations or address the class biases of the de facto political economy of juridico-state triangulation (health insurance, property transmittal, contract legitimacy, etc.) accorded all married couples, though only those with health insurance, property to transmit, and so on benefit. The admission that a love-sex-property union can be formed equally unremarkably by two people of the same sex, however, jettisons the requirement of heteronormativity. In other words, to the extent that same-sex marriage is the same as opposite-sex marriage, it loses the political posit of essential alterity that motored its difference and political standing in the first place. If any two people can marry, then the foundational categories opposite-sex/same-sex and the laws based on them lose their differentiating power. "Gay" and "straight" likewise lose their saliency—at least for purposes of hierarchizing every *body*'s formal juridico-social relationship options.

To the extent that the politics of identity formation is based on the protest against exclusion, it repudiates the universalistic fiction of inclusion as inadequate.[6] Identity politics has sought to differentiate itself against the erasure of liberal universalizing of human rights and the Marxist universalizing of class struggle. Ironically, Marxism has proven no more hospitable to the demands of some self-identified groups than liberalism. The proliferation of politicized identities is in part a reaction against a Marxism viewed as legislating the ontological boundaries of what counts as "the political" and making metanarrativizing, anachronistic, single-variable economistic claims that subsume gender, race, and other loci of oppression. Our contemporary postsocialist condition[7] can be seen alternately as a rejection of a comprehensive vision of a unified struggle for social justice or as a micropolitical deconstructionist embrace of historically excluded cultural narratives in a modest politics of multicultural coalition. However, both political paths are strewn with epistemic dangers: the totalizing metanarrative of social unity homogenizes and assimilates diversity while the skeptical fragmentation of identity formation can devolve into ahistorical essentialism and a politics of authenticity. The search for recognition that drives all identity politics (civil rights struggles, the women's liberation movement, the lesbian and gay movement, disability activism) accomplishes differentiation at the price of reinscribing essential unity, ontological fixity, or ossified identification.

Purnima Bose and Linta Varghese's counterreading of the authenticity of the portrayal of "real" South Asian diasporic identity in *Mississippi Masala* continually resists criticisms of the film's lack of representativeness by insisting on the nonhomogeneous nature and culture of South Asians as diasporic subjects and as viewing communities. They argue that immigrant identity is "a product of multiple national formations" that South Asian discourse of the "real" occludes, and they scrutinize the basis on which the film is criticized for distorting the "real" life experience of the diasporic female subject. Bose and Varghese note that criticisms of *Mississippi Masala* for the unrepresentativeness of its particular set of representations do no more than replace one set with another competing set of representations. Given the paucity of representational capital and the enormous diversity of South Asian experience "there" as well as "here," replacing one partial, interested "truth" with another hardly constitutes the trumping of distortion by "truth." The authors insist on the shifting diversity of the South Asian "experience": "a common, unified South

Asian diasporic culture does not exist in the United States, insofar as the South Asian immigrant population is comprised of regional, age, linguistic, caste, class, gender, and age diversity that has been exported from the subcontinent and has mingled with local U.S. contexts to produce multiple dynamic, hybrid, diasporic subcultures."

Bose and Varghese's essay demonstrates how oppositional identity elaborations have been produced by late modern liberalism and postcolonialism, effecting social recognition of subaltern or micronational groups along with a politics of separatism or reparation. As such, testimonial narratives claim a reconfigured representational power and agency as culturally and discursively immanent or, as Wendy S. Hesford says in her essay, "as embodied negotiations and material enactments of cultural scripts and ideologies."

Trauma as Telling What *Really* Happened

When realist discourses of testimony, autobiography, or documentary are utilized to narrate tales of surviving trauma or oppression, they generate the additional problem of representing the essentially unrepresentable psychoanalytic "Real" of trauma. Although all experience is inseparably enmeshed in the telling of it,[8] as conflicts between reception of textual performance and intention often show,[9] trauma is paradoxical in its tenaciousness and its belatedness, both of which contribute to its resistance to narrativization. The traumatic event resists cogent narration and appears "unreal" to the person experiencing it because it occurs in such extraordinary circumstances as disrupted time, space, causation, or scale.

The subsequent narration or documentation of trauma by survivors of historical events such as combat, torture, the atomic bomb, and the Holocaust or interpersonal events such as rape, sexual abuse, and incest paradoxically perform the impossible task of bearing witness, forging community, and/or inciting political resistance to the erasure, invisibility, or denial that often exacerbates the original traumatic event. At the same time that disciplinary categorization may reinscribe subjects in networks of domination by "realizing" them, the absence of mooring identity categories as the template that coheres one's experience is equally problematic because traumatic experience is delegitimated as the exceptional unreal. Writing of the paradox of bearing witness to the Holocaust, the psychoanalyst Dori Laub writes:

> The trauma is thus an event that has no beginning, no ending, no before, no during and no after. This absence of categories that define it lends it a quality of "otherness," a salience, a timelessness and a ubiquity that puts it outside the range of associatively linked experiences, outside the range of comprehension, of recount-

ing and of mastery. Trauma survivors live not with memories of the past, but with an event that could not and did not proceed through to its completion, has no ending, attained no closure, and therefore, as far as its survivors are concerned, continues into the present and is current in every respect. ("Bearing" 69)[10]

Perhaps the ability to imagine radically different futures from one's past entails embracing past experience as neither hyperreal nor unreal but as a making and a being made that one can tolerate having happened and dream of not having to be repeated.

Survivors of historical and familial trauma utilize narrative forms like the testimonial to invoke a witnessing that confirms the reality of their suffering and allows them to transcend it.[11] Leela Fernandes's reading of *I, Phoolan Devi*, for example, enlists this paradox by transcending the binary opposition of the untranslatable truth of the exotic Third-World subaltern woman and her necessarily partial rhetorical fictions of self-presentation. The paradoxical status of testimony about trauma, however, is never simple for two reasons: it reproduces a representation of the trauma that it attempts to transcend, and it invokes a "real" that it is hyperinvested in deconstructing itself as being over and no longer threatening. Yet the process of retelling one's story, of constructing a narrative that re-externalizes the event, cannot take effect without explicating the intertextual dimension of testimony: interpellating a listener. Laub notes the importance of articulating and transmitting one's story to another in order to reassert and re-externalize the traumatic event ("Bearing" 69). Survivor narratives thus articulate what cannot be said, what defies believability, but what must be avowed to finally transcend the experience.

Put another way, the genre of the testimonial, through its creation of solidarity and validation, can facilitate a transformation from victim to agent by the facing and working through of loss, not by restoration of what is irrevocably lost but by achieving the solidarity of witness to one's own and others' suffering. The "reality" recaptured by the testimony, however, is not that of nostalgic, minimizing, or static identity but, according to Laub, "The testimony in its commitment to truth is a passage through, and an exploration of, differences, rather than an exploration of identity, just as the experience it testifies to—the Holocaust—is unassimilable, because it is a passage through the ultimate difference—the other-ness of death" ("An Event" 91).

Even the most apparently unfettered agent is equally imbricated in networks of disciplinary power and complicity. In this volume, Leslie Bow's analysis of Le Ly Hayslip's autobiography *When Heaven and Earth Changed Places* understands that "the issue is not about Hayslip's specific agenda, Vietnam War representation, or even about the status of the subject of autobiography but about rhetoric and the multiple political uses that experiential narratives authorized by claims of alterity can serve in their appeal to the real."

Bow charts Hayslip's activist account of Le Ly's traumatic Vietnamese past— her torture, rape, abuse, and prostitution—and her transcendence of her past to arrive at the advocacy of a maternalized pacifism, forgiveness, and capitalist economic development. She argues that Hayslip's narrative performs a dual function, criticizing militarism and also reopening "questions about the other forms domination may take." Specifically, Bow notes that Le Ly's sexual agency is double-edged, determining and betraying national identity, colluding with neocolonialism and resisting it. Even bartering sex for survival signifies "her refusal to be victimized."

Wendy S. Hesford raises related questions about agency by exploring the dialogue between a material "real" and the psychoanalytic resistance to it in Strosser's documentary film *Rape Stories*. In so doing, she addresses the tensions between realist political representation and postmodern skepticism toward all experience by resisting the ascendancy of either, richly complicating both agency and resistance.[12] Hesford's analysis repeatedly enacts the problem of and conflict between political and epistemic honesty through her careful consideration of the film's representation of the material effects of one survivor's rhetoricization of the body. Continually straining against existing models of agency, including feminist ones, Hesford rues the many limitations of complicity while celebrating the varieties of resistances, ultimately showing that agency "does not exist outside of culture and its discourses" and that resistance is not inherently oppositional.

Stated more politically than psychoanalytically, Wendy Brown's discussion of the politics of revenge notes its reiteration of "the existence of an identity whose present past is one of insistently unredeemable injury. This past cannot be redeemed *unless* the identity ceases to be invested in it, and it cannot cease to be invested in it without giving up its identity as such, thus giving up its economy of avenging and at the same time perpetuating its hurt" (73). Anyone interested in power, justice, or equality must weigh issues of difference and sameness, of individual memory and group survival. The essays in *Haunting Violations* understand from a variety of disciplinary perspectives and methodological commitments that the "real," like the "truth" about the self or society, is not so much discovered as it is crafted within the limits, in the interests, and for the agendas of contemporary political, scientific, and social projects. Or, as Wendy S. Hesford and Wendy Kozol put it in their introduction, "the 'real' is not a fixed essence but a historically formulated epistemology that responds to localized needs and expectations." The question of adjudicating the referent of the "real" is a question of rhetoric and power rather than literal correspondence.[13]

The postmodernist suggestion that all access to the "real" is mediated by language, culture, and history has provoked a monumental crisis of representation and generated much epistemic and personal anxiety. As the cyberculture critic Sadie Plant notes about the ubiquity of discontinuity and indeterminacy, "the revolutions in telecommunications media, intelligence gathering, and information processing they unleashed have coincided with an unprecedented sense of disorder and unease, not only in societies, states, economies, families, sexes, but also in species, bodies, brains, weather patterns, ecological systems. There is turbulence at so many scales that reality itself seems suddenly on edge" (45–46). Criticism of traditional representations of "objectivity" as acontextual, universal, and cross-cultural is the result of much politicized argument and evidence. Out of critiques of mainstream canonicity, scholarship, and epistemology were born new disciplines and methods that acknowledged their filiations with power and interest: cultural studies, women's studies, critical race and ethnic studies, and lesbian and gay studies. Work in these areas has shown how the articulation of difference in liberal discourse often produces not acceptance but domestication, not equality but neutralization.[14]

Identity as the Claiming of Who One *Really* Is

Politicized identities describe individuals or groups who have ontological status. They are stably and objectively "out there" in the world, and they are thought to occupy exhaustively and self-evidently their identity. Really, however, subject positions are the complexly constructed, performed, and maintained effects of ever-shifting personal and historical acts and events—contingent, historical, and normative. Feminists, for example, often question the acceptability of phallocentric standards by counterposing examples of sexual difference that legitimate women's real experience of gender inequality or exclusion, recommending strategies of differential special treatment or opposing sex discrimination. Whether this invocation of the "real" is advanced as a self-conscious strategic intervention or as a consummate political "truth" matters much. Legal and ethical arguments for special or compensatory treatment, reparation, or affirmative action are based on redressing women's or people of color's gender or race specificity and difference erased or denied by the equality model's privileging of the white male position as norm.

For what is feminism but the argument—in a multitude of cacophonous registers—with liberal universalism that the default position of "the human" (formerly "man") does not embrace feminine sexual difference? In the words of the feminist legal theorist Drucilla Cornell, "Sexual difference is recognized and valued, even if at the same time deconstruction also challenges the inevitability of the current division of sexual beings into only two genres, male or female" (282). Feminist appeals for gender specificity, difference, and uniqueness—and race theorists' insistence on race specificity, difference, and uniqueness—often invoke a counterreal or an essential difference shared by the oppressed group and install new modalities of normativity, albeit at a higher level of abstraction. Indeed, as Linda Nicholson notes, "'a feminism of difference' tends to be 'a feminism of uniformity.'"

Such countercanonical appropriations of the "real" by oppressed people, however, often trade the arrogance of objectivism for the uninterrogated moralizing adulation of the "real" experience of oppressed constituencies. Susan Sánchez-Casal's essay on *I, Rigoberta Menchú* illustrates the problem of equating "truth" with the literal. Her love of and loyalty to the text she analyses does not compromise her insight that its realist conventions "present us with as many critical, theoretical, and ethical problems as they solve." At the same time, Sánchez-Casal admits that her text discursively dismantles the unity of its autobiographical subject, acknowledging its multiplicity and indeterminacy. Her analysis doggedly pursues the ways in which "truth" and "authenticity" are effects rather than conditions of her text's veracity. Her rich examples of multiple textual performances illustrate her text's production of new definitions of native selfhood and community, the representation of "the unmaking of the 'authentic' native world posited by realist strategies of reading and writing and portrayed in the introduction and in segments of Menchú's narrative."

Likewise, Wendy Kozol's study of U.S. archival photographs of interned Japanese Americans during World War II teases out the representational struggles of U.S. government photographers and their subjects to assert the situated practice of agency against hegemonic idealizations. To this end, she reads the ambiguities and complexities of archival photographs depicting relocated Japanese Americans as normalized, unraced, and ungendered Americans. Her examination of the idealized photographic images produced by the World War II War Relocation Authority's photodocumentation project of Japanese American internees argues that its refiguring of identity, experience, and agency also gets refigured by its own strategies and reception.

Kozol shows "how the images participate in constructing the historical narrative" of the forced relocation rather than how these photographs document a singular historical "truth" or univocal identity. Because the government-sponsored photographic project shows Japanese American internees in poses, attitudes, and contexts of citizenship, domesticity, and recreation, its propagandistic effects are complicated. Kozol's analysis of the photographs allows us to understand "reality" as a multiply and complexly (and often contradictorily) constructed site by gender and race configurations. As such, "reality" is always particular rather than an objective fixed referent to which the documentary form could accord an inquirer privileged access.

The essays in *Haunting Violations* do not presume that realist discourses of autobiography, testimony, documentary, memoir, or ethnography are inherently either hegemonic or resistant. The speaking or representation of experiences that have been marginalized or undervalued by hegemonic accounts does not automatically authenticate them simply because they are other. Neither position (objectivist universalizing or its trumping by subjectivist discourse of the oppressed essential Other) ultimately challenges the binary thinking shared by naive subjectivists and realists: the belief in the authenticity and purity of discourse as the unambiguous and transparent conductor of unified subaltern subjectivity as epistemic guarantor of truth or authenticity. On the contrary, if less consoling, the essays in *Haunting Violations* provide rich case studies of reconciliations of philosophical and methodological rigor with committed political agency and interest. They work with postmodernist conceptions of the self as decentered, multidimensional, and mutable, reconfiguring foundationalist conceptions of agency.

Although political outcomes can never be known in advance, the multiple imaginings of a radically democratized world that does live up to liberalism's most capacious dreams can be nudged onward by reading *Haunting Violations*.

Notes

1. The physicist Karen Barad argues for accountability both for "the particular exclusions that are enacted and in taking up the responsibility to perpetually contest and rework the boundaries" (104).

2. Debates about and reflections on the relation of fictional and other literary techniques to the historical event foreground the memoir as "one of the defining artistic forms of our era" (Paola 45).

3. See Hayles's essay that tracks one instance of privileging the abstract as the real against embodiment or materiality.

4. Writing of the emergence of post-traumatic stress syndrome, Bessel van der Kolk et al. note: "Amazingly, between 1895 and 1974, the study of trauma centered almost exclusively on its effects on white males" (60–61).

5. Many feminist political theorists have noted the problems that essentialism poses for theory and activism. Kristie McClure, for example, argues that politicization of

excluded spheres ultimately confirms rather than disrupts traditional conceptions of "the political" as the management of the social (347).

6. The political theorist Wendy Brown discusses this dilemma: "politicized identities generated out of liberal, disciplinary societies, insofar as they are premised on exclusion from a universal ideal, require that ideal, as well as their exclusion from it, for their own continuing existence as identities" (65).

7. The phrase is Nancy Fraser's, from *Justice Interruptus*, a canny theoretical attempt to fuse cultural politics of recognition with visionary socialism by pumping up identity politics to include political and economic institutions.

8. According to Derrida, reading "cannot legitimately transgress the text toward something other than it, toward a referent (a reality that is metaphysical, historical, psychobiographical, etc.) or toward a signified outside the text whose content could take place, could have taken place outside of language, that is to say, in the sense that we give here to that word, outside of writing in general. That is why the methodological considerations that we risk applying here to an example are closely dependent on general propositions that we have elaborated above; as regards the absence of the referent or the transcendental signified. *There is nothing outside of the text*" (89).

9. Sánchez-Casal's essay attends to the multiple ways that *I, Rigoberta Menchu* works to subvert its declared intentions of validating an essentialist episteme of the "real."

10. The literary critic Naomi Morgenstern notes the same phenomenon in her analysis of "neoslave narratives": "Testimony inevitably troubles the opposition between a pure repetition of the past (trauma) and representation through narrative. Because it must reproduce the past it purports to represent, it always risks re-traumatizing both victim and witness" (117).

11. In an interesting theoretical move that aligns the "real" with the postmodern, the philosopher Charlene Spretnak argues that rehabilitation of a violated "real" (ecology) is "truly postmodern," recommending attending to "the dynamic physicality of the cosmos" and connecting "anew with our larger context: the Earth, the cosmos, the sacred whole." She argues that deconstructionist denial of access to the "real" has "thrown out the baby with the bathwater" (66).

12. As Riley has said in regard to identity politics and women, "The question of the politics of identity could be rephrased as a question of rhetoric. Not so much of whether there was for a particular moment any truthful underlying rendition of 'women' or not, but of what the proliferations of addresses, descriptions, and attributions were *doing*" (122; emphasis added).

13. Brown theorizes this process of normalization, locating it in politicized identity's desire.

14. Brown notes the problem with invoking identity as essential: "what kind of political recognition can identity-based claims seek—and what kind can they be counted on to want—that will not resubordinate a subject itself historically subjugated through identity, through categories such as race or gender that emerged and circulated as terms of power to enact subordination?" (55).

Works Cited

Barad, Karen. "Getting Real: Technoscientific Practices and the Materialization of Reality." *differences* 10.2 (1998): 87–128.

Brown, Wendy. *States of Injury: Power and Freedom in Late Modernity.* Princeton, N.J.: Princeton University Press, 1995.

Cornell, Drucilla L. "Gender, Sex, and Equivalent Rights." In *Feminists Theorize the Political.* Ed. Judith Butler and Joan W. Scott. New York: Routledge, 1992. 280–96.

Derrida, Jacques. "The Play of Substitution." In *The Truth about the Truth: De-Confusing and Re-Constructing the Postmodern World.* Ed. Walter Truett Anderson. New York: Putnam, 1995. 86–91.

Foucault, Michel. "Strategies of Power." In *The Truth about the Truth: De-Confusing and Re-Constructing the Postmodern World.* Ed. Walter Truett Anderson. New York: Putnam, 1995. 40–45.

Fraser, Nancy. *Justice Interruptus: Critical Reflections of the "Postsocialist" Condition.* New York: Routledge, 1997.

Hayles, N. Katherine. "Toward Embodied Virtuality." In *How We Became Posthuman: Virtual Bodies in Cybernetics, Literature, and Informatics.* Chicago: University of Chicago Press, 1999. 1–24.

Laub, Dori. "Bearing Witness or the Vicissitudes of Listening." In Shoshanna Felman and Dori Laub, *Testimony: Crises of Witnessing in Literature, Psychoanalysis, and History.* New York: Routledge, 1992. 57–74.

———. "An Event without a Witness: Truth, Testimony, and Survival." In Shoshanna Felman and Dori Laub, *Testimony: Crises of Witnessing in Literature, Psychoanalysis, and History.* New York: Routledge, 1992. 75–92.

McClure, Kristie. "The Issue of Foundations: Scientized Politics, Politicized Science, and Feminist Critical Practice." In *Feminists Theorize the Political.* Ed. Judith Butler and Joan W. Scott. New York: Routledge, 1992. 341–68.

Morgenstern, Naomi. "Mother's Milk and Sister's Blood: Trauma and the Neoslave Narrative." *differences* 8.2 (1996): 101–27.

Nicholson, Linda J. "Interpreting 'Gender.'" In *Race, Class, Gender, and Sexuality: The Big Questions.* Ed. Naomi Zack, Laurie Shrage, and Crispin Sartwell. Malden, Mass.: Blackwell, 1998. 187–211.

Paola, Suzanne. "Truth or Consequences: A Nonfiction Symposium." *Bellingham Review* 22.1 (Summer 1999): 45–46.

Plant, Sadie. *Zeros + Ones: Digital Women + the New Technoculture.* New York: Doubleday, 1997.

Riley, Denise. "A Short History of Preoccupations." In *Feminists Theorize the Political.* Ed. Judith Butler and Joan W. Scott. New York: Routledge, 1992. 121–29.

Scott, Joan W. "Experience." In *Feminists Theorize the Political.* Ed. Judith Butler and Joan W. Scott. New York: Routledge, 1992. 22–40.

Shohat, Ella, ed. *Talking Visions: Multicultural Feminism in a Transnational Age.* Cambridge: Massachusetts Institute of Technology Press, 1998.

Spretnak, Charlene. *The Resurgence of the Real: Body, Nature, and Place in a Hypermodern World.* Reading, Mass.: Addison-Wesley, 1997.

van der Kolk, Bessel A., et al. "History of Trauma in Psychiatry." In *Traumatic Stress: The Effects of Overwhelming Experience on Mind, Body, and Society.* Ed. Bessel A. Van der Kolk, Alexander C. McFarlane, Lars Weisaeth. New York: Guilford Press, 1996. 47–74.

White, Hayden. "The Value of Narrativity in the Representation of Reality." In *The Content of the Form: Narrative Discourse and Historical Representation.* Baltimore: Johns Hopkins University Press, 1987. 1–25.

Contributors

Purnima Bose is an assistant professor of English at Indiana University, where she teaches courses on feminism, cultural studies, and postcolonial studies. She has published or has forthcoming essays on these topics in *Passages, Boundary 2, Genders,* and *SAMAR* and is the author of the forthcoming book *Organizing Empire: Individualism, Collective Agency, and India.*

Leslie Bow is an assistant professor of English at the University of Miami, where she specializes in Asian American literature, ethnic autobiography, writing by women of color, feminist theory, and theories of race and ethnicity. The author of *Betrayal and Other Acts of Subversion: Feminism, Sexual Politics, Asian American Women's Literature* (forthcoming), she has also published articles in *Cultural Critique, Profession, Prose Studies, Dispositio: American Journal of Comparative and Cultural Studies,* and *Forkroads: A Journal of Ethnic-American Literatures* as well as several book chapters, including one in *Who Can Speak?: Authority and Cultural Identity* (ed. Judith Roof and Robyn Wiegman).

Patrick Brantlinger is a professor of English and Victorian studies at Indiana University. His most recent books are *Fictions of State: Culture and Credit in Britain, 1694–1994* (1997) and *The Reading Lesson: Mass Literacy as Threat in Nineteenth-Century British Fiction* (1998).

Malathi de Alwis is a senior research fellow at the International Centre for Ethnic Studies, Colombo, a visiting assistant professor of anthropology at the New School for Social Research, New York, and a cofounder of the Women's Coalition for Peace, Sri Lanka. The coeditor, with Kumari Jayawardena, of *Embodied Violence: Communalising Women's Sexuality in South Asia* (1996), she has also published articles in South Asia and North America on gender, nationalism, militarism, and humanitarianism in various parts of the globe and is a regular contributor to "Cat's Eye," a feminist column on current affairs in the *Island* newspaper.

DION FARQUHAR, a political theorist, poet, and prose fiction writer who divides her time between Santa Cruz and New York, is a lecturer in women's studies at the University of California at Santa Cruz, Hunter College, and New York University and is on the Graduate Faculty of the New School for Social Research. The author of *The Other Machine: Discourse and Reproductive Technologies* (1996), she is working on projects that take her in two different but related directions: cybercultures and gamete traffic and its vicissitudes.

LEELA FERNANDES is an assistant professor of political science and women's studies at Rutgers University, New Brunswick, N.J. The author of *Producing Workers: The Politics of Gender, Class, and Culture in the Calcutta Jute Mills* (1997), she is working on a book on the Indian middle class in the context of economic reform in contemporary India.

WENDY S. HESFORD, an assistant professor of English at Indiana University, teaches courses in cultural studies, composition, and literacy studies. The author of *Framing Identities: Autobiography and the Politics of Pedagogy* (1999), for which she received the W. Ross Winterowd book award, she has also published essays in numerous journals and anthologies, including *College English*, *JAC*, and *In Other Words: Feminism and Composition Studies* (1998; ed. Susan Jarratt and Lynn Worsham). She is working on a book titled *Auto/biographical Spectacles: Trauma, Transnational Feminism, and Pedagogy*.

WENDY KOZOL is an associate professor of women's studies and history at Oberlin College. The author of *Life's America: Family and Nation in Postwar Photojournalism* (1994), she has also published articles on television news, documentary photography, and news coverage of domestic violence in anthologies and journals such as *Genders* and *Signs*. She is working on a book about government agencies' reliance on visual media to represent histories of social dislocation and disruption within the nation.

SUSAN SÁNCHEZ-CASAL is an associate professor of Spanish and women's studies at Hamilton College in Clinton, New York, where she teaches courses on contemporary Latin American and U.S. Latino literatures. Her published articles include "Testimony as Writing: Criticism, Representation, Reception" (1993) and "In a Neighborhood of Another Color: Latina/Latino Struggles for Home" (1998), and she is coeditor of *The Feminist Classroom for the Twenty-first Century: Pedagogies of Power and Difference* (2000), a critical anthology of interdisciplinary essays.

LINTA VARGHESE is a graduate student in cultural anthropology at the University of Texas at Austin. Her research focuses on the use of sexuality and gender in the South Asian Diaspora and South Asian racial positioning in the United States.

JULIA WATSON, an associate professor of comparative studies at The Ohio State University, is a coeditor, with Sidonie Smith, of *De/Colonizing the Subject: The Politics of Gender in Women's Autobiography* (1992), *Getting a Life: Everyday Uses of Autobiography* (1996), and *Women, Autobiography, Theory: A Reader* (1998). She has published several essays on autobiography and is working on a book on autoethnography.

Index

Abel, Elizabeth, 39n
Abeydeera, Priyangani, 206
Abu-Lughod, Lila, 69n, 195, 197, 198, 199, 211n; *Veiled Sentiments*, 199
Academy, 76
Achugar, Hugo, 106n
Activism, 2, 7, 10, 11, 24, 31, 92, 95, 103n, 137–63, 182–83, 207, 269; antirape movement, 21, 37; cultural politics, 150, 151; disability, 266; guerilla, 93; indigenous, 81, 96–97; and representation, 137; South Asian, 137, 138, 151, 153, 162, 163, 254; women's grassroots, 10, 151, 153, 165n. *See also* Manavi; Mothers' Front
Adams, Ansel, 228, 248n; *Born Free and Equal*, 228, 248n
Adams, Timothy Dow, 133n
Addiction, 118–20, 123, 125, 126, 130, 132
Adisa, Opal, 38n, 40n
African American, 140, 159, 229, 243, 244, 245, 248n; men, 20; women, 21
Agency, 2, 6, 7, 18, 19, 22, 23, 24, 25, 29, 30, 50, 62, 67, 78, 86, 88, 89, 92, 93, 99, 102, 137–63, 174, 175–76, 184, 185, 187, 218, 219, 242, 259, 260, 261, 268, 269, 272; cross-cultural, 84; and embodiment, 220; fractured, 238, 240; hegemonic, 240, 246; of narrator, 87; situated practice, 241, 245, 264, 271; social, 138, 154
Aguilar-San Juan, Karin, 137; *The State of Asian America*, 137
Ahmad, Aijaz, 71n
Alarcón, Norma, 47
Alcoff, Linda, 6, 14, 17

Alegría, Claribel, 104n; *No me agarran viva*, 104n
Allen, Beverly, 35, 41n
Allen, Chadwick, 117, 118, 134n
Alloula, Malek, 8, 52, 54; *The Colonial Harem*, 52
Alonso, Ana, 142, 143
Althusser, Louis, 199
Amar Sánchez, Ana María, 105n
Amerasekere, Damayanthi, 205
Amin, Idi, 138, 139, 143, 144, 145, 156, 157, 158, 254
Anderson, Benedict, 152
Anthias, Floya, 190n
Anzaldúa, Gloria, 71n, 232
Appadurai, Arjun, 71n
Appelbaum, Richard, 180
Appropriation, 19, 85, 88, 99, 107n; governmental, 113; mimicry, 23; symbolic reappropriation, 117
Argentina's Dirty War, 28
Arias, Arturo, 101, 106n
Aristotle, 203
Armor, John, 247n
Arpilleras, 77, 103n
Asian American: autobiography, 182; literature, 171, 181, 187, 188, 190n; women's movements, 151
Atwood, Margaret, 15
Audience, 125; analysis of, 52; colonizer/reader, 85, 86; consumption of texts, 56; middle-class, 61
Authenticity, 2, 3, 6, 7, 9, 10, 32, 50, 52, 54, 62, 66, 76, 77, 78, 80, 82, 86, 87, 112, 116, 122, 137, 141,

Capitalism, 4; in India, 61
Carby, Hazel, 40n
Carey-Webb, Allen, 76, 103n, 104n; *Teaching and Testimony,* 76
Carr, Robert, 50, 54, 64
Carter, Daniel, 40n
Caruth, Cathy, 17, 25, 26, 27, 28, 124, 126; reading of *Gerusalenime Liberata,* 25; *Unclaimed Experiences,* 25
Caste, 252; class relations, 66–67, 156, 159; gender, 54, 60, 66; hierarchies, 66; inequalities, 54, 61; patriarchy, 55
Catholicism. *See* Religion
Censorship, 59
Ceylon, 200
Chakrabarty, Dipesh, 211n
Chan, Sucheng, 220, 224, 233, 239, 247n
Chaudhury, Sarita, 139, 148, 159, 161
Cherniavsky, Eva, 39n
Chicano, 229
Chief Joseph, 130
Chief Seattle, 111
Chow, Rey, 47, 52, 57; *Writing Diaspora,* 47
Christerson, Brad, 180
Christopher, Warren, 189n
Cigelj, Jadranka, 35, 36, 37
Citizenship, 10, 217–46; and race, 242
Civil rights, 266
Clark, Colin, 165n
Class, 83, 147; middle, 5, 9, 50, 51, 60, 145; and racial conflict, 158, 159; social, 83, 206. *See also* Caste
Clifford, James, 48, 80
Clinton, William J., 170
Cloud, Dana, 18, 38n
Cock, Jacklyn, 30
Coehlo, George V., 165n
Coeur d'Alene Indians, 117, 121, 122
Cohen, Hal, 253
Collins, Jane, 8, 219
Colonialism, 8, 48, 56, 84, 113, 119, 120; anti-, 143, 144, 263; narratives of, 54, 157–58, 159, 164n, 186, 200, 212n, 264; neo-, 10, 119, 263
Comaroff, Jean, 211n
Comaroff, John, 211n
Commemorative practices, 37, 131
Commodification: of differences, 47; of identity, 147, 148. *See also* Autobiography
Community, 114, 153; cross-cultural, 91; ethnic, 114; heterogeneous, 92; imagined, 24, 152, 243; ladino, 89; Native American, 121; pueblo, 87; Quiché, 87, 88, 92; subaltern, 76; "telling on,"

119, 122; transpersonal, 130; universalizing women, 24, 84. *See also* Culture; Identity
Conceit, 197–98, 199, 204, 205, 210n, 258
Concentration camps, 247n, 255. *See also* Internment camps
Confession, 14, 113
Connolly, William, 208
Consciousness: collective, 88, 89, 90, 91; *concientización,* 88, 91, 97; double, 148; revolutionary, 93
Consumer, 48
Cook-Lynn, Elizabeth, 133n
Cooper, James Fenimore, 257
Cornell, Drucilla L., 271
Crisis, 8; abuse, 132; of American identity, 133; definition, 3; migrancy, 132; narrative, 3, 113; national, 101; poverty, 132; racial difference, 128; as trope, 3
Crowley, Sharon, 38n
Culbertson, Roberta, 16, 17, 22
Cultural: amnesia, 119; capital, 52; criticism, 142, 162, 163, 253, 262, 263; discourse, 11; ideologies, 18; politics, 2, 31; practices, 11; scripts, 18, 23, 24, 115
Culture: Indian, 54–56; Native American, 119; Quiché, 77, 84, 88, 91–101, 107n, 253; visual, 7; wars, 2
Curtis, James, 225

Daly, Mary, 209n
Daniel, E. Valentine, 212n
Daniel, Pete, 225
Daniels, Roger, 223, 224, 225, 226, 234, 247n; *Prisoners without Trial,* 223, 224, 234, 247n
Das, Veena, 203, 212n
Das Gupta, Monisha, 145
Das Gupta, Sayantani, 146, 147, 152, 153, 154
Das Gupta, Shamita, 153
Daston, Lorraine, 203, 212n
De Alwis, Malathi, 7, 10, 195, 200, 202, 208, 210n, 212n, 257, 258, 260, 265; *Maternalist Protest,* 195, 200, 202, 208, 210n, 212n
De Bonafini, Hebe, 104n; *Historias de vida,* 104n
De Certau, Michel, 196
Deely, John, 104n; *Basics of Semiotics,* 104n
Delacoste, Frederique, 23
De Lauretis, Teresa, 7, 20, 27, 39n; *Technologies of Gender,* 20, 39n
Dementia, 196
Departicularization, 142, 143
Depression, 196
Derné, Steve, 161

Typeset in 10.5/13 Minion
with Helvetica Neue display
Designed by Dennis Roberts
Composed by Jim Proefrock
at the University of Illinois Press
Manufactured by Thomson-Shore, Inc.

University of Illinois Press
1325 South Oak Street
Champaign, IL 61820-6903
www.press.uillinois.edu